AF265013

MY PEACE

THE AUTOBIOGRAPHY OF BRANDON A. ROWELL

Published in the United States by:
JTB Capital
Atlanta, GA.
jtbcapital.com

Library of Congress Control Number 2019902406
Hardback ISBN 978-0-692-14997-3
Paperback ISBN 978-0-578-47010-8
Ebook ISBN 978-0-578-47377-2

Final Edition

To those of you who helped and inspired me,
you know who you are.

Some of the quotes contained herein have
been edited for grammar, clarity, and flow.
The originals and other supporting documents
can be found on my website, jtbcapital.com.

CONTENTS

Prologue xi

1. Growing up Minnesota....................................1
2. Off to College 19
3. A Small Market 45
4. The Next Level 73
5. Falling 95
6. Temptation 121
7. Exit Strategy 147
8. New Life... 181
9. The Storm 213
10. In-Dependency 241
11. Calibration 265
12. Misrepresentation 287
13. Survival 307
14. Dreaming 321
15. The Eleventh Circuit................................339
16. Home 365
17. Finding Paradise 377
18. Reflection 393

PROLOGUE

Like most people, whether we acknowledge them or not, I wouldn't be here without my family.

My dad, Alex Rowell, came from humble beginnings. His mom found work as a cook while her husband served in the navy, but neither of his parents studied past the eighth grade. He, however, was gifted in athletics and was offered a scholarship to Notre Dame. At a friend's request though, my dad joined him at Luther College in Decorah, Iowa.

My mother's dad was a car salesman whose income depended on his sales. Her mom took care of the home. Driven to succeed, my mom, Saundra, graduated from high school at sixteen, got financial aid, and joined my dad, who was starting his sophomore year.

Having earned starter roles for both basketball and baseball his freshman year, Alex was becoming known as a standout athlete. The Dallas Cowboys took interest, as did USA Basketball, but he decided to continue his baseball career. The Minnesota Twins selected him in the first round of the 1968 draft.

My mom faced adversity at college her sophomore year when her dad passed away, but she received support from stepbrothers and stepsisters, who accepted her as family. She found herself having to explain to her classmates why she changed her last name without having gotten married. Not necessarily a fan of athletics, but of my dad, she got over her disinterest in sports and attended his games regularly. He made good on his word by marrying my mom after she graduated in 1969.

Together in Minnesota, they shared hard times, including the loss of their first child, Carolyn, who was stillborn in 1970. Baseball salaries were low in the minor leagues, and my dad left the sport after two years to pursue a career in teaching and coaching. My mom found employment as an English teacher in the public school system.

Despite apprehension from Carolyn's death, my parents tried again, and six years later my brother, Derek, was born. In 1978, tragedy struck again when my parent's second daughter, Alexa, was diagnosed with DiGeorge syndrome. With congenital defects of the heart, parathyroid, and thymus, she lived for five months before also passing away.

I was born in 1980, and from what I've been told, I was a happy baby, calling people to my crib just to smile and laugh. The name given to me means "from the lighted hill" and expressed my parents' hope for a healthy baby.

They put hard times behind them, and my dad changed careers from education to sales. My mom became an administrator. They placed a high value on studies and led by example with each earning master's degrees.

Thanks in large part to the good salaries in the pharmaceutical and medical device industries, steady paychecks from Minneapolis schools, their discipline for savings, and the 1990s stock market surge, my mom and dad found themselves in the upper middle class. They promised my brother and me that in addition to the necessities, they'd provide us with a college education and down payment for a home. They, however, went much further. My dad told me at one point that they'd sacrifice everything they had in order for us to be stable, and they have.

Act I

CHAPTER 1

GROWING UP MINNESOTA

I clocked in at a hospital in Golden Valley, Minnesota, on March 27, 1980, at nine pounds and eleven and a half ounces. My mom later told me that she cried, not so much from the pain of my birth, but from the realization that she then had two African American sons in a predominately white state.

My parents brought me to our home in Brooklyn Park, where my brother was excited to have a playmate. He and the two German Shepherds were not only my friends, but my guardians. My parents enrolled my brother and me in private schools as toddlers, where we were exposed to foreign languages and advanced learning techniques. A few years later, my parents decided to move to Minnetonka, a highly rated school district. The downside of the move wasn't just being farther from the city, but relocating to an area that was ranked one of the whitest in the nation.

I enjoyed the half days of kindergarten, but my world changed in first grade after being assigned a seat next to a transfer student from Iowa. During the math portion of our class, we were asked a question, and both of us raised our hands. Our teacher pointed in our direction, called "Brandon," and by responding at the same time with the correct answer, Brandon Stech and I were bonded for life.

During the next two years of elementary school, there were school boundary changes and my new school was less welcoming. More importantly, I was separated from Stech. To make matters worse, it was the beginning of the name-calling phase of childhood. I was called nigger and because of my glasses, "four-eyed brownie." I did, however, find relief as I began participating in organized basketball for the first time in third grade.

The following year, we moved to Chanhassen, the home of Prince. My parents did their best to keep our family connected with the black community, and so they enrolled my brother and me in an organization named Jack and Jill of America. It had monthly activities to develop cultural, educational, and social experiences for African Americans.

Although those experiences were helpful, my everyday life as a fourth grader led to frustration when I auditioned for our school's civil rights play. I wanted to be Martin Luther King Jr., but I was passed over in favor of another student. As the only person of color in the production, I received the role of a reporter whose sole job was to point to a headline. My mom, bless her heart, said that I would be the best reporter I could be and took pleasure in outfitting me with a sports coat and brimmed hat.

Family Matters became a popular TV show when I was in fifth grade. It was about an African American family and a neighboring boy who wore oversized glasses, colorful suspenders, and talked in a high-pitched voice. He and I had a similar haircuts, but I didn't find it amusing when other students and teachers called me "Urkel."

The next year, I earned a role on Minnetonka's traveling basketball team, which kept me busy all winter. We practiced throughout the week and played in tournaments that mostly started on Friday nights and went through Sunday afternoon. The fifty-two games that season forced organized religion to take a backseat. Although we finished with forty-two wins, the all-black teams from the Boys & Girls Club and South Minneapolis accounted for most of our losses.

As students in the seventh grade, we were given the opportunity to study a foreign language. I was thinking that I would elect study hall instead when a friend told me that I already knew Spanish. Puzzled, I stared at my classmate who counted off "uno, dos, tres," and with newfound excitement, I signed up to learn more.

Despite attending different schools, Stech was a member of most basketball teams that I played on. And when given the opportunity to choose a friend to spend a week with him at his grandparents' house in Illinois, he picked me consecutive summers.

His aunt drove us in her convertible, and being in a car with its top down was a new experience. I fell in love with the feeling while en route to Deerfield. There, I met Stech's grandfather, an executive at a toy company, and his grandmother, who owned a store. They welcomed me as one of their own and provided my favorite donuts every morning.

After sleeping in, Stech and I would wake up to watch a movie or explode firecrackers. In addition to the free time, we went to an amusement park and also to his grandparent's country club. We were also given the opportunity to earn money. It was tradition that each of Nana's grandkids and their friends went to work in her store.

She delighted in making newcomers guess which business was hers. As we approached, I was afraid to say the one that caught my attention. Deciding to play dumb, I read each and every name at least once before saying, "Hooker's Nook." I was relieved to learn that it was a store specializing in knitting and framing instead of erotic accessories. After we completed our tasks, we were given the option of splitting $40 or a coffee mug full of coins. Stech's recommendation of the accumulated change wound up being the wiser choice and paid several dollars more.

During summers, I participated in basketball camps, including one run by a former player of my dad's. The six-foot-eight Ben Coleman was a student at North High School and went on to play in the NBA. The camp was located in the inner city, where everyone was new to me. I quickly settled in, however, to play some of my best ball.

At the end of camp, I was surprised to receive the "Best Camper" trophy, but was struck that there was no ceremony for parents. Every other basketball camp that I had attended, paused to perform an exhibition for parents. Not Ben's, which made his camp my favorite.

I believe that was also the same summer when I had my first unpleasant encounter with the police.

It wasn't uncommon for my dad to bring me along to play basketball, but on that occasion, there was a scheduling conflict. My dad decided that we'd wait in the parking lot to inform others that the gym was unavailable, when suddenly we were surrounded by squad cars. Guns drawn, the police ordered us to our knees. Gravel dug into my skin as I feared a deadly miscalculation. It turned out that kids observing from a distance decided to play a prank and falsely reported a robbery. They had given the authorities our description.

The Stechs, by then, had purchased a house on the cul-de-sac opposite ours. Mrs. Stech, a physical therapist, set her own hours. She often drove the neighborhood kids to and from basketball camp. One day, while I should have been preparing for my ride, I went off to visit a girl and lost track of time. Then, I ignored it. I knew that Mrs. Stech had been by, but I didn't think much about it until I returned home.

I could sense my parents' displeasure and began to plead with my mom as my dad left the room. Those pleas grew stronger as he re-entered. He had his belt.

I gave one last futile attempt, saying, "I'll never do it again."

My dad responded, "I know you won't."

In eighth grade, I noticed another black kid walking

around school. We hadn't met. One of my previous teachers had gone to Central America on a bike ride and recorded the adventure on CD-ROM. The media, at the time, was expensive, and the disk left in the library for students to use had gone missing. The vice principal called me to his office and explained why I was there. Noticing the lack of expression on my face, he realized it was the other black kid who had taken it.

My mom enrolled me in classes that summer as I prepared to enter the high school from which my brother had just graduated. The first day went as one would expect, but another black student showed up on the second. He introduced himself as Rashad, and at first opportunity, I pulled him aside to explain what he might expect from his new surroundings. He had moved from Atlanta for the same reason that I was attending summer school, to stay out of trouble.

The two of us hit it off and were each other's bright spots in classes that we had no desire to attend. It wasn't long before he invited me to his uncle's house. While on our way, Rashad had a good time with me by suggesting his relative was famous. The name of baseball player Kirby Puckett was floated, but it wasn't until we almost arrived that Rashad confessed his uncle was Darrin Nelson.

The fact that his uncle was one of the Minnesota

Vikings' great running backs held little importance to either of us. His name, however, did help when Rashad was pulled over while driving his uncle's Jeep. We weren't as lucky in our next encounter with the law.

We had started to collect BB guns and joined friends at a nearby lake. We found cover under trees and had just started shooting into the water when a neighbor threatened to call the police. The consensus was to leave, but one of our friends lived in the area and wanted to "piss the guy off." As a group of us walked ahead, he lit a firework fuse at the base of the man's driveway.

Apparently the guy recognized Matt, and officers showed up at a nearby park asking for him by name. Rather than avoiding the encounter, he responded, "Yeah, that's me. What did I do now?" To complicate matters, he gave the police my name. By the time I returned home, an officer was waiting for me. I hoped to plea bargain, but my parents laughed at the notion.

Rashad and I were charged with discharging firearms in a public place. We showed up at court with my parents and his guardians. My dad asked the court to change the language from "firearms" to "BB guns." The judge agreed and was about to give us probation when my mom interrupted. She recommended that Rashad and I perform community service. We wound up visiting my previous middle school teachers to talk to their students about gun laws and our mistakes.

Well into our freshman year, another black kid, whose Afro and tank tops made him stand out, arrived from Houston. Already close friends, Rashad and I were skeptical, but befriended him anyway. As the three of us walked the hall one day, we passed by another friend of mine, Jake, who was flanked by a group of seniors. They were much bigger, known to be prejudiced, and wore cowboy hats in solidarity.

Their leader, nicknamed "Gandhi," was about my brother's age and had dated a good friend of his. Jake later pulled me aside to say that Gandhi had pointed to my friends and said they were trash. Referring to me, Jake inquired, "What about him?" Gandhi's response was "He's cool. He's a Rowell."

Rashad traveled back to Atlanta for the summer and I got a visit from Matt, who had lit the firework fuse. He caught a ride with another friend who had just gotten his driver's license and a new pickup truck. The three of us coasted to the other end of the street to pick up Stech and set course to play basketball. With space for only two in the cab, Matt and I rode in the bed. After working up a sweat, Matt and the driver somehow convinced us that jumping from a cliff into a nearby lake was a good idea.

We were headed downhill and approached a right-hand turn that the driver cut too close. The passenger side tires hit gravel, which caused the truck to fishtail. At that point I began to lose consciousness. I recall the truck skidding while trying to straighten out and the back of my head dragging against the pavement. The truck had rolled and thrown me in the process.

When it settled, I staggered to the side of the road and took a seat as my friends tried to turn the truck upright. I attempted to evaluate my damage and saw blood on my fingers. Sirens approached, and through the commotion I was told that Matt had escaped unharmed. I was secured, placed on a stretcher, loaded into an ambulance, and taken to a hospital.

My parents brought me home, and I stepped into a bathroom to get a better look. There was no discernible difference while looking straight ahead, but my profile grew when I turned sideways. The wound on the back of my head had swollen to the size of a medium orange.

Despite these events, I remained close with Matt until I visited his bedroom one day. Directly above his mattress was a rebel flag that included a skull and caption that read, "The South will rise again." An act of such prejudice coming from a close friend helped me to begin seeing beyond people's exterior.

Sophomore year showed just how connected Stech and I were. We were both studying Spanish and our teachers had allowed us to choose nicknames. After reviewing the list, I picked "Domingo" because the listed translation was "Dominique," and the most ethnic sounding name on the list. Stech, however, picked "Domingo" simply because he thought it sounded cool. We were both surprised to later learn that "Domingo," is most commonly translated to the seventh day of the week, "Sunday."

In Spanish class together for the first time, our teacher wanted to avoid confusion and asked us to pick new names. Stech selected "Yemo," I chose "Memo," and we became known as *Doyemo* and *Domemo*.

Apart from Stech, I was spending most of my time with Rashad and the transfer from Houston. The circumstances that brought them to Minnesota bubbled up, and they again found themselves in trouble. Rashad was the first to go, and my friend from Houston left months later. It was difficult seeing people I so closely related to move away.

I continued to find solace in basketball, but I began to feel wear that summer. There was tightness and swelling behind my right knee. My dad took me to a doctor friend of his, who requested X-rays. They revealed bone chips caused by a lack of cartilage. At the age of sixteen, I was diagnosed with arthritis, scheduled for arthroscopic surgery, and told knee replacement was in my future.

The health warning didn't stop my love for the game, and I signed up for fall league. It would be my first time playing without a coach, and our top players were instead participating in football. I linked up with the guys with whom I had the most chemistry, and it turned out to be the most fun I'd ever had. We played unselfishly and were dominating most of our competition. Then came the kids from the Boys and Girls Club and South Minneapolis. They had merged and were playing for Minneapolis North.

The game became intense as my opponent called me names like "Oreo" and "Uncle Tom." I was too black for some of my classmates, but not black enough for them. The verbal attacks spurred me to play harder, and the box score revealed that both Stech and I had each scored twenty-seven points in the win.

That same year, I began to take note of polite behavior as opposed to genuine actions. The rap group Bone Thugs-N-Harmony was approaching the height of its popularity. Most of their lyrics are unintelligible, and it was fun trying to decipher what they were saying.

One word was unmistakable though: "nigga." I was in a classmate's car as my peers rapped along. They went silent as the word approached then continued afterwards. I appreciated what felt like respect, but was surprised on the next occasion when I was the only one who stopped rapping. It was clear to me they had forgotten I was in the car.

In the spring of that year, I inherited my dad's Lincoln Continental, which already had been driven more than two hundred thousand miles. It was supposed to get me to school and a job he had arranged for me at his friend's law firm. Most kids with driver's licenses in my school had their own cars, which caused the district to issue parking permits. I missed the cutoff to purchase mine, but Andrew, a classmate, was using a scanner, color printer, and laminator to make counterfeits. He gave me one that I hung on the rearview mirror. It worked until the warming days caused it to curl. A security guard, whom I had gotten to know, approached me and asked if I knew about anything inappropriate. I eventually confessed to the violation and started parking down the street.

I didn't have a girlfriend, but I was spending study hall with a girl I was growing fond of. Many well-to-do black men seemed to date white women as if to say they had "made it." Black women, as a result, were missing out and my mom repeatedly expressed her desire that my brother and I date someone of color. I had made several attempts, but really liked Rachel. We hung out a few times that summer, and our group of friends often got together on the weekends. I was unsure about how to proceed, but did my best to remain close.

With the start of senior year came football and more racial tension. Upon going to an opponent's school, a couple of black kids were walking in front of our student section. A classmate jumped the railing, got in their faces, sagged his pants, turned his hat sideways and did his best impression a "homeboy" dance. The black kids walked away, and my classmate left the area. It was fortunate for him because the black students returned to confront him with a mass of people.

I had been neglecting my studies in favor of basketball and realized as much when sitting next to my class's co-valedictorian. Report cards were handed out, and I reviewed my grades that had improved from Cs to Bs.

I glanced over at my neighbor to see straight As and naively said, "Whoa, are you going to Harvard?"

He replied, "Maybe, but you're obviously not."

With a preseason basketball rank of number one in

the state, college was a concern, but my priority was winning a state championship. Early into our season, we prepared for what was sure to be our greatest test, playing against a nationally ranked team from Kentucky. I came off the bench to score a handful of points and guard their seven-footer. We wound up winning, and a picture of me getting fouled on a shot attempt was in the paper the next day.

The win propelled us to a national ranking, but my role diminished as the season carried on. My parents suspected that race was a factor, but I believed our head coach was simply developing younger players. Besides, my focus was winning.

My prayer life to that point consisted of before I ate, and I decided to give it a shot during my pregame stretch. My groin was never tight, but while sitting with my feet together, I bowed my head and prayed for a win. If we were to lose, I asked that it be for a greater cause.

Our next big test was against Minneapolis North. They came to our gym, and during warmups, a loose ball bounced in with their parents. I went to collect it, and one of them said, "You know you should be a Polar [Bear]," the name of their mascot. What most of the people in the gym didn't know was that my dad led North to their first playoff berth two decades prior. With our complete rosters, we had never beat them, but that night we went to 8–0.

Next on our schedule was Armstrong, a team that never really gave us any trouble. They came to our house and beat us. I figured it to be a fluke and kept praying. Our rivals, Hopkins, visited our gym days later and gave us another loss. Reeling, I considered abandoning my prayer, but thought about the "greater cause" and put my faith in the process.

We got back to our winning ways, and more importantly, I got the news that I was hoping for. My life plans to that point ended with a state championship, and I had just walked into the house after practice when my parents welcomed me with applause. I had considered applying to a small school in the area and the local university, but had my sights set on the historically black Morehouse College. My brother was preparing to graduate from there, and I submitted paperwork that he guided for early admission. I knew by my parents' reaction that I had been accepted.

Our basketball team streaked into the conference finals, where we had lost twice in the past three years. Considering our team camaraderie and number-one ranking, losing in my junior year was especially bitter. In order for our season to continue, we would have to win a rubber match against Armstrong in Hopkins's gym. Our team clapped in rhythm as we walked from the locker room to the court. I was surprised to see two of the previous year's teammates in our path and offering support. Knowing how much they wanted us to win, I said, "This is for you."

We won the game to advance to the state tournament, where the coaches asked me to read the sportsmanship pledge. As a persistent mumbler, I was a bit apprehensive, but walked to mid-court. There, I was handed a mic and felt comforted by knowing that my voice was barely audible over our cheering fans.

We squeaked out a win to face Minneapolis North in the semifinals. It was a close game with its fate decided in the final seconds as our six-foot-six, three-hundred-plus-pound all-state center was brought crashing to the floor by an opponent. The flagrant foul awarded us free throws and possession of the ball, which sealed our victory.

Shane, our star player, had struggled in the tournament, but he carried us to a nice lead in the championship. I hadn't played any meaningful minutes in what felt like a month, and with about seven seconds left, I joined Tom Erickson and three other seniors to finish the game. The state tournament would be changing venues in the coming year, so we were the last winning group on that floor.

Minnetonka High School announced its annual awards night for students. I was invited, but never entirely learned why. There were three players on our team who had earned all-state honors, so I tuned out when the presenter began talking about basketball. About halfway through his speech, something clicked and I realized that he was talking about me. In addition to my team naming me Mr. Hustle, I was awarded the US Army/Navy Reserve Athlete and Scholar of the Year.

CHAPTER 2

OFF TO COLLEGE

In the spring of my senior year, I traveled to Atlanta for Morehouse's pre-student seminar, or PSS. I had been to campus each of the previous four years visiting my brother, but I was still apprehensive about the environment. The neighborhood had a bad reputation and was filled with more people who looked like me than I had ever been around. PSS gave prospective students the opportunity to acclimate, but a poor decision nearly got me kicked out.

Our hosts had arranged activities and icebreakers, but I didn't want to do or say the wrong thing, so I kept mostly to myself. By the time PSS came to a close, I had identified two other students with a disposition like me, and we became fast friends. One was from Philadelphia and chose Morehouse over the school where my high school co-valedictorian had enrolled.

The other, Johnny, lived in California and grew up in an area with demographics similar to mine. We continued to find things in common, like his mom was also an English teacher, his basketball team had comparable success, and we both needed a roommate.

As PSS was ending, the organizers threw a party for attendees. My brother was invited to another gathering on the same night. Thinking I had solidified the start to my college experience, I decided to join him, without telling a chaperone. I knew something was wrong when I later attempted to rejoin the seminar.

There was more organization than I expected and word of a head count caused me to panic. I nervously approached our event's coordinator, an ROTC instructor who wore his military uniform with pride, and said, "I think you're looking for me." He confirmed my name and then threw his arms up in exasperation. I told him that I had been with my brother, and he responded, "You don't belong at Morehouse." I returned home and waited to hear of consequences that never came.

In the meantime, I had resumed work at the law firm. I had gotten to know the partner, Larry, who was a member of my dad's Friday night poker game. Larry helped teach me how to properly answer phones, track files, and deliver documents to the court.

With the summer coming to a close, I was determined to fit in at college. I wasn't sure what people would be wearing and bought clothes that I really didn't like just so that I wouldn't stand out. A friend later told me that a shirt I was wearing "hurt" his eyes.

Morehouse, an all-male institution, was one of six historically black colleges or universities making up the Atlanta University Center. The other five schools co-located in southwest Atlanta were the all-female Spelman, coed Clark Atlanta, Morris Brown, the Interdenominational Theological Center, and Morehouse's School of Medicine.

Morehouse's dorm rooms were rectangular with cinder-block walls and closets on either side that doubled as overhead storage. They were connected to twin beds, followed by adjoining desks that butted up against the exterior wall. The air-conditioning unit came courtesy of the 1996 Olympics, when the school converted the dorms into athletic residences.

My roommate, Johnny, supplied a TV, and I brought a cordless phone, which had to be disconnected for us to dial into the Internet. The resident assistants, who both happened to be pastors, were the only ones on the floor who were allowed microwaves. My friend, whose eyes I had hurt, was a fellow Jack and Jill'er from Minnesota and happened to live next door. The only real inconvenience we had was the plumbing. It was connected to the cafeteria, and if dishes were being washed, we'd only have cold water.

There were two infamously long lines at Morehouse, the ones for financial aid and registration. To sign up for classes, students went to Forbes Arena, another addition from the Olympics. There, I sat long enough to fall asleep before being called to select my first four college courses. Most of the other students were selecting five, but the probationary condition of my acceptance placed a limit on my workload.

My first class was English. I took my customary seat in the back of the room and struggled. I was required to take precalculus, which I found to repeat much of what I had learned in high school. With the help of a high school teacher, who had also tutored me, I tested into advanced Spanish. The class I enjoyed the most, however, was history and was taught by a self-identified radical.

After seeing Morehouse buckle to the corporate backlash of having had Louis Farrakhan on campus, the professor of my new favorite class, History, correctly predicted that his tenure wouldn't last. He taught us about "Lucy," whose skeletal remains were found in Africa and dated back 3.2 million years, of how Napoleon ordered a twenty-one gun salute on the nose and lips of the Sphinx to destroy the most telltale signs of its race, and about how slave owners used a pear-shaped torture device that was inserted into the rectum and blossomed like a flower.

About two months into the school year, I exited my dorm and was surprised by the energetic activity on campus. It was homecoming weekend and unlike anything I had ever experienced. There were people, food, and music all over the place. Fraternities had rented tents and provided refreshments while calling chants and doing steps. Ms. Maroon and White was coronated, and there was a fashion show, numerous parties, and even a football game.

Of everything that was happening, it was my brother's return to campus that most excited me. I had a surprise for him. A floormate had a gift for drawing and sketched a large letter "D" with a "B" inside. Design in hand, my brother and I traveled to Atlanta's West End for our first tattoos.

Still adjusting to my new environment, I had no issue with spending Friday and Saturday nights in my dorm, where I played games, socialized, and studied. Johnny and I both received care packages, but I got none greater than the one sent by my Aunt Betty. It was busting at the seams with canned and packaged goods. She lived in Chicago, married into our family through my mom's half brother, Clifton, and had an arrangement with all of her nieces and nephews. Upon receipt of a letter, she'd send a care package. In a nearby suburb, I had the opportunity to get home-cooked meals on Sundays at my cousin's house. With all of the familiarly of home, I started getting comfortable and made the honor roll for the first time in my life.

At the start of my second semester, I made what proved to be a smart social, but poor academic decision. I brought with me to college my Nintendo 64. Included with the system was James Bond's *GoldenEye*, a first-person shooting game where up to four people could compete on the same screen. I quickly learned that I wasn't the game's only fan and competed against my peers for hours at a time.

Johnny, my roommate, didn't like the crowd in our room, so he often grabbed the phone and left. Our game was moved down the hall, but that didn't help my already fraying relationship with Johnny. He was jealous of my acceptance to Jack and Jill, my family's finances, and he resented his father's absenteeism.

With the lock on our room's door in need of repair, he often maneuvered it so I couldn't enter without permission.

Although Johnny and I were losing, the third floor of Mays Hall was gaining and became known as the "Third Ward." I was friendly with all of my floormates except Rawle from Brooklyn. He was about my height, wore his hair in cornrows, and had a long, gold chain that swayed as he walked. I tried to initiate conversation by making eye contact, but decided it was useless. There was a day when it was just the two of us in the hallway, and we crossed paths without uttering a word.

I was having a lot of fun, but my grades soon slipped as I started not to study, read, or attend classes regularly. My goofing off came to a head when I got food poisoning after eating takeout. The vomiting, hot flashes and cold sweats were eased by my high school friend, Rachel. We had finally started dating, and although she was attending school in Montana, her voice helped me to correct course.

Fitness classes were required for graduation, and I signed up for basketball, but I also played pickup in my free time. Members of the Third Ward were going to an outdoor court, and I went with Johnny. Included in the bunch were the Brooklyn, New York native

Rawle, and Rickey, who was born in Hope, Arkansas and spoke with a country accent. The shorter, Johnny, served as point guard. Taunts were exchanged, and we finally came to see that we were all talented.

The year was coming to a close, but rather than immediately returning to Minnesota, I opted for six weeks of classes in Mexico. With the additional credits, I would be two-thirds toward a minor in Spanish. There was a total of fourteen of us signed up to study in Oaxaca: seven from Morehouse, six from Spelman, and one from Morris Brown. In Oaxaca, we were greeted by our host families. My family, the Cruz Yescas, consisted of the father, who was an attorney and spent half his time in Mexico City; his wife, who took care of the house; two sons, who had moved out; and two daughters, who all befriended me.

Classes were taught at a language center that was also open to locals. They were accustomed to having visitors and were eager to share their culture. Men commonly greeted women with a kiss on the cheek, and I began getting friendly with another student from the area. She showed me around, taught me to salsa, and invited me into her home. The two of us began hanging out with another male student who was a year older, but much shorter than me. People began referring to her as my wife and him as our son.

She respected my distancing relationship with Rachel, but said that if we were both single in four years, we should get married.

Our class took several field trips, and when I missed the group bus to Monte Albán, I realized that I could communicate in Spanish. Survival mode had kicked in, and I pushed myself to ask for directions. Another late-arriving classmate and I arrived at the attraction shortly after our peers.

After the summer courses, we traveled to the coastal city of Puerto Escondido to unwind. Our next destination was Pinotepa Internacional, and from there we prepared to drive to a town settled by slaves. The ship they were on had crashed, which allowed them to swim to shore and settle as Afro Mexicans. After a long, bumpy ride on a dirt road, the woods gave way to a pristine area with cows, farms, and an ocean view. Two shacks were set up to serve lunch, and for $5, we were able to choose shrimp or lobster.

I returned to Minnesota for the remainder of the summer and took a higher-paying job as a drywall taper. As an hourly employee, my boss taught me the meaning of *time is money*. It was my first day on a construction site when he asked me to find a specifically sized piece of wood. When he didn't think

I was moving fast enough, he yelled at me. He later explained that my delay was coming out of his pocket.

Having my buddy Stech as a coworker made the job fun. We learned to hang drywall, trim edges, and fill holes with plaster. We advanced to working on scaffolding and used stilts to scrape plaster from ceilings. Lastly, we sanded. Jobs weren't finished until a halogen light showed nothing but smooth texture, ensuring the walls and ceilings were ready for paint.

Upon returning to school after an eventful summer, I was tasked with finding off-campus housing. I hoped to follow in my brother's footsteps and rent the room where he had stayed. Unfortunately, his former landlord no longer had space available. He suggested that we contact his friend, and my dad drove me to her nearby home.

My prospective landlord shared a four-bedroom house with her cousin and young son. She offered me the smallest room by far, and because I hadn't planned ahead, I reluctantly accepted. My new landlord made me feel a bit better by touting her pool, cable television, and relationship with a well-known basketball player.

I was happy to be back on campus and spent

time between classes in Rickey's room. To support his newborn daughter, he had joined the US Army Reserves and was living on campus as a resident assistant. The position paid for his room, and because Rickey had gotten to know the cafeteria staff, he ate for free.

My grades toward the end of my third semester weren't as good as the first, but better than my second. With the As that I earned in Mexico, I decided to pursue dual degrees in economics and Spanish. I applied to another study-abroad program in Madrid, Spain, for the fall of my junior year.

I returned, as usual to Minnesota for the holidays and was invited by another Jack and Jill'er to a New Year's Eve celebration. He was good friends with Jesse "the Body" Ventura's son, who was an aspiring director, and my Jack and Jill'er friend became a go-to actor.

Jesse Ventura, a former wrestler, was Minnesota's governor, and his son made plans to host a party. My friend and I met at the governor's mansion, where a group of us took a limo to the reserved venue. We returned to the mansion afterwards, where I later woke up in the new millennium.

Upon returning to Atlanta, I was starting to get a feel for the community and wanted to get involved. I went to the installation ceremony for the Freedom Bell at Stone Mountain, which was inspired by Dr. King's "I Have a Dream" speech. I was elected president of Morehouse's Spanish club, and used the platform to organize activities with Spelman.

Knowing I was single, a good friend of mine, Marcia, wanted to introduce me to someone she had grown up with. She was a student at the University of Texas, and the two of us quickly got to know each other. She happened to be the great niece of Jesse Owens, the famous Olympic sprinter. My friend said that she'd be passing through Austin during spring break, and I tagged along.

Marcia and I reconnected for the fourteen-hour drive back to Atlanta, and I was exhausted after dropping her off. It was early in the morning when I got home, and the garage door that normally served as my entry was shut. I was never given a key to the front door and there was no activity inside. Frustration set in as I thought about the pool, which was full of debris, the cable that had been disconnected, and that I hadn't heard anything more about my landlord's famous friend. With my hand wrapped in a T-shirt, I punched a hole in the glass near the front door, which allowed me to unlock it.

My dad paid for the damages, and I later attempted redemption when the neighbor's house caught fire.

They had come to me for help, and I noticed that their pit bulls were chained in their yard. I suggested that they be released, and the dogs crossed the street to where another was tethered. They snapped, then attacked the restrained dog. My intervention resulted in permanent bite marks in my wrist.

After school ended, I began a summer internship that had been lined up by another friend of my dad's, who was a high-level executive at a major company. They relocated me to La Crosse, Wisconsin, but I didn't have to look long or hard for a place to stay. A friend from high school, Jarvis, was enrolled at a local college and offered me a room in the house he was renting.

As a grain merchant, my job was to learn how corn and soybeans were moved around and generated income. It started with farmers, or aggregators who committed to a delivery that our facility evaluated. The load was shifted to silos while awaiting a barge to be taken by a tugboat down the Mississippi River. Ultimately, they would arrive at port for worldwide shipment.

To start my junior year, I flew seven hours across the Atlantic to Madrid. For the first two weeks, a group of almost two hundred other students and myself visited Toledo, Córdoba, Granada, and Sevilla in what seemed like a blur of cathedrals, mosques, and museums.

Our group did our fair share of hanging out, and while I saw anti-immigrant graffiti, I never thought I would be targeted. A handful of us attempted entry into an open-air bar, but I was denied for "wearing brown shoes." As I turned to walk away, a white student from the program got my attention and pointed to a patron who was dressed in similar footwear.

Fortunately, that sentiment didn't extend to the program's administrators, who had identified another student and me as proficient in Spanish. Most of our peers were to be placed with host families, one or two to a room. The other student and I were offered a three-bedroom apartment with a señora living upstairs. She was to cook us dinner and do our laundry.

Getting to school required a short walk to the train, a straight shot to our stop, and another walk to school. While en route one day, I had just exited the metro station and was walking downhill toward school when I felt something hit the back of my head. I thought that it might be a rain drop, or worse, bird droppings, but reached to feel that my hair was dry. There was no one around me, and in the same moment, I heard sirens. An ambulance then crossed the street from right to left bearing the word *angel*. I took it as a sign of a higher calling, but kept it to myself as I continued my day.

I was between classes when a yellow shirt caught my attention, and I looked to make eye contact with the exotic, five-foot-eight, long-haired, voluptuous-figured woman wearing it. She introduced herself as Mariah, a student at the Ivy League Brown University. She said that she had passed multiple times and was wondering when I was going to notice.

I had always wanted a wife, but I came to see relationships as more drama than they're worth. As a Dominican, she was raised as bilingual, but had also learned French. Mariah played the piano and flute, was considering a triple major, and her well-to-do family owned the first company to wire funds from New York to Central and South America.

We started hanging out with a group of people and found ourselves waiting outside of a nightclub. The metro had stopped running at 2 a.m. Options for getting home included hailing a cab or waiting until six when the train started running again. It was starting to get cold, as she pressed her body into me. In that moment, Mariah convinced me to give a relationship with her a chance.

The classes I elected were phenomenal and included the topics of literature and cinema. In History of the Women in Spain, I learned about a group called the *Taliban* and their oppressive practices. Women were forbidden to drive and were subject to bone-breaking discipline for showing too much skin. My favorite class, though, was Economics of the European Union. The professor taught us about the EU's strict rules for entry and local businesses.

On my way back to my apartment, I stopped in a local market. It displayed produce and parts of animals that I had no desire to eat. A Bahamian woman in our group was excited to see cherimoyas. The green-skinned, white-pulped, large-seeded fruit was unlike any I had ever tried, and I quickly fell in love with their taste.

The highlights of being abroad came with trips during three-day weekends. For my first, I joined classmates going to the island of Mallorca. A couple from the Atlanta University Center wanted to visit Morocco, and we took a train to Algeciras then ferried across the Strait of Gibraltar. Once docked in Tangier, we met a guide, who walked us through the market. I was on the hunt for a shot glass to add to my collection, and he led me to a man willing to sell a teacup of similar size.

For my first trip with Mariah, we traveled to Paris. There, we encountered more trouble than we expected. We paid too much for a taxi, were booted from a restaurant for sitting next to each other, and were fined $80 for not keeping our metro receipt. Seeing the Eiffel Tower with its strobes flashing in the night, however, made the trip worthwhile.

My family planned to spend Thanksgiving with me in Europe, and my brother arrived a week early. He, Mariah, and I took a train to Barcelona, where we rode a double-decker bus around the city. I was excited to see La Sagrada Família, designed by Antoni Gaudí. The layout was in the shape of a cross. There were four bell towers on each side and four more at the bottom. Each one of the twelve represented an apostle. Gaudí planned four taller towers in the center as the four evangelists, with a fifth for the Virgin Mary. The middle, and tallest tower yet, symbolizes Jesus Christ.

My parents and paternal grandmother then arrived, and I brought them to stay at Madrid's Puerta del Sol. From there, they were able to explore before we later flew to Rome. My mom, brother, and I really enjoyed the food and wound up eating from three different restaurants in one night.

After my family left, the semester was drawing to a close when I was with Mariah in my apartment. Out of nowhere, she started yelling at me. The energy from her aggression welled up inside me until I released it by snatching a water bottle off of the table. I had always been relatively easygoing, but my reaction revealed to me something I didn't know I had, a temper.

Any apprehension I was feeling about my new relationship was not put to ease when the two of us met my friends in Atlanta. Mariah had developed a relationship with my former roommate, Johnny, and they got along, but she showed no tolerance for Rickey. Rawle had dealt with similar personalities, so he wasn't bothered, but overall the meeting was very uncomfortable.

I didn't want another roommate, so with my $1,000 monthly allowance, I followed Johnny's lead. He had moved to a community with affordable one-bedroom apartments, and I chose a unit downstairs from his. It was nice being close to him while still having separation. His actions after knocking on my door, however, started becoming a problem. He was typically waiting with a phone pressed to his ear; then he would walk directly to my refrigerator for something to eat.

Continuing my relationship with Mariah was

dependent on a low-cost airline. For $39, young adults could fly standby, and I often traveled to Providence for long weekends. With a larger, greener, and better-kept campus, Brown University gave me insight into unfamiliar wealth. I was accustomed to seeing chicken and hot dogs being grilled, but in front of their frat houses, students were preparing lobster.

At the close of my junior year, I continued my internship with a placement near my parents' house. Instead of waterways, my new grain facility used rail for transportation. I was given the responsibilities of creating bids, handling orders, and completing miscellaneous tasks. The work was fun, and I began staying late to get ahead. At the conclusion of the summer, my supervisor said that I was the best intern he ever had and wanted to know if I would come to work full time. I didn't see myself with a career in agriculture, so I declined.

Before returning to college, I met with the assistant coach of my high school basketball team. He filled me in on our star player, Shane, who had been kicked off his college team and had since encountered trouble with the law. The signs that Shane could be going down a bad path had been present for some time. I knew that his behavior could have been altered by restricting what he cared about the most, but the head coach, Hedstrom, prioritized winning.

My assistant coach went on to say that there were several occasions when he suggested that I get more playing time. His boss ignored him. After Hedstrom and my dad argued over my lack of mid-season development, they ceased to speak, and my assistant coach had a suspicion as to why. The black dad of another talented player who transferred in a year later was treated similarly. My mom referred to my work as tilling the field, and my assistant coach confirmed that Hedstrom was, in fact, prejudiced.

I spent the first month of my senior year as I did the end of my junior, traveling back and forth from Atlanta to see Mariah. She had a car accident over the summer that made it difficult for her to drive. When a craving struck, I drove her family's Pathfinder to get bagels. While waiting in a parking lot, another car shifted into reverse and crunched our bumpers.

Her family appeared fond of me, but I was intimidated by her dad and not eager to tell him about the accident. With a road trip planned to her home in Teaneck, New Jersey, I waited to explain in person.

With his loud, deep voice, he asked for confirmation. "She, reversed into me," I repeated. He later told me that the other driver gave her insurance company a different story. He went on to explain that a friend was able to fix his car for less than his settlement. He had a big smile on his face, and I understood that my ordeal had made him money.

Mariah's mom treated me like one of her own and took me along when she traveled to her old neighborhood of Washington Heights. On our return, she began telling me additional details of their family business. Dealing with cash, they brought large deposits to the bank, but they had to take precautions along the way. They privately filled shoeboxes with their earnings, and security both led and trailed as Mariah's mom walked. If stopped by a friend, she was able to conveniently demonstrate shoes located at the top.

I was just settling into my senior year and sitting in my labor economics class on a Tuesday morning. I had heard about a disturbance in New York on my way to school, and a classmate turned around after looking at his two-way pager to say, "A second plane just hit the World Trade Center." Commotion quickly spread around campus and classes were cancelled. Not quite knowing what was happening, I stopped to talk with professors. They didn't seem to know anything more than I did. I decided to go home, where I sat to watch news for the first time.

Cell phone traffic caused the networks to go down, but I was able to reach a panicked Mariah by landline. Her mom was scheduled for a meeting that morning in one of the two towers. After a day of worry, she arrived home that night. Her meeting had been delayed, and with roads closed, she had to walk home.

The Georgia World Congress Center was scheduled to have its annual career fair a month later. I spent much of my first semester in the career-placement offices, hoping for leads. It was a contrast from the online searches that Brown provided, which gave me an idea. I approached Morehouse's webmaster and asked if they'd be willing to publish the interview schedule if I collected it. Not only did they agree, but they paid me for my service.

Mariah came to one of my intramural basketball games a few weeks later. I wasn't necessarily playing well when Rawle checked in. At first opportunity he came directly toward me, saying, "Yo, B! Watch your girl." I looked up in the stands to see a guy talking to Mariah. Distracted, I later missed a rebound that caused my left eye to slam into the back of Rickey's skull. With blood dripping, I walked off the court as she joined me to get a handful of stitches.

The second semester arrived quickly, and while my job prospects hadn't improved, I began to feel relief from my hard work. I needed 120 credit hours to graduate, and a heavy workload left me just nine credits away. Mariah had promised to help me with a thesis to complete my Spanish major, but our relationship had turned toxic.

Prior to meeting her, I had lost self-control just once. It occurred while playing in a fall league basketball game when I tried to pin an opponent's shot to the backboard. I missed, which caused my hand to slap the glass. The referee called me for a technical foul, which surprised me. "That's bullshit!" I said. He gave me another technical foul, which should have disqualified me, but he was going to let me finish the game. I, however, needed to make a point. With two technical fouls, I argued, I should be ejected. The referee agreed and allowed me to sit.

Mariah and I were fighting more than we were getting along, and things came to a head in my apartment. She was needling me over something, and I just wanted her to stop. I got up and went to lay facedown on my bed. Frustration boiled over, and I sent my palm through the wall. I used the skills I learned as a taper to fix the drywall, but Mariah and I were finished.

As graduation approached, I realized that as my comfort level increased, I had moved from the back of the classroom to the front. In turn, I was getting better grades and began receiving recognition I didn't know I was eligible for. I earned the E. B. Williams Award for exceptional student performance, was named an outstanding senior economics major, and was inducted to the Omicron Delta Epsilon Economics and Sigma Delta Pi Spanish Honor Societies. I graduated with a 3.6 grade point average in economics and 3.8 in Spanish, finishing fifth and second in my class respectively. My thesis earned me honors in Spanish, and they came in economics, as well.

The accolades, though, didn't help my job prospects. As graduation came to a close, I only had three job offers. The first was from Mariah's mom, who was trying to resurrect her family business, which had come under pressure from MoneyGram and Western Union. The second was selling career fair space in a down economy. Last, and what seemed to be most promising, was a company named Primerica. In order for me to get started, I would have to provide a list of personal contacts and pay a fee for training. I told my dad about the meeting, and he angrily said that he had just spent $100,000 on my education, and it shouldn't cost him anymore.

Most seniors were enrolling in graduate school. I knew of just five who had found work. Operating on a hunch, I stopped by campus and saw the ROTC chaperone from PSS. For my first time since enrolling as a freshman, I didn't avoid him. The reason for my visit to campus was to see a professor who had taught my brother. He was well connected with companies and said MetLife was looking for a couple of graduates.

CHAPTER 3

A SMALL MARKET

I got contact information for a sales manager working in MetLife's Atlanta office and reached out. I didn't immediately hear back, and my parents then gave me the choice of moving back home or to Chicago with my brother. The sales manager then responded, and we scheduled an interview at his office, where the first thing I noticed was a framed scorecard. I looked closer to see a hole in one, which he said wasn't indicative of his golf game.

He explained that his job consisted of driving around Georgia and Alabama, making friends, and discussing college football. He was well-paid and said that new hires had to earn at least $100,000 by the end of their first three years or they'd face termination. If brought on board, I would be enrolled in MetLife's million-dollar training program, paid a base salary of

$35,000, and receive reimbursement for relocation in addition to an expense account.

The next step was to be interviewed by a regional vice president in MetLife's latest attempt at breaking into the market for groups having fewer than five hundred employees. The company had tried several times before, but it was only successful in targeting corporations with more than one thousand workers. The regional vice president's assistant arranged my flight to Houston, where we met in an airport lounge before his business trip.

My interviewer told me that hiring for the season had finished, but he was impressed by the diversity of my résumé. He was Caucasian, had married an African American woman, and had taken on her children as his own. I was already intrigued by what MetLife was presenting, and the mention of his alma mater amazed me. He had graduated from Luther College, the same school as my parents. He then said there wasn't currently an office for me and that I'd miss the first training, but if I promised to be successful, he'd take a chance on me.

I returned to Atlanta and started packing for my relocation to Dallas. While in the midst of getting my things together, I crossed paths with my former roommate, Johnny. It was time to discuss our strained relationship. At the top of my list was why he had suggested to Mariah that she break up with me. He had insinuated that my newfound freedom would help his social life. I said his actions were more selfish than friendly, and he nodded his head in agreement.

My mom came to help me move, and before leaving town, she requested that we explore the National Black Arts Festival. There, she bought me my first painting, a teary-eyed black boy restrained by a chain-link fence titled, "Forbidden Innocence."

Days later, we were on the road to Texas, when it dawned on my mom that we would be passing by our family farm in Mississippi. Her mother had grown up there, and my mom wanted to stop by. As we approached Yazoo City, however, the sunny skies turned dark, and rain began to pour. We were forced to press onward.

Upon arriving in Plano, a suburb of Dallas, the managers introduced me to the staff and I began learning the difference between sales and underwriting. Most everyone was nice, and some began taking me under their wings. One rep gave me financial tips, another introduced me to his wife, a third made it a point to see me socially.

My first training took place in Kansas City, where I bumped into another Morehouse alumnus. Aside from us, there were just two other African Americans in our hiring class, which brought the total number of our group to twenty-one. We took a bus the next morning to the local headquarters, where conversation revolved around "STD and LTD." I had no idea what my coworkers were talking about and found it best to be quiet.

We were served a buffet-style breakfast and got ready to listen to presenters. The goal of the training was to establish a base of understanding for short- and long-term disability insurance. During breaks, we were served selections of snacks that never seemed to repeat. At the end of the day, we were taken for a group dinner with an open tab at the bar.

A couple of days into training, I glanced across the room to see Tony, another African American hire. He was keeping himself entertained by making a series of funny faces. He caught me looking at him, and we both laughed. It was an icebreaker and moment of levity to begin a journey that we understood might be especially difficult for us four African Americans.

Upon returning to our local offices, our training class kept in contact by conference calls and applied our learning in role plays. We were scheduled to meet three weeks later in Tampa, but Tony, the fourth black rep, and I flew in early. The upcoming training was for dental insurance, and with Tony's notes, I was able to catch up on my missed life-insurance classes. I was finally starting to understand my job, which consisted of marketing MetLife's four core products to brokers that had companies as clients.

While in Dallas, an African American pre-sale underwriter warned me to keep my eyes open. Despite her knowledge of the product and people skills, she had been passed over multiple times for the lucrative role as a sales rep.

Prior to our final training, the regional vice president told me of three cities that needed a rep, and gave me the scenarios. I could choose Los Angeles or Houston, but he recommended Cleveland, where a rep was said to be on her way out. Her departure would leave a semi-developed territory.

The last training was in White Plains, New York, where I received insight as to why I was hired. When MetLife failed to secure Coca-Cola's business, the feedback was that MetLife lacked diversity. The result was MetLife's largest single hire of corporate minority reps in the company's history. It brought the national total to eight. We represented just 3 percent of the sales force.

I flew to Pittsburgh in October, where I interviewed with the sales manager, Stan, and his boss. I instantly connected with the two as Stan was a former athlete and, his boss, like my ex-girlfriend Mariah, had gone to an Ivy League school. Before leaving, Stan, who managed northeast Ohio, western Pennsylvania, and West Virginia, took me on a tour of the city. He offered me the position, with the caveat that I had to be moved in by Halloween. His boss, a regional vice president, wanted me in place and ready to work.

On the morning of Friday, October 25, I started my drive north and later approached Cincinnati, where I had planned to spend the night. For fifteen hours I had been on the road, but I was still energized. Two hours later, I was in Columbus and decided to complete the nineteen-hour trek. I found a hotel at my exit and checked in before waking up to cross the highway and sign a lease for my new apartment.

I was curious to see the surroundings and quickly moved in before taking a drive. It was my first time in northeast Ohio, and my familiarity was limited to the area's hometown rap group, Bone Thugs-N-Harmony. I sought action downtown, but was disappointed. It was a Saturday afternoon and the city was like a ghost town.

A senior sales rep with management aspirations, invited me to her family's dinner that Sunday night. I showed up at the office the following day and was pleased to meet Jim, Joe, Lori, Tracey, and the departing rep.

With no more than fifteen workstations, our office covered benefits for companies having up to twenty-five thousand employees, school district sales and administration, e-commerce, employee paid benefits, 401(k), and individual disability.

An underwriter helped me to see who got along and who didn't. Lori was the outsider. She flirtatiously cozied up to me, and I tried to return the favor. She was late for a weekly call and had previously asked us to tell Stan that she was in the restroom. When the line connected, I blurted out, "Lori's in the bathroom." There was silence before Stan said that Lori had called to say that she wouldn't be in the meeting. He later pulled me aside and said that he hoped that we could build a relationship based on trust.

We were required to physically attend meetings once a month. The 7 a.m. start had us awake three hours prior, and we weren't dismissed until 4 p.m. It already made for a long day, but those Monday nights offered the best pickup basketball.

I was starting to settle into my new environment, but was also tasked with getting licensed to sell insurance and securities. I put in what I thought was the necessary work, but was shocked to fall short of earning my life and health license by two questions. After studying a bit harder, I returned for redemption and then prepared to become a registered representative. Classes for the Series 6 and 63 financial certifications were offered, and I used mock exams for practice.

The computerized test presented a survey before the exam, which asked my race and gender. Hours later, I submitted my work to the proctor, who accessed and provided my failing score. I returned home to change my study tactic. Instead of memorizing answers, I learned why they were correct. When my next exam asked for my race and gender, I entered "White Male," which I suspected might generate easier questions or a more forgiving score. Either way, I earned my licenses.

As Thanksgiving approached, Stan told me that the transitioning rep was leaving and I'd be getting her territory. I became responsible for all brokers in a 3,500-square-mile territory that ranged from Akron to Dover's Amish country. I was also assigned an agency in downtown Cleveland. It was owned by Arnold Pinkney, who ran Jesse Jackson's campaign for president in 1984.

Stan helped me transition by riding along for meet and greets, but my first solo appointment was with a broker named Bob. He candidly said that he couldn't offer me much business, but we got along well. His good friend was a minority owner of the Cleveland Cavaliers and got us a meeting at their arena. The vice president of human resources wasn't in a position to change their insurance, but offered me tickets whenever I wanted them.

It was with Bob that I closed my first deal, and it led to a major decision. As a trainee, I was guaranteed income designed to carry me until I began generating sales. With business in the pipeline, I elected to go on "draw." MetLife continued providing regular paychecks, but bonuses came when sales exceeded my pay. Falling short, however, would put me into a deficit.

The rep who had me over for dinner, desired a warmer climate and was promoted to be an associate manager in Houston. I hoped to inherit her office, but Stan reserved it for a new hire with more experience. The rep came on board in time for my first national sales conference. The entire team traveled to Florida's South Beach. We were supposed to use the time networking and sharing best practices, but coinciding with MTV's spring break made it a party.

I was invited to a get-together that summer in Cleveland that helped me understand how small the city could be. While there, I exchanged numbers with a great niece of Rosa Parks. Her ex called shortly thereafter to ask about the "new guy from Morehouse."

As I was beginning to question Cleveland's social scene, the city began to buzz in anticipation of the NBA's draft lottery. Then, on May 22, the Cavaliers were awarded the number-one pick, which meant that LeBron James would be staying put. I called my contact at the arena for tickets, but she couldn't even get them for herself.

As 2003 was coming to a close, I was within reach of my sales goal, which meant validation and a bonus. I scoured my opportunities and came to one that would put me over the top. The group wanted to begin on January 1, but working through the broker, we offered additional savings for them to start on December 31. The next call I remember came from Stan, who opened the conversation by congratulating me on making the leader's list. In addition to the nearly $20,000 bonus I would get for reaching my goal, I would also be traveling with other top performers to Phoenix, Arizona.

Two thousand three was a good year, but 2004 arrived with a larger sales goal. To make insurance plans easier, most businesses renew their group insurance on January 1. With the energy I had exerted to reach my goal, I had neglected the industry's busiest date and was behind to start my second year in the business.

The newest rep my manager had hired took another offer, and Stan again declined to give me the vacant office. I took the snub as motivation to develop *milk runs*. The designated routes ensured that I could see everyone in an area. I had one for Akron, Canton, and the southern suburbs of Cleveland that stretched into downtown.

I packed my bags to join the other leaders in Phoenix, which was a conference similar to the one in South Beach. The primary difference was that awardees were allowed to bring their significant others. Meetings were scheduled and attendees were given a list of activities from which to choose. Only one appealed to me, and I spent an afternoon riding in a hot air balloon.

Our group came together for organized meals and Maria Morris, head of MetLife's group and individual disability businesses, took a seat at my table. I explained to her how multiple lines of distribution based in the Cleveland office provided a ripe environment for selling across platforms.

MetLife provided denim shirts for us to wear during our final night, which complimented a cowboy-themed meal. Horse-driven carts picked us up from our hotel, and I rode with a group of people, including the rep who had introduced me to his wife in Texas, and the president of US insurance and financial services, Rob Henrickson.

The rep from Texas was catching me up on his Nissan when another attendee took interest. He asked me what my dream car was, and I paused before responding, "A Mercedes Benz SL 500." With my peripheral vision, I noticed that future CEO Henrickson was visibly uncomfortable. I determined his fidgeting had to do with my response and/or presence.

Prejudice at the company's highest levels apparently didn't extend to Maria, who subsequently launched an initiative requiring reps to partner across divisions.

When I returned to Cleveland, I knew it was time to get serious about my career and extended my office hours. I sat in my cubicle until early evening, where I memorized every promotional flyer that I had available. The stress was palpable as I could feel my hairline beginning to recede. The change marked my transformation from a layman into a professional.

My newfound confidence and ability brought more sales and the ability to replace my often-breaking-down

SUV. I bought a used Lexus GS300 as Lori, who continuously lobbied for additional territory, was saddled with a large sales goal and was struggling to keep pace. She may have seen it coming, but she was still surprised when Stan fired her. The turmoil continued as Stan was demoted and my regional vice president stepped in as the interim sales manager.

Around that same time, my brother became disgruntled with his most recent promotion. He was living in Philadelphia, but was eager to get back to Chicago. We started talking about my experience at MetLife, and he was interested in coming aboard. I passed his résumé to the area manager, who scheduled an interview. When my brother told me that he was offered downtown Chicago as his territory, I was a bit jealous.

I was complaining about my inability to find a good girl in Cleveland when, Lynette, a woman who was helping me learn the city, took offense. She then organized an icebreaker at her downtown loft. I walked into a room full of people and she introduced me to several attendees, including a pleasant young lady. As our conversation progressed, I noticed another young woman in the corner who appeared to be frustrated. Lynette pulled me aside to say that was Leslie, the woman I had been invited to meet. I went over to talk with her and asked if she wanted to take a walk. We strolled past bars and lounges before returning to the get-together. With the Fourth of July approaching, Leslie invited me to her family's house for the holiday.

It seemed a bit forward, but I knew her intentions were good and accepted the invitation. I drove to her neighborhood two days later, where I met her dad, mom, grandparents, uncle, and two sisters. After we ate, Leslie and I prepared to leave to see a fireworks show, but were stopped by her dad, who suggested taking Leslie's baby sister along. Leslie's youngest sister seemed put off, but she joined us nonetheless. Meeting so much of her family on our first date felt like a bit much, but we continued to see each other as she prepared for her senior year in college.

I was working in my cubicle when my former coworker, Lori, surprised me with a phone call. She hadn't been nearly as kind since the reps she wasn't getting along with were replaced, so I knew she had an agenda. As I refrained from engaging, her voice began to tremble. She confessed that she needed witnesses for a lawsuit alleging religious discrimination and asked that I support her claim. I recommended that she contact someone who wasn't employed by MetLife.

My regional vice president then hired Stan's replacement, who became my fourth direct supervisor in three years. About the same time, the rep who was in the office I coveted submitted his resignation. At first opportunity, I requested the space, which my new manager granted. He also hired a former employee to help cover the market.

Having had transitional supervision, I made a habit of figuring things out myself, which landed me in trouble. Bil-Jac, a pet food company, was shopping for disability insurance and asked if MetLife would cover payroll tax on a disabled employee. My affirmative response gave me the sale, but MetLife refused to honor what I had promised. To make the situation right, I offered to personally pay the tax. The disability came to an end, but not before my manager heard what I had done. Fearing it could have been mistaken for a kickback, he placed a negative note in my file.

With 2004 coming to a close, I got anxious to lay roots and get a tax deduction, so I started house hunting. My parents had pledged $50,000 toward my down payment, but they had recently moved and needed the cash. They instead promised to pay the balance on a second mortgage, so I started looking in suburbs with better access to my territory. A realtor showed me a place under construction, and I made an offer that was accepted. My mom and her sister Sharon, my favorite aunt, flew in to help me choose furnishings. I took business calls as they sat with the builder, and they then joked with me about how they were spending my money.

I exceeded my numbers two years in a row, but I started 2005 even farther behind and needed a way to catch up. MetLife was shifting its focus to employee-paid benefits, so I started pitching supplemental life and short-term disability insurance. If I did a good job, brokers would invite me into their groups, where I could explain the advantage of having additional coverage. To avoid adverse selection, underwriting required that the greater of ten employees or 25 percent of the population enroll, so I began to hone my pitch.

After 9/11, the powers at MetLife got together to discuss contracts and determined they weren't liable to pay. By doing what they thought was right, however, they waived the clause excluding terrorism and honored the claims. More impressive was the strength of their business, which allowed them to recoup the paid claims in a quarter.

Leslie occasionally sat with me to stuff marketing envelopes. The materials helped me successfully achieve participation in both one-on-one and group presentations. None challenged me more though than meeting with young adults at a water park. I arrived in a suit and tie and successfully pitched employees at their workstations.

I knew that my life and career were becoming one when I arrived for a long overdue dentist's appointment. On my last visit, I was told that I needed eleven fillings, but I couldn't see the cavities on the X-rays. My new doctor said that I only needed a few, but he began to complain when he learned that I worked for MetLife.

As a participating dentist, he agreed to discount services, but he argued that other carriers were more generous. I knew from my training that low reimbursements kept prices competitive, but with a large MetLife clientele, he felt cheated. I attempted to explain that his volume led to stability, which fell on deaf ears. The topic returned to my fillings, which he suggested that I do without Novocaine. He assured me that they weren't deep, and I got the feeling he was enjoying the pain he was putting me in until I could take no more.

I reserved Monday afternoons through the close of business Thursday in my territory, which helped me get a feel for it. I occasionally took my brokers to lunch, but I also used downtime to explore. I discovered a winery that had a variety of wines, homemade cheese, and peppered bacon. On any given day, I would drive anywhere from fifty to 150 miles. To that point, my Lexus had been a magnet for traffic stops, but my encounters with police started to slow. For every ticket that I dodged, I looked up toward heaven and said, "Thank you."

Most of my competition seemed to be spending their time calling on big agencies, but I was making my living with the smaller ones. While driving east in a suburb of Akron, I saw a strip mall with office space and an insurance sign above it. I pulled in to meet a middle-aged guy who was smoking a cigarette. I asked if they sold group insurance, and Scott said, "I do."

Another agency had an impressive building, but I wasn't having any luck inside. Another assistant, whom I had gotten to know, claimed to be good friends with one of their agents. She introduced me to an attractive older lady who had a lot of small business.

Outside of work, I spent a good amount of time around Leslie's family, who I came to understand was well connected. Her mom was a teacher and her dad partnered at an international law firm. They introduced me to the late congresswoman Stephanie Tubbs Jones, and when a plant owned by BP exploded in Texas, Leslie's dad handled the litigation.

My life appeared to be heading in the right

direction, but I felt something was missing. While driving Leslie to a party, I was in a funk that caused me to pull over. Unable to control my emotions, I started to cry. Leslie tried to console me, but to no avail. I eventually realized that I missed my friends.

The two of us were later going out for the night when I was feeling indifferent about her presence. I was driving through a residential neighborhood when a car ran a stop sign. It slammed into my doors, knocked us off the street, and my first instinct was to be sure that she was okay. The event caused me to realize that I still cared.

My insurance company gave me the option to repair my car, but its damaged frame was a safety concern. I shopped around for a highly reliable, luxury sedan and narrowed my focus to Acura's TL. A broker of mine knew the lot's owner and negotiated on my behalf for a great price.

My brother's assignment of downtown Chicago was too good to be true. His opportunity consisted of brokers not already doing business with MetLife. He had left a job paying six figures for door-to-door sales. He confided with the underwriting manager that he was also dealing with depression. What he thought was a private comment eventually became office chatter. It created an environment where he couldn't stay.

I was seeing and speaking with the fourth black rep from my hiring class on a regular basis. He came to visit, and I was content hanging out one-on-one, but Leslie wanted to spend time together. To make the accommodation, she asked her childhood friend, Cheryl, to join us. She had a boyfriend, but the rep's flash of money at dinner inspired her to order a drink called "Gold Digger."

With tickets to a Cav's game, I sat watching the action on the court while Leslie was preoccupied with the rapidly forming couple. That night, Leslie told me about Cheryl's plans for his money. I thought I would be a good friend and called to relay the comments. I was near exhaustion with warning when he responded, "I kinda like that."

Since my car accident, I had been seeing a chiropractor for whiplash and was having episodic pain in my back. Relief came with treatment, but a doctor's visit to address my discomfort seemed impractical. When I was next experiencing symptoms, I drove to a furniture store and reclined in a massage chair. It helped. With a doctor's note, I convinced my insurer to include the $2,000 piece of furniture, along with an ergonomic chair in my settlement.

Then came news that I feared, but didn't expect. Rickey had received his orders and would be deploying to Iraq. Dealing with shock, Rawle and I began making plans to see our friend off. I flew to Atlanta, and we went shopping for what we thought Rickey might enjoy. I suggested getting tattoos, of which Rawle already had several. Rickey didn't have any, and after some convincing, we rolled up our sleeves for *Never Alone*.

When the drinking and clubbing had concluded, we were at Rawle's sister's house when reality hit. Ricky was using the computer in the den, and Rawle and I found ourselves at her dining room table. We broke down. Rawle had previously verbalized what we feared, "Rickey might die and shit."

My sales year was coming to a close, and I knew that if I really pushed I might be able to make my numbers, but I didn't have the energy or desire to try. I flew to Minnesota for Thanksgiving and Christmas, but was in Cleveland for New Year's Eve. There, Cheryl and her new boyfriend were among a group organized for dinner.

I rolled the business that I normally forced at the end of the year to go effective in January and started 2006 in great shape. Separate bank accounts that came as a recommendation from a rep in Texas served me well, and on my brother's urging I maxed out my 401(k) contribution. I had also learned a trick of my own. Using an Excel spreadsheet, I began keeping track of my monthly expenses. I locked the document with initials to a phrase that inspired me, as I thought "this is Just The Beginning."

My personal growth wasn't reflected in my new circle of friends, whom I was told were circulating the rumor that I was gay. It apparently originated with a girl I knew from Jack and Jill, and was passed to Leslie's friend, Cheryl. She and her friends were gossiping about it during our New Year's Eve dinner.

The emotional disturbance didn't compare to what I was feeling physically. Without notice, a debilitating pain began shooting to the center of my brain. CAT scan results were inconclusive, and fearing that an aneurysm was coming, I decided to purchase life insurance.

Stan, who was an overqualified rep, decided to change companies, but he pulled me aside before he did. He warned me to be careful, saying, not everyone who appears to be a friend, is. He cited Lori as an example. When under pressure, she attempted to deflect attention to me by saying that I wasn't returning to the office after sales calls. She claimed to be concerned about my work ethic. Stan knew she was lying, though, because I was calling him from my cubicle when I was trying to learn the material.

His vacancy left an opening in Pittsburgh, which shifted rep's responsibilities. Cleveland was traditionally handled by three people, but my new manager wanted to proceed with two, and nearly tripled my territory. Despite carrying a cell phone, Blackberry and laptop with Internet connection, voicemails and emails piled up.

Even with new brokers to meet, I wanted to spend time with the people who had helped me succeed. Scott was easily my best broker, and he reduced his compensation to write cases when my rates weren't competitive. On a trip to Pittsburgh, year-end numbers were presented, and his production rivaled major firms.

The attractive older lady I had met serviced a lot of groups and put all of her eligible clients with me. We would often meet for an early happy hour, then drink into the night. She was frustrated with her bosses continuously reducing her commission; so to supplement her income she developed plans to market products through a website. The contractors, though, were both slow and expensive.

I had heard that my high school friend, Andrew, was quite good at it, so I put the two in contact. They entered into a working relationship, which lasted until the company's owner called to say he was unaware of the project. In turn, he fired Andrew for stealing company resources. I saw no affect to our friendship and made multiple calls to say so. He never answered.

I was spending an increasing amount of time with a broker who started swinging big cases my way. He entertained me as much as I did him, which included bringing me to restaurants that I had never heard of. We spent time in his home, and he told me about his plans for another. He introduced me to the maître d' at Morton's Steakhouse, where we ate and drank before sitting in his seats for Cav's games.

With the addition of my new territory, I knew I had to meet new people and took a seat next to Tonya. She was employed to support a broker, and despite being surrounded by staff, I instantly felt comfortable and opened up.

Although servicing my accounts required me to spend an increasing amount of time at my desk, I was selling more business than I ever had. For my performance, I was selected to attend a sales academy with other top reps. A few other Clevelanders and I were flown to Chicago, where we met at the McDonald's Hamburger University building. During that time, we were presented with high-level concepts and plans for MetLife's future.

For the first time since 1998, the Cavaliers earned a playoff berth. I invited Scott, my broker, to the opening game. He came to my house with marijuana. It was my second time getting high, and I laughed uncontrollably as Scott drove us downtown. He dropped me off that evening with several pre-rolled joints.

I hadn't spoken to my high school friend, Rashad, in years, but my mom ran into his aunt. She said that he was living in Japan. His contact information was passed along, and I excitedly reached out. His Marine enlistment placed him in Okinawa, I promised to visit, and I arrived to meet his three-year-old son, *Brandon*. I didn't want to jump to conclusions, and Rashad put any doubt to rest when he said that he had named him after me.

It was good to see Rashad, but I fell into the trap of childish behavior. We went to a club where I met a girl, and I sent Rawle an email about how I wanted to make her more than a friend. I was plotting on how I might make that happen when I got an angry message from Leslie. She was staying in my house and I had left my inbox open. I apologized profusely and assured her that nothing had happened. When I landed in Cleveland, she picked me up, but refused to look in my direction. I knew that I was wrong and rededicated myself to our relationship.

I enjoyed the company of most people that I met through work, but was also tasked with others I didn't care for. One of the first people Stan and I had called on, proceeded to go on a tirade about everything he thought "sucked." When an internal wholesaler wanted to see brokers, I found myself back in his office and was reminded of my distaste.

The last time I was there, he insisted that he had slept with my girlfriend. Sitting there again, he recalled my home state and that the former wrestler Jesse "the Body" Ventura was governor. Thinking that I'd share, I told him that I had spent the night in the mansion. He replied, "What were you doing there, shining shoes?"

I was content not to see or deal with him again and was afforded the opportunity when my manager announced that he was leaving. The rep he brought over was underperforming, and his expenses were out of line. My regional vice president initiated an investigation, which turned up receipts from a gentleman's club. With cause, he terminated the rep as turmoil reigned in the market. Through the disruption, Jim, who worked with accounts having 1,000 to 25,000 employees, was promoted to manager. While I was unaware of it, he had been grooming me since my arrival and asked if I'd come work for him.

CHAPTER 4

THE NEXT LEVEL

Although apprehensive about my new opportunity, I no longer wanted to be in the small market. Aside from building relationships, my job was about getting to the right price. For any case that had less than one hundred employees, underwriting provided rates that were based on demographics. Using percentages, I was allowed parameters for discounting. In the middle market, the groups would be rated by their performance. The new math would give me a chance to exercise my brain.

My start date was set for September 1, but I was having a stellar sales year and hoped to hit my goal before the transition. I took to eating lunch at my desk as I sifted through my opportunities and came across a $250,000 dental case controlled by one of my best brokers. We closed the deal and celebrated at Morton's with ribeye, hash browns, and creamed spinach.

I then traveled to Minnesota, where my dad had planned his sixtieth birthday party with a friend exactly ten years younger. My girlfriend, Leslie, her mom, and dad were invited. He was a big Ohio State fan, and one of my dad's friends had a connection through his job. As vice president of Jostens' sports marketing division, part of his responsibility was meeting with championship teams to help design their rings. He carried authentic samples for demonstration in a briefcase containing upwards of $750,000 in precious metal and jewels. He brought the case to my parents' house, and in addition to letting us try them on, he presented Leslie's dad with a poster of Ohio State's 2002 championship ring. It was personalized with a message from the head coach.

Back in Cleveland, my new manager, Jim, tasked me with learning how to develop rates by hand. Joe, who was preparing for retirement, had more than thirty years of experience and encouraged me to pick his brain. He had stacks of files strewn throughout his office, but he always seemed to know where everything was. Tracey, who had worked almost exclusively with Jim for years, served as a coordinator and would have her finger on the pulse of all of my cases. MetLife ranked its employees on a bell curve, and she perennially earned a top score.

For my first official duty, Jim asked that I travel to MetLife's customer service center in Aurora, Illinois. It housed the underwriting and account management teams that Jim said would be instrumental in my success. He charged me with developing relationships.

Both Joe and Jim had earned numerous awards throughout their careers but worked in different capacities. Jim acquired new business with at least 1,000, but no more than 25,000, employees. Any case with 3,000 or more went to Joe, who was paid to focus on sales, retention, and profitability.

Although I had been with Leslie for most of my career, our relationship plateaued. We took a break, but started again before the holidays and traveled together to Minnesota. Prior to visiting the Mall of America, I noticed her phone charging and was bringing it to her when she snatched it. Once in the car, I attempted to take it back but she wouldn't hand it over. Leslie confessed to an ongoing conversation with someone else. In the end, she was more interested in spending time with her coworkers. I was disappointed more than heartbroken and said, "I hope you know what you're doing."

MetLife successfully grew their small market

business thanks, in part, to requiring that their reps make at least twenty-five sales calls each week. The original manager and four reps had grown to twenty-seven offices. The manager was promoted, reps became regional vice presidents, and their pressure on the middle market forced realignment. Instead of eight overlapping regions, seven were established. My regional vice president resigned and Rebecca was hired to replace him.

I was coming into my own and created a folder for emails that documented my growth. My first sale in the middle market came from a broker I had gotten to know early in my career. He previously worked for MetLife and enjoyed telling a story of brokering on the side. When his manager found out, my broker played the role of his boss and fired himself.

That deal was followed with an acquisition made by an account based in New Orleans. It counted toward my goal and paid commission. I was then able to get a meeting with a company whose employee paid-life program had stagnated. Tracey showed her capability during the presentation, but it was Jim who guided me through the process.

He helped me make the case to internal partners for co-branded re-enrollment. The effort normally saw a revenue increase of 14 percent, but on that deal we doubled participation, increased the coverage by a multiple of five, and the premium jumped 350 percent. In addition to other regional successes, the news that I had closed my third deal in five days was communicated to senior management. Maria Morris, whom I sat next to in Phoenix, sent a note reading, "Outstanding results and momentum!"

As I wrapped up a day in the office, I listened to a voicemail from my mom saying to call her back; it was about my dad. I immediately tried, but she didn't answer. I reached out to my brother, who didn't have any additional information. She eventually called to explain that while performing a demo in an operating room, my dad began having heart palpitations. A doctor recognized the symptoms and told him to "lie down."

He pressed his luck on a trip to Alaska. With just weeks until retirement, he and a group of friends went fishing and were golfing when my dad again tempted fate. He had just hit a ball from the woods when a partner told him to *run*. Behind my dad was a bear that my dad said "...could have had [him] if he wanted to."

With my dad's scares and Rickey's announcement of a second deployment, I began looking at life differently. I started allocating resources for travel, and it was time for homecoming. While tailgating, Rawle introduced me to a woman who questioned the wisdom of our *Never Alone* tattoos. In response, I told her, "The only way that he and I wouldn't be cool anymore is if I did something to intentionally hurt him, and I wouldn't do that."

My relationship with Tony, who joined MetLife around the same time as me, evolved from emails and phone calls to texts and visits. He had no problem driving across Pennsylvania and had recently recommended that MetLife hire his former college teammate, Moe. The two ex-football players began sharing an apartment and New York office with my fellow Morehouse alumnus. The trio made for three brown faces in an office rampant with inappropriate jokes.

They had few business opportunities and my former classmate was first to resign after gunshots erupted in his territory. He was replaced by an Arab American, and Tony overheard a manager saying that he would "never see the streets." It was a clear sign of prejudice.

A Caucasian rep hired after Moe was given a more lucrative territory, so Moe left for a competitor. Tony hoped for the best, but counted seven reps hired after him who were placed in better positions. He contacted a regional vice president who had left during MetLife's realignment, and Tony took a job in LA.

He continued traveling to see me and caught me by surprise with an email. Attached was the beginning of a story that he was writing. When he asked my opinion, I told him just how incredible I thought it was. He said, "Good, because you're going to help me write it." I didn't want to ruin what he had going and was assured that I wouldn't. Through exchanges of ideas, phone calls, and an intense session in Cleveland, we put the finishing touches on a screenplay titled *War of Angels*.

The drives across town to play basketball and fouls that counted as defense were starting to wear me down. My workout partner moved away, and I started hanging out with another guy on weekends. We were meeting women, and I was having a good time when things came to a halt. While playing basketball with my manager and his friends, I dropped my left foot back in preparation to intercept a pass. Upon pushing off, I felt a pop, which was followed by a curl up my calf. I let out a yell and dropped to the ground before shuffling to the sideline. There was no doubt in my mind that I had just ruptured my Achilles tendon.

I was physically stronger than I had ever been, but I knew I would be disabled for quite some time.

Hoping for surgery in the morning, I fasted that night. The physician couldn't immediately operate and an upcoming prospect meeting led me to postpone getting better.

To make my recovery easier, I moved my home office downstairs. Bob, my broker, brought me to the hospital, waited during surgery, filled my prescription, and took out my trash before leaving. I wasn't very useful the next day, but I checked in with the office while progressively using my phone and email. My mom and Aunt Sharon, who looked for excuses to get together, returned to town to make me more comfortable. Tracey sent me a variety pack of gourmet ice cream. Our voluntary benefits rep, nagged me until I went grocery shopping with her. Though not a fan of the attention, I appreciated their support.

For the first time in my life, I had to slow down. Given the numerous women I was dating, that was a good thing. I joked with my bosses Jim and Rebecca that the only reading I did was for work and street signs. On Tony's recommendation, however, I picked up *Harry Potter*. With my recovering leg draped over the side of my whirlpool or the couch where I slept, I dove into the world of magic.

As my confidence in *War of Angels* grew, I pondered what I'd do with the proceeds. My brother and I had talked in years past about creating a scholarship at Morehouse. With funds mentally allocated, I considered opening a franchise and started shopping for a convertible.

I had plenty of free time and focused my attention on how to develop insurance rates. At Jim's request, I also worked to improve my written communication. I could see the dividends start to come as I began closing larger deals. The first of which was the Ohio Turnpike. They wanted Administrative Services Only, or ASO, which asked a company to manage their costs while they paid the claims.

Because ASO cases limited MetLife's financial reporting, the company preferred fully insured business that counted total premium. When we got notice of the sale, I sent a thank you note to our team. Jim followed by saying, "Brandon did a great job of setting the data up with me… And with a few suggestions, we decided which elements were important to the buyers. This really helped the consultants cut to the chase and determine that we were making a good and fair offering… Brandon has done a very nice job in putting forth the effort to understand what goes into MetLife's pricing and thus how to best position it against competition and ASO. It changes this case from a $40,000 ASO sale for January 1 to about $500,000."

I was simultaneously working on keeping an account that hadn't received bids for years. They had grown quite profitable. The client requested that their agent get competitive pricing, and we were forced to relinquish their data to the market. Another carrier offered to undercut our rates by 10 percent, guarantee them for two years, and promised a rate cap in year three.

We were given a chance to save the business, and my underwriter allowed me to structure a similar deal. Having built a relationship with the broker, I learned that the client would accept a 5 percent decrease for one year with limited increases in those that followed. I then sent an email to the team explaining how MetLife would get at least $50,000 more revenue than they had expected. The underwriting manager responded, "I will not tire of using this statement. This is yet another awesome example of underwriting and sales working together to ensure a win-win situation. Without both of your engagement, this could have easily turned to a lose-lose. The customer is happy because we were able to meet their pricing needs and allow them to maintain the service they have come to expect. MetLife wins as we were able to maintain a profitable customer that is happy. These are the wins that we must have to be successful as a region. This note made my month."

I made it a point to treat everyone as equals, and it reflected in the survey the customer service center conducted. On a range of one to seven, I got a four, two fives, three sixes, and eight sevens. It included comments like: "Brandon is easy to work with... follows through with the fine details... has great people skills and partners well... is becoming very knowledgeable of our products and is a quick learner... Communicates clearly and effectively. Provides complete documents in a timely manner. Negotiates collaboratively. Demonstrates high-quality work... is always upbeat and very pleasant... works to solve problems for the best of the customer and MetLife... has successfully (and quickly) built relationships with his internal partners, which [will] help ensure long-term success." To me, it was more of a reflection on the culture that Jim, Joe, and Tracey had built than my addition to the team.

I wouldn't, and didn't get all of the cases I worked on, but I learned how to take premium, claims, and employee counts, then project them forward with expenses, margin, and inflation to create numbers that were sustainable. I developed a spreadsheet that automatically calculated the numbers and shared it with Jim, who responded, "Great job. I would say that you took your 'Year 2007 Topic' of underwriting to heart and certainly have mastered how dental is underwritten." After my first year as a middle-market rep, I was named runner-up to the region's Account Executive of the Year.

I was finally able to play basketball again, and Jim asked if I would be willing to help coach his son's team. While it was a no-brainer, my underlying goal was getting back to Atlanta, and Jim knew it.

The company that my former regional vice president had gone to work for flew me in for an interview. I didn't want to start over and declined to proceed. I did what I thought was next best by pricing vacations. Rio was first, and I found a penthouse located just blocks from the beach. Tony's paperwork didn't arrive in time, but I was joined by my brother and Moe.

I was settling in Brazil when Express, the apparel company, made a decision to accept my proposal. It was a running joke that Jim sold cases while on vacation, which left Tracey to pick up the pieces. I relished following in his footsteps and asked if I could relocate and work from Rio. Rebecca, my new regional vice president, responded, "If it means that you sell a s***load of business, ABSOLUTELY!"

Jim then broke the news that he had spoken with Robert Johnson, the regional vice president in Atlanta. He wanted help managing MetLife's partnership with

Morehouse. Jim suggested that I reach out to him so there would be an established relationship if an opportunity presented itself. Rebecca chimed in with, "It would be a travesty to lose you to our competition. If you are able to hang on, something will open up… [I] just hate to see you start over again with another company when your career is on such an upswing."

My next social trip was to Phoenix, where I met my dad, who had joined a group of black golfers. They called themselves the Eagles. They originated out of Minneapolis and had been taking the trip each March for several years. The aging group was looking for "young blood" to carry on their tradition. I wasn't sure what to expect, but I wanted to spend time with my dad.

We arrived in time for a Wednesday practice round, and I was happy to see members of his poker group. Most everybody there was a better golfer than me, so I did my best not to get frustrated. Part of the weekend's expense went toward hospitality, which began with drinks handed through the fence of the eighteenth fairway.

I then traveled to LA, where Tony had gotten to know the city. We toured from his place in the Valley, which included trips to Las Vegas. Another former teammate of his bounced at nightclubs and put us on

VIP lists. I had previously only observed roulette, and without really knowing what I was doing, I placed a bunch of chips on a number that had always brought me luck, six. It hit.

Being single allowed me to get a feel for things that I enjoyed, and they centered around watching the Cavs. With alerts programmed in my calendar, I watched them grow and develop. They reminded me of my high school team. On nights when they weren't playing, I smoked a joint and played a game similar to *GoldenEye* on my Xbox.

I was told that every small market rep who had attempted moving into the mid-market had failed. My sales were solid enough for me to feel as though I was succeeding. With enough income for a second car, I skipped over Mercedes because their constantly changing models would quickly date my purchase. I liked a BMW 645 I had seen, and found three online that were in my price range. None of them were in state. I ultimately played the dealers against each other but wasn't sure that I'd buy one until I drove to the airport and purchased a one-way ticket to Chicago.

My last trip out of Cleveland was both social and professional. I flew to Atlanta for a visit with Rawle and a scheduled interview. I met with Jeff Trinkwon,

MetLife's mid-market manager in Atlanta. He said that he didn't have a position for me, but suggested that his overloaded reps could use relief. He offered me a job like Joe's, a client executive, and said, "I could use some diversity on my staff."

I already owned everything I wanted, but I was concerned about the dress code in my new office. Jeff's promise to match my earnings for the previous twelve months spurred me to order custom suits. I had been working out and the tailor remarked at the size of my biceps. I didn't think much of it, and selected four suits at a cost of $1,500 each.

I hired movers, loaded a U-Haul, and drove behind my dad, who led the way to my new apartment in Atlanta. My suits later arrived in a box and I was excited to open the package. The euphoria quickly faded after trying on the first jacket. The arm space was several inches too large. I called the tailor, but he offered me no relief.

In my first week on the job, I received Jeff's offer letter and immediately noticed a mistake. It read as though I would be paid a salary in addition to my guarantee.

He said that I was mistaken. My paycheck that month, however, was $5,500 too much. I asked Jeff to correct it.

I began building relationships with other reps in the office by going to lunch as often as they invited. One of the reps, Remus, pulled me aside to say that Jeff had asked his reps to relinquish cases and that one claimed he was going to give me his "shit." A second rep said that his opportunity was reduced and goal increased, which made reaching his numbers impossible. Had he not found another position, he would have been terminated. He warned me to watch my back.

Even after being armed with this knowledge, I wasn't concerned because I had been successful in everything that I had ever committed to. Jeff called a meeting and provided a short list of cases for me to manage. Then, he tacked on three additional responsibilities. He asked that I assist with MetLife's recruiting effort at Morehouse, manage a relationship with the African American-owned Atlanta Life, and call on a broker who happened to be black.

I had assisted at Morehouse in years past and was happy to share potential job opportunities. The Atlanta Life assignment was odd, but my parents knew the former CEO. What bothered me was the broker assignment in a job dedicated to clients.

Concern over being singled out was alleviated by being back in Atlanta. I was seeing Rawle almost daily, but Rickey had returned to war. He left us dog tags that included nicknames. Mine was "Minnesota's Finest." I was comfortable in a small circle, but Rawle had branched out. He began introducing me to his new friends. Across from my apartment was a cigar bar, and we started gathering to watch Monday Night Football. Most of the guys were still looking for a career, and I joked that MetLife couldn't fire me unless they wanted a multimillion-dollar lawsuit.

The first challenge of my new role came when Cherokee County Schools' policy came up for renewal. I was pitted against their actuary, whose job was to minimize his client's costs. As I learned to do in Cleveland, I went to underwriting for their walkaway price. By playing with the math, I was able to earn an additional $24,000 in profit. Robert, my new regional vice president, sent a note saying, "Outstanding!! Best of all, better than the profit (and I certainly appreciate that!!), the partnership and credibility with underwriting you gained through this. Terrific Job!!"

The next client, Gwinnett County Schools, casually wanted their employees reimbursed for dental expenses. MetLife had only one other such arrangement, and it was administered by national accounts. With 25,000 employees, my case was at the border between the two markets. When my new manager, Jeff, saw how I addressed their needs, he wrote, "As we discussed, I was very impressed with the way you handled this situation… You presented multiple potential solutions, ultimately the one that we will go with, and positioned/tested the waters with the broker in a way that gave us direction and maneuverability that was just first rate… Damn impressive, actually, and clarifies that you have learned your craft well, and that we made a fantastic decision when we moved you down to the ATL."

Word then came that the fourth African American rep in my hiring class got caught trying to cheat underwriters for better rates and was fired. Six years into my employment, I was now the longest-tenured minority in the division.

My house in Cleveland sold and my parents had access to money, so I started shopping for a new home. My brother was living nearby, and we entertained purchasing a place together. Atlantic Station, once a steel mill in the heart of the city, was repurposed for mixed used. There was a home under construction listed at $600,000. Having been trained to negotiate large deals, I pushed the price down by using everything from time on the market to the builder's stock performance. I went to lunch with my brother to discuss an offer and had just returned to my office when he called to say that he was laid off.

In the market on my own, I enlisted the help of a realtor, who sent multiple options. I had strict criteria, including spacious living within the perimeter of the city. We narrowed to three options, and I happened to fall in love with the cheapest. It was a townhome in North Druid Hills.

March rolled around and I convinced my brother and a friend to join us Eagles in Phoenix. Members of the poker group included my former boss Larry and Woody, who piloted for Delta. Beck, who had recently sold his business, was staying in his nearby vacation home and also joined us. As Beck had been diagnosed with cancer, I made a point to ask for any wisdom that he cared to share.

A lazy afternoon in Atlanta brought a bunch of reps and myself to a strip club. Jeff, my manager, was golfing, but he arrived after being rained out. He had been drinking and told me that he was earning upwards of $500,000 and that his boss, Robert, was taking home closer to a million. I, however, expressed concern over reaching my numbers. He told me not to worry and keep doing what I was doing.

MetLife decided to consolidate office space and bring small and middle markets together with national accounts. My commute would be reduced, I was assigned an office, and an icebreaker was organized. We gathered at a local park, where other reps began playing basketball. I hesitantly joined them and later knew I had made a mistake. While at home that night, I lost feeling below my knees. I feared a trip to the emergency room, but felt better in the morning.

What started as an occasional escape from reality became a full-blown habit. I used marijuana to focus, feel good, and relax. My only concern was losing what I had worked for by getting caught trying to replenish my supply. I shopped online for a hydroponic kit, set it up in my attic, and used bag seeds to start my grow.

I returned home from work to a pre-filled bowl, then smoked through bedtime and all weekend long. I didn't believe that drug use was hindering my performance and felt further validated by a response to my efforts. A coworker asked me to pitch a product, then responded, "This is an excellent email, thoughtfully presented and frankly a template for an overview of Retirewise to institutional accounts."

I was high when I got a call from Tony. On the line was Sharkie, whom he had previously described as a "bad-ass white girl." I understood that she was moving to Atlanta, but I wasn't interested in anyone who couldn't relate to me on multiple levels. He asked that I help her transition, and while they thought I was shocked from being high, I was actually taken by how sexy her voice was.

Rickey was due back from Iraq in time for my birthday, and I was planning a party when I got a message from Milla. She worked as a mortgage broker upstairs from my office in Cleveland. We had explored dating, but had never gotten very far. She bought a ticket to Atlanta, and I drove us from the airport to a café, where she gave me a Gucci watch. I saw her off two days later, and a feeling came over me. I then messaged my mom, "I'm going to get married in the next couple of years."

CHAPTER 5

FALLING

Because Sharkie wasn't familiar with the Atlanta area, I suggested she look for an apartment in Atlantic Station. I then found one for her, without knowing $1,000 was too expensive. In fact, she and a roommate were already signing a lease.

I could tell that Sharkie was attractive from pictures Tony had shared, but I still wasn't interested. She asked me to join her and some friends at a lounge, so I asked Rawle and his friend Kareem to join me. The three of us arrived before they did and stood just feet from the bar. A trio of women entered a moment later, and just after they walked past I said, "That's her."

They stopped on the other side of the bar, and I got a message directing us to their location. We began to talk, then separated before coming back together.

Conversation turned to the coming summer, and I said that I wasn't looking forward to the heat.

Sharkie had been to the place once before and claimed the bartender remembered the brightly colored shoes she had previously worn. She had an electric personality and bright smile, and said that I resembled her ex-boyfriend. While playing arena football, he, too, had ruptured his Achilles tendon. I responded by saying that she looked a lot like my former girlfriend, Mariah. We presented pictures to prove our claims.

The meeting led to phone calls and on one I told her that Tony and I had worked on a project. Sharkie said she was from Chicago, where she had started dancing professionally. Her career had brought her to LA, and finally Atlanta. Her dad was from Ecuador, her mom Guatemala, and Sharkie was raised speaking Spanish. In fact, she was *Latina*.

About a week later, Rawle told me that he and his friends were going out for the night. A friend of his was promoting a club, and I invited Sharkie to join us. She brought another dancer and the topic again turned to the weather. Preferring it warm, I said that I was looking forward to the cold ending. Sharkie quickly reminded me of my previously stated preference. I emphasized my desire for a moderate climate, but was shocked that she had remembered my preference, and likely everyone else's too.

She texted me a few nights later, asking for permission to come over. Though a weeknight, I was happy to have company. She showed up wearing basketball shorts and a T-shirt. I welcomed her inside. We walked past the dining room and into the kitchen, where she set her phone.

We settled on the couch in the living room as her cell phone began to sound. She occasionally got up to check it, then put me at ease by saying the notifications weren't people trying to reach her, but club promotions. Sharkie said that she had started working as a go-go dancer at age sixteen, and worked at retail stores until dancing supported her. She had met all sorts of people, including professional athletes. One expressed interest, and I asked why she didn't date him. Sharkie responded, "He couldn't string two sentences together."

She talked about going to an actor's house in LA, whom I had heard was known for hosting wild parties. I was comforted to learn that Sharkie kept her clothes on. She claimed to hang out with a lot of guys, but explained that most of them were gay. She then excused herself for prearranged plans.

We were talking by phone a day or two later when

she confronted me with information that Tony had given her. Sharkie said that the "project," as I called it, was a movie script and that I had a thing for strippers. What he said was true, so I didn't deny it. More importantly, she wasn't bothered.

Sharkie only drank clear fluids, having water without ice as her favorite. When drinking alcohol, it was Patrón or Grey Goose on the rocks. She had stopped eating animal products, which some people found strange. My brother, however, had experimented with veganism so I thought about recipes to share.

She occasionally swapped her contacts for glasses that had a cracked lens, had a tongue ring, wore mismatched socks, burped louder than anybody I knew, and liked coloring books. If she caught you looking at her funny, she was quick to say, "Don't judge." Sharkie avoided paying for a mixer in her drinks, could tell when a cheaper vodka had been poured, had a flesh-colored accessory that concealed her piercing, and didn't see the value in fixing her glasses or taking the time to match her socks. She was a free spirit.

Sharkie swore off pirated media because it reduced revenue of the artists she depended on, and was happy to learn that I had cable television. Any time the conversation stalled, she posed a question or presented a YouTube video. Comedies were her favorite, and in return I queued SportsCenter commercials that had made me laugh.

Her visit was getting late, and I invited her to stay in my guest room. She declined, and made herself comfortable on the couch. I could see she was nestled and kissed her on her forehead. She smiled and adjusted. Sharkie had over a thousand friends on Facebook, but was spending an increasing amount of time with me. I finally broke down and asked what was going on between us. She responded, "I don't spend that kind of time with just anyone."

Sharkie demonstrated self-sufficiency and uniqueness. Her theme song was "She Got her Own" by Ne-Yo, Jamie Foxx, and Fabolous. Her given name was Jessica, but she earned the nickname by biting her classmates' ankles during swim class. If having drinks at a bar, she covered her glass when turning her head to avoid tampering. She was quick to refuse gifts, bypass compliments, and kept her address secret. Jessica was the first person in her family to graduate from college, and she financed it herself. I asked about her grades and she said that she had earned As and Bs. They confirmed what I already knew: she was the smartest person I had ever met.

Anytime I started getting serious with someone, I

asked what they'd do if they won the lottery. Jessica gave the best answer: she pledged to help her family. Her penetrating questions came to my acts of charity. Before answering, I frustratingly said, "I don't tell people this stuff."

We were on the phone when the topic of death came up. I told her how I had previously answered a Myspace survey. She paused, asked for my screen name, and verified that I wanted to die "years from now, at the same time as my wife."

The relationship between her parents had stalled, so she didn't think partnerships could last. Her view was giving me pause when she said, "I want to settle down at some point." I allowed my guard to fall, and we talked about our idea of a perfect wedding.

I was no stranger to beautiful women. Mariah told me how a guy had tapped her bumper in an effort to get her number. I dated an exotic dancer who was featured in a Lil Wayne video. During a stand-up show in Cleveland, the comedian Paul Mooney called out Leslie while we sat in the front row. He asked me what I did for a living, and I told him "sales." He responded, "You must be selling some shit." Milla had a lovely face, body that rivaled Kim Kardashian, and the credit of rejecting one of the NBA's biggest stars.

Jessica, who looked gorgeous with, but best without, makeup, blew them all away.

As we got up from the couch, she took the long way around the coffee table. I cut her off before she could pass. We were stopped in front of the fireplace, where I grabbed her and got close. She looked at me. I went in halfway, and she continued to stare. I couldn't help but to laugh as I moved even closer. Her lips then came to meet mine. She led the way to the door, and I was feeling light on my feet. I was brought back to reality, though, when I tripped as she was crossing the threshold. Fortunately, Jessica was stopping to turn around and grab my shirt for another kiss before leaving.

My guaranteed income that provided about $2,000 of monthly surplus was nearing its end, and I had no prospects. With renewal money arriving toward end of the year, I decided to borrow $15,000 against my 401(k) to fill the gap.

Middle market reps flew to Chicago each year for account planning. My meeting about the construction company Caterpillar presented a problem. They had formed an association for their dealers to save money, but the better-performing ones were anchoring the costs. If the profitable dealers decided to leave, the association's rates would rise and likely terminate the relationship. The program was designated *At Risk.*

To give them a reason to stay together, I asked underwriting to offer discounts on dental. I talked with the broker, who provided contact information for the program's managers. I then created a presentation, to which my manager Jeff responded, "This could be a really nice opportunity. I like the creativity and positioning you did on this and look forward to your implementation on the strategy."

Less than three weeks had passed since I first saw Jessica, and I knew that I wanted to see her more. Since moving into my townhome, I had hosted several gatherings and decided on another for Easter. With my tightening budget, I knew it would be my last for a while. During the event, I wound up standing next to Jessica and whispered, "You're beautiful, inside and out."

As people began to settle, I directed them to my shot glass collection and asked that they choose one. Only two of my nearly two hundred were off-limits. One was a $70 pewter elephant that came from my parents' trip to South Africa. The second was oversized and came from Morehouse's bookstore. I poured caramel apple shots and raised a toast.

As I entered my twenty-ninth year, I hoped to see all of my friends. Having spent time with Rickey and Rawle, I looked west. My childhood classmate, Stech, had moved to LA after college. I told Tony that I wanted Sharkie to join us, but couldn't afford her ticket. He paid for her flight.

With a later departure, Sharkie gave me a ride to the airport while joking about a similar trip. Another friend of hers, Jason, also needed a ride. Upon arriving at the airport, Jessica refused compensation. To her dismay, he threw cash in her window. I smiled. When she dropped me off, I opened my backpack to reveal payment in the form of a Morehouse sweat suit. I dropped it on the seat and turned to walk as she laughed.

In LA, Tony was preparing a cookout, so we went to a store. I wanted to ensure Jessica wouldn't go hungry, so I bought oranges and pistachios. The barbecue coincided with the opening of the NBA playoffs, which prompted me to start my chores so that I could watch the Cavs. Sharkie arrived with her friend, and we were asked to transport items to the adjacent park. To reserve our place, Jessica and I sat in lawn chairs. I was a bit nervous, but she soothed my feelings with world-stopping conversation.

Invitees began to show, and I watched as she laughed, joked, and held a baby as if it were hers. She told stories that were genuinely funny. Most joyful for me, though, was seeing her eat the fruit and nuts that I had provided. As things began to quiet down, I saw Jessica doing the dishes when she didn't think anybody was looking. I wasn't feeling any special attention, though, as she left with friends.

Fearing that my growing feelings were one sided, I reached out to a woman with whom I had a relationship that most people wouldn't understand. Despite what we did physically, Melissa and I were just friends. We had previously discussed a finale, and I let her know that I might have found someone.

The Lakers were on TV when Sharkie messaged me about who she knew was my least favorite player, Kobe Bryant. She could see the game on TV from the bar where she was and thought it would be funny to needle me. She returned later to spend the night on the futon. I made myself a bed on the floor in front of her. Although my mind was unsettled, my body was changing. I could feel that my stomach was tight and I reached under my shirt to get a sense of it. My motion drew a comment from Jessica, and I then understood that she was watching me.

I continued looking for clues the next day, but got no read. Jessica was alone in Tony's room when I finally cracked. I walked in and poured out my feelings. Her eyes changed shape, and she responded with a kiss.

We were happy when we met, but happier together, so I said, "You and I have a shot at happiness." Having been in serious relationships in the past, I knew there would come a time when her focus would be elsewhere and stated, "I'm going to tell you everything while you're listening." Opposite me, she had broad friendships, but not deep ones. I predicted, "You'll thank me in five years." Understanding her reluctance to get involved, I promised, "I'm gonna fight for you."

Back at work, the Fruit of the Loom company inherited MetLife's coverage through an acquisition. The transition was presenting a challenge, and I was told that the company might cancel their policies. The broker asked us to schedule a visit. It would be an easy drive for me, but the new account manager, MiChaela, was permitted to travel just once per year. I asked the broker's assistant to submit the request in writing. MiChaela later responded, "Great news! It has been approved for me to go... Thank you for your support… It helped… as well as Brandon going to bat for me."

I was getting ready for my annual negotiation with the actuary, but that was less concerning than my group, Cobb County Schools. Its broker had been in the business for a long time and was politically connected. Their $6 million annual premium paid him about $100,000. Once installed, the coverage required little work, and the broker collected a check whenever Cobb County paid the bill.

Charles, the black agent whom I was assigned, happened to be competing for the business. Instead of commission, he proposed a fee for his service. He told me that the previous rep had failed to provide timely reports, then faxed illegible documents. Caught in the middle, I felt the right thing to do was provide what had been requested and allow the client to choose.

I sent a note to my team saying, "Cobb County is going out to bid for their dental again this year… It's my understanding that they bid last year, as well. Normally this would mean that a) they have issues with the carrier, or b) pricing is a concern… but not in this case. There are three main reasons for the bid this year: 1) Cobb wants to make sure they have the best product for their money… that doesn't necessarily mean a decrease to their current rates. 2) Cobb wants to make sure that their plan is in alignment with their competition… 3) Politics."

My life was taking shape. Since leaving Atlanta, I knew that I wanted to come back, and I was happy to find a home with a career that I enjoyed. I owned everything I wanted, knew how to cook, clean, and maintain a home. I, however, was missing a wife. I figured my financial lean time would be short, and with a quality movie script in my back pocket, I told Jessica, "My life is about to take off, and I'm happy that you're in it." I asked for three things in exchange: the freedom to smoke, play Xbox, and watch the Cavs.

We went for a meal that cost less than $10, and it was the best date I had ever been on. Understanding people were important to us, I shared my desire to own the house next door. That way, our family and friends could visit without intruding.

We laid on my sectional couch with our heads pointed toward each other and arms rested underneath. Our elevated hands slowly drifted until making contact. They then held for the first time.

Sharkie told me about her "three-month rule." It went that whatever I had done to get her interested had to be continued past ninety days. I agreed that the initial months of a relationship tended to be the best, but I had learned to say "I love you" in six different languages, so I wasn't concerned.

I noticed that she was making purchases that could be deducted on her taxes and said, "Save your receipts."

Sharkie responded, "You're looking out for me."

I then told her what I knew to be true, "I'll always tell you what's best for you."

Upon returning from an outing, I got a craving for a donut. I wasn't in my best shape; I had been overweight before and didn't much like it. Knowing that it was only a matter of time before I firmed up, I looked directly into her eyes before taking a big bite and told her to "trust me." Her brother, as she said, was a big guy, so weight wasn't a problem. She was concerned for my health. Jessica claimed that I was going through a midlife crisis, which I didn't believe. She put me at ease, though, by saying, "Don't worry. I got you."

I later stopped by her apartment. Sharkie was packing. In disbelief, I asked where she was going. She said that she had booked a gig on a cruise ship. For the next handful of days, she would be surrounded by swingers. The environment bothered me less than the time we'd lose. I asked if she might call me when she got back. Not realizing the numbers matched my birthday, she said that she didn't care if it was "3:27" in the morning, I'd be getting a call. It was just another hint of the magic that we were beginning to share.

I knew I loved her and began telling her so without expectation of reciprocation. To me, she was the most beautiful person in the world, but she didn't believe me when I told her so. Jessica asked which celebrity I considered to be most attractive, and I said, "Roselyn Sanchez." Her demeanor changed as she told me about a photo shoot in Los Angeles. The photographer had also taken pictures of the Puerto Rican actress. He said Sharkie was prettier.

Jessica wasn't looking for a relationship, was having difficulty accepting ours, and began to fight me. Although on the phone, I did the only thing I thought might settle the dispute. I asked her to marry me. With no response, I continued to talk and asked again. Finally, she said, "The answer isn't *no*."

Jessica wasn't always able to express her feelings, but we found a bridge with music. I started to play a list of songs that I had been curating since entering Morehouse. She captured her emotions with "Lions, Tigers & Bears" by Jazmine Sullivan. It talked about what she wasn't scared of, but why falling in love was terrifying.

It didn't bother me that Jessica had few possessions. We felt good together. Almost too good. I stopped myself to avoid ruining what was sure to be a positive experience. Sharkie didn't earn much money, which was only important because it might cause her to take a job that she otherwise wouldn't. A three-month gig in China presented itself. I was excited for her, but let down when she booked it.

To complicate matters, Rickey was being deployed again. I was now being forced to decide whether my life or career was more important to me. I had done everything MetLife had asked of me and was in a position to succeed, but knew that I could start again if I had to.

I wanted to have my relationships *and* financial stability. In that moment, I believed that I knew how to get both. I didn't have much confidence in my manager, his boss, however, seemed quick, empathetic, and we had bonded over basketball. To get the process started, I called my regional vice president, Robert, who redirected me to my manager, Jeff. He didn't answer my call. With the beginnings of a solidly established track record, I emailed Jeff:

> I know that we didn't get a chance to connect yesterday, but in short, this is what I wanted to talk about. I hope that you are okay with the job that I am doing

as a Client Executive, because I want to be the best CE I can be. I know that we've talked in the past about me doing bigger and better things at MetLife, but things have changed a little. I've come to find out that I really enjoy the job that I do. I enjoy helping people with their problems and selling insurance! I understand that I'm still relatively young in my career. I want to let you know that I don't see myself changing jobs… ever. I love this job and will do it as long as MetLife will have me as an employee.

Secondly, I think that I made a mistake. I reached out to Robert before I reached out to you. I'm all about relationships and should have started this dialogue with you first. Considering all of the major changes in my personal life, I couldn't wait any longer to talk. I hope that you understand. If not, here goes.

I never fully disclosed why I wanted to move back to Atlanta. It was a matter of friends and family, but there was a trigger.

One of my best friends, who lives here in Atlanta, is a soldier. He went to Iraq for the first time a few years ago. I flew in from Cleveland to show him a good time before he left. He came back and received a call to return. That time I was unable to come down before his deployment. For a solid year, it disturbed me that I couldn't see my best friend of eleven years off. This same friend has returned from Iraq, but is now weeks away from going to Afghanistan. At the same time, the woman I plan to marry is getting ready to go away for three months. The sad part is that I am so committed to doing a good job for you that I won't visit her unless my work schedule permits.

The moral of the story is: I love my job and I love being in Atlanta. I also appreciate you giving me the opportunity to come and work for you. Trust me, I want to earn a lot of money, and I want to do a phenomenal job for you, but what's most important to me is my work–life balance. After all, I was making good money in

Cleveland. I will do whatever it takes to be successful at this job, I will put the time in, I will build relationships, but most importantly, I will do what's best for this company. All I ask in return is the understanding that the people in my life don't necessarily work nine to five. From time to time, after my work is completed, I would like the opportunity to spend time with them.

I bring this to you because I don't want you to ever question the dedication I have for this job and company, whether I'm in the office or not.

I was at Sharkie's apartment, just a month or two since we had first met, when the first test of our relationship came. We were sitting next to her futon as her roommate, who resembled Amber Rose—a socialite, came to the doorway. She was wearing loose-fitting shorts and sat crossed legged with an opening in my direction. The challenge of keeping my eyes level was nothing compared to the fight that later broke out. Sharkie and I disagreed over something, the details of which escape me, but it caused her to stop talking and me to ask why she was acting like a "bitch."

Apparently I chose the wrong word because our communication got no better. The incident forced me to leave. I had just exited the freeway when she texted me and I immediately turned around. With a face wet from snot and tears, I asked her to tell me why I came back. She didn't answer. After a pause, Sharkie attempted to change the subject. I wasn't asking her to divulge her feelings about me, but to affirm what I had been telling her.

"Say it," I repeated.

Jessica's voice cracked as she said, "You love me."

She had promised herself that she would never again stay with someone who called her a bitch or made her cry. I immediately eliminated the word from my vocabulary. She went on to say that she didn't need me to be miserable. A song by Musiq Soulchild, titled "Teachme" was popular at the time. In it, the artist was pleading with his partner to help him understand how to care for her. With that as inspiration, I promised to *teach* Jessica how to love.

At the office, I had been content doing my work without anybody paying attention to it, but had invited prying eyes. I realized as much when Robert stopped in to see me. I knew from my training in Cleveland that my knowledge could help the team. There were four other mid-market reps in the Atlanta area who reported to Jeff. Blackburn was a perennial leader, Skelley was both tough and experienced. Vietri had been hired a month before I moved back, and Ryan had given me his "shit."

Robert asked how I was doing. As I continued typing, I said, "Good." Then I took a break to look up and asked, "And you?"

He puzzledly walked away and later emailed, "You're a complex dude."

I wasn't exactly sure how to take his comment, but it didn't matter. Robert was paying me more attention than I cared for. I had brought it on myself. His management style of making subliminal comments for the entire office to interpret became personal office visits, emails, and even drunk texts. He was determined to learn more about me, and I began telling him, "You don't know me very well."

Robert, so I was told, was the champion of his golf club and had invited other reps to play. I heard that my name was brought up as he boasted that I was poised for a strong sales year. His rationale was that I needed to pay for a wedding. The comment confused me, because Robert's hands-on approach should have revealed my limited workload.

No matter what was happening at the office, nothing made me happier at the end of the day than seeing Jessica. While we had been nearly inseparable since becoming a couple, our jobs had been pulling us apart. We finally got to the living room, sat down on the couch, and opened our mouths to speak. I wanted to provide an update on my day, and she wanted the same. I made the conscious decision to let her go first.

At Sharkie's suggestion, we went to a margarita bar. She was wearing a shirt that didn't much cover her bra. While walking to the restaurant, she asked if her outfit bothered me. I enjoyed looking at her, but didn't necessarily want others to, as well. Feeling especially connected, she asked if I felt like we were in a bubble. I did.

We had just gotten back to my place when I was rambling. Jessica got my attention and slowed me down until I stopped. She looked me in the eyes and for the first time said, "I love you."

She warned me not to let too much space get between us. I didn't want anything between us. The next step in our relationship, as I saw it, was updating Facebook. I was "friends" with most everybody I knew. Sharkie, who used her account primarily to keep in contact with people she had met on jobs, was concerned about people trying to tear us apart.

She continued status quo, and I updated to *in a relationship*. Jessica was everything that I had ever thought, said, and never knew I wanted. I made my standing wish, "May all of my dreams come true."

We began using the couch as our base and were happy to provide for each other when getting up. Sounding phones were passed without a glance, and updates were given when conversation concluded. We exchanged passwords and morning kisses. I even found a place to tell her that writing in ALL CAPS, was cute at first, but made me feel like she was always yelling. We reached such a level of comfort that I noticed she had forgotten to shave under her arms.

Before we knew it, her departure for China was upon us. I had done my best to give her a good send-off. I bought her an external hard drive that I filled with entertainment, gave her access to my media accounts, agreed to take care of her car, and drop off her rent. As we embraced at the airport, we signaled the Holy Trinity on each other before bringing our fingers to the other's lips, saying, "Bendición" or *blessings*.

Sharkie began sharing a hotel room in Macau, China's version of Las Vegas. My finances had gotten no better, so I agreed to roommates of my own. My brother was working to start a business, and he moved into my basement with his dog, Charly. My high school friend Stech's little sister was beginning a career, needed a place to stay, and claimed the room down the hall from mine. They asked about rent, and without a number in mind I said, "Donations."

Between the two of them, I was getting $700 a month. I kept to myself while adding a mini-refrigerator to my bedroom. Their best opportunity to see me was as I binge-watched the counterterrorism television show *24* from the couch. Jamy liked to bake and made treats for the house. My brother and I shared one-on-one time as I gamed from his loveseat in the basement.

The communication that flowed with Jessica got difficult after she left. We were separated by the diameter of the earth and in opposite time zones. An invitation from my brother's girlfriend made matters worse. While out for dinner, she showed me a picture of her friend, who was wearing a bikini. My brother's girlfriend said that her friend spoke Spanish and proposed a meeting. Neither Sharkie nor I appreciated the gesture. Jessica encouraged me to get out nonetheless.

A friend of my brother's, who I understood to be

a swinger, invited me to her party. I didn't want to go, but she had thought enough of me to extend the invitation, so I felt that I should at least make an appearance.

I was cordial, but quiet and nearly out the door when a group of women asked, "How would you like to take three blondes to the W [hotel] in Buckhead?"

"My girlfriend's in China," I calmly responded.

As I turned to leave, I heard one of them say, "He really loves her."

As part of her contract, Sharkie agreed not to gain weight. The casino where she was working comped her meals, but the cafeteria cooked mostly with meat. A dancer had already been dismissed and Jessica was limited to eating tomato and cucumber salad. As stress began to mount, she placed the relationship in my hands. I decided that we should wake to emails summarizing our days. They became love letters.

I had kept in relative contact with my realtor, who asked that I speak with his friend. She was charged with writing articles on home buyers in Atlanta's premier newspaper. I sat with her to discuss the three homes I had considered. On May 17, 2009, an article was printed under the headline "Morehouse Man Returns."

My relationship with Jessica was continuing to

strengthen, but my arrival in Macau produced a hiccup. I exited the baggage claim expecting to see her, but she wasn't there. I started walking toward a landmark and then recognized her in the distance. Sensing my displeasure, she ran toward me and threw her arms around my neck. Jessica kissed me until my mood changed.

She took me on a tour the next day and used some of her newly acquired Chinese. I was introduced as "boyfriend." We walked the area, sampling food, and I saw the mosaic of a shark tiled into the street. I pointed to it, but Sharkie had already seen it. I realized that she had already evaluated everything that I was seeing for the first time. I was accustomed to being in the lead, but I allowed her to show me around.

Days passed and I felt the need to check in with work. I hadn't really taken a vacation since starting with MetLife, so when Jeff offered to cover for me, I thought I would have some time off. A dated message revealed an unaddressed issue. I handled it and shut down my laptop. Jessica saw that I was disturbed and asked what I wanted. Without hesitation I replied, "Time, money, and you."

CHAPTER 6

TEMPTATION

My first week in China consisted largely of fighting jet lag. To mark the beginning of my second, I removed my career as a priority. Sharkie worked six days a week, which gave me time to read the news and review songs on my iPod. When not working, Sharkie and I walked the streets, where on multiple occasions people called me "Kobe Bryant." She found it amusing, and I paid her back in chivalry. As I understood it, gentleman walked on the curb side of the street to shield their companion from danger. It was also a sign that the male's companion was a respectable lady. I hopped to Jessica's outside every time we changed direction until we agreed that it had gotten annoying.

We came to a lady who was selling clusters of a pinkish fruit, called lychees. She offered a sample, and their shell gave way to a delicious white flesh. We bought a bundle and stopped for lunch. I was craving a crêpe while deciding between desserts. The waitress came to take our order and Jessica surprised me by ordering both. On our way back to the hotel, she pointed to an image that she liked. The poster had rings looped together, diamonds around each, and one in the center. It was Jessica's ideal engagement ring.

On a day off, Sharkie, her roommate, and I rode a bus to visit the Chimelong Safari Park. I had become a fan of the Animal Planet channel while living in Ohio, and was excited to share what I had learned. I began to maneuver between Sharkie and her roommate, which led to an attitude, fight, and my realization that Sharkie had a looser definition than me of the word *friend*.

For meals, I had access to the cafeteria, but I couldn't identify most of its selections. As a result, I drifted to the food court. A burger chain advertised a veggie patty topped with bacon. They called it a *hypocrite*. Jessica and I traveled off-site to both a Thai- and safari-themed restaurant for dinner. It was my first experience with Tom Yum soup and pineapple fried rice. Macau Tower offered a buffet atop its 360-degree rotating platform. It allowed a view of the world's highest bungee jump. We frequently ended nights at a hotel café for dessert.

To get away, Jessica surprised me with a day at the spa. It included couples' massages and refreshments. She had scouted the casino's pool area and later led me to a place where kids weren't allowed. I was in the water when she started snapping my picture. Then, I noticed her taking selfies at an angle. She was trying to capture her smile. To me, it was an indication that she was still on a journey to discover who she was.

Jessica depended on her laptop to connect with her family, and it wasn't recognizing its DVD-ROM. Skype didn't need it, but I had experienced similar issues and thought I could fix her computer by reintroducing the hardware. While Sharkie was dancing, I munched on lychees as I worked.

The drive came out and slid in rather easily, but the computer presented an error message when I tried to restart it. I made another attempt, but the problem persisted. I was beginning to panic when Jessica and her roommate returned. I told Jessica that I might have broken her computer. She took the news better than I had expected. I promised to buy her a new one, and then began cleaning up as they started downstairs to meet other performers. I found Jessica at the bar, where she had ordered my favorite drink, Hennessy and Coke with lime. She wanted not only to tell me things were OK, but to cheer me up.

At our first opportunity, we set off for Hong Kong to sightsee, shop, and find her a new computer. It required a forty-five-minute ferry ride. A bit exhausted, the two of us settled into lower-level seats, where I put my hand between her lower thighs. She laid her head against my shoulder, and I rested mine on hers as we comfortably fell asleep.

On my last day in China, Sharkie took me to a restaurant where she had befriended the chef. I wore a pair of my better jeans with a polo. She draped herself in a silky dress. We took our seats, and I did several takes, unable to believe what I was seeing. Finally, I stopped and said, "You're hot." Without effect, she kept smiling and cracking jokes. We ended the night at Morton's with dessert and a drink.

I was hoping for the exit row and would have settled for an aisle, but got I stuck in a middle seat for my commute home. Knowing that I'd be cramped for the long ride, I was a bit depressed and treated myself to a back rub in the Hong Kong airport. Upon arriving in my house, I was pleasantly surprised with my roommates' *donation* of a patio set.

Once settled, I fell into my routine of smoking and cleaning. I found that marijuana caused my mind to race as I digested information. Peace came from putting things in order. I made adjustments in iTunes, digitized old photos, and placed housewares where they belonged. My Blu-ray player was overheating, so I gave it airflow by drilling a hole in the adjacent cabinet. With every action, I remained focused on my mission of eliminating detractions from quality time with Jessica.

I returned to my office and was amused that a recent cover of *Sports Illustrated* had been hung from my credenza. The Lakers had just won another championship and Kobe Bryant was featured. I knew it was a gift from my regional vice president, Robert. He too knew that I wasn't a fan of the NBA player. Before unpacking my briefcase, I went to a drawer, grabbed a red marker, and suppressed my laughter as I drew horns on Kobe's head.

For every kernel of wisdom I gave Robert, I reinforced my belief in work–life balance. When something was needed, I reminded him that we were in a relationship business and to "pick up the phone." A phone call, after all, was much more personal than email, especially when you were asking for something. He referred to our communication as "wordsmith," or the ability to always use the appropriate word.

The office would be constituting a group of "masterminds," top reps charged with sharing best practices. Each sales channel was supposed to be represented by one rep. There was already a client executive in the group, but Robert added me anyway.

One of my accounts, the administrative offices for the Presbyterian Church in America, or PCA, asked about increasing its life insurance offering. It turned out to be a small sale that got rolled into their larger policy. They elected a participating contract in lieu of a traditional one, which would potentially give them a refund.

PCA collected premiums from locations nationwide and then paid the bill. Their plan had run quite profitably. For each of the past few years, PCA received a check from MetLife for about $100,000. Despite the fact that parishioners were paying the premium, the lawyers for PCA said the organization could keep their money, and it did.

My job as a rep consisted of many factors, which included staying abreast of the happenings in the market, ensuring that customers were happy, and evaluating opportunity. Learning that a church organization was keeping money that rightfully belonged to its members was enough to cause stress, but unfortunately for me, the issues with Cobb County Schools were coming to a head.

Cobb was insured with MetLife for multiple lines of coverage but was only concerned about their dental insurance. They offered a base plan at minimal cost and a premium one that employees could buy into. The low plan was fully insured, but the high had $5.3 million in claims that would translate to a $6 million sale. I knew that it would be my best opportunity to reach my 2010 goal, and that their agent of fifty-four years, T. W., had insight. He said that Cobb budgeted four to five years out and would only consider the proposal if it aligned with their budget.

Dental rates could be volatile and were standardly guaranteed for just one year. Two-year options were becoming popular and underwriting was starting to approve three-year deals. I pulled Cobb's financials for a better look. MetLife had banked almost 25 percent on the $1.25 million that Cobb had paid for their low plan in the prior year.

Three hundred thousand dollars of profit wasn't enough ammunition to convince underwriting, so I dug into the metrics. I learned that the population was stable, located in the most saturated area for participating dentists in the country, and that claims were being processed at an escalating rate in network. In short, my conclusion was that there was no better population or location to take a chance on.

I sent my analysis to my bosses, Robert and Jeff. They asked the financing division in New York for approval. Their response was, "No."

I asked Robert for an explanation, and he said, "The person hired to make those decisions is conservative."

Jim taught me that when it comes to cases, "You've got to be like a dog on a bone." I wasn't about to let up.

I continued to ponder and thought about capping future rate increases. I sent an email to the team after business hours, and the underwriting manager responded. His engagement set off an exchange that had me working through 2 a.m.

Later that morning, Jeff inserted the following thoughts:

> Call my cell after the two of you talk, and we will lay out the strategy point-by-point. Be thinking, and present to me your entire strategy. Thanks for your hard work here. Also, in thinking thru new alignment for our team, I might need you to take on some new responsibilities. I

know you are up to the challenge. It's a little too early to discuss, but I think you will like my ideas. I will bring you up to speed when I am able.

T. W. then called and opened with small talk in the southern drawl that I had come to expect. He began crossing the line with questions about Charles, his competition.

His accent then faded, and he clearly stated, "I want you to treat him like he's your friend, but he's not. He's the enemy, and everything he tells you, I want you to come back and tell me."

I dropped my posture and held the phone in one hand with my head in the other before responding as diplomatically as I could. Our call finished, his drawl was restored, and he attempted a joke before laughing and hanging up.

I immediately walked past Jeff's office to knock on Robert's door. He welcomed me. Still a bit startled by TW's comments, I took a seat while attempting to recap what had just happened. Robert asked for clarity and I recited T. W.'s exact words. Robert offered advice that finished with "That way you don't have to lie."

I got home to see Jamy, who, along with most of my friends, didn't really understand what I did for a living. My days primarily consisted of taking orders and solving problems. A rare few provided thousands of dollars in commission. I summed it up by saying, "I have good days and bad."

Jeff called me into his office a few days later and explained that Skelley, a mid-market rep, was considering a transfer to national accounts. Her move would free up territory that Jeff wanted me to take. Since I had expressed my desire to have both a career and a life, I was hoping to be a client executive, like Joe from Cleveland. To me, that was the perfect blend, and I wanted to do it for the duration of my career. Further, the complications of my living circumstances forced me to decline. He asked why, and I began talking about difficulty that I was having with my knees. He again offered the position, and knowing how much walking it would take to establish myself in a new territory, I declined for "medical reasons."

Jeff summoned me to his office again the next day, saying a rep had never previously refused him additional responsibility. The offer was repositioned, with the caveat that I could "take it or find another place to work." With no real option, I asked for additional details, which he promised to provide.

At the time of our scheduled follow-up, I went

to his office, but he wasn't there. His absence wasn't atypical, so I emailed him and asked if he still wanted to talk. Jeff responded, "On calls for the rest of the day… Really just need to know if you can or can't assist. The accounts are kind of non-important."

Given my "shit" assignment, I knew the accounts, *were* important, but I ultimately said that I would take the new job and title. Feeling as though I owed my bosses an explanation, I wrote:

> I know that I floored you with my initial response to the opportunity that you proposed. But, just so there's no question about it: I've always wanted the account executive job in Atlanta. As you know, I'm handling some personal issues at home right now. But those should be cleared up in the next few months. I understand that when you make a hire or job change, MetLife expects a commitment. As an example of my level of commitment to you and this business, I've needed surgery on at least one of my knees for over a year (my knee makes noise when I stand and sit, I have trouble going up and down stairs, and at times simply walking or

standing). I haven't had this surgery yet because I wanted to establish myself in this market and with you. I'll most likely wait until spring, when the sales cycle is slow and the weather is good. Then I'll take the time I need to get healthy. I just wanted both of you to know that I am 100 percent committed.

Regardless of my managers' opinions, I had work to do. One of my accounts was having issues with their billing that required manual reconciliation. I could have asked my assistant to help, but she was more interested in seeking the attention of top performers.

Knowing that the data entry needed to be done quickly, I forwarded calls to my cell phone and went home. I was busy with my keypad when Jamy entered. I halfway looked in her direction and snapped, "Really bad day."

To recap, MetLife had come to the campus of Morehouse College looking for black men after receiving a diversity complaint from Coca-Cola. They had hired me into a territory and expected me to leave it when they needed minority representation. Upon my transfer to Atlanta, my prospective manager explicitly said that he needed diversity. He then assigned me roles outside of my job duty. The first time I told them "no," they threatened to fire me. When I next had the opportunity, I pulled Jamy aside to explain my frustration as "MetLife's Nigger."

Jeff called me into his office and said that Gwinnett County Schools was having technical issues. He had attended at least one meeting without me and questioned whether or not I was "into" my job. Prior to my transfer, I had heard that Jeff wasn't a terrific manager. I was now seeing evidence firsthand. Unable to believe what he had just asked, I suggested that an *invite* to future meetings might be helpful.

I was typing when Robert entered my office. He wanted to discuss my presentation on Cobb County. We were deep into the weeds of underwriting when he stopped to say the approach had to be in layman's terms.

"It is," I responded, flipping my screen around and saying, "I've already started writing it."

I gave him a moment then said, "Tell me you see what's going on here." Due to my timing and delivery of the double entendre, I could see him wondering if I was referring to the case or Jeff's management style.

He called a subsequent meeting so that Jeff and I could air grievances. I entered Robert's office with only one target in mind. The conversation got underway and I locked in on Robert, who said, "This isn't wordsmith."

For me, it always had been.

I smoked when I got home with the hope of relieving stress, but I thought about Jamy's frequent conversations with her mom. Mrs. Stech was connected with many parents who had watched me grow up. I began to feel the happenings of my once-private home were being shared. I couldn't discuss the best parts of my life with my brother, for fear that it might trigger a deeper depression. Seeking an outlet, I sat next to him for a gaming session and mashed the controller until my fingers hurt.

Feeling residual pain, I resorted to pecking letters on my keyboard with the digits that hurt the least. Sharkie, still in China, didn't understand that I was in pain and became dissatisfied with the quality of my letters. A bartender had gifted her several bottles of Grey Goose, and she was becoming more social. My concern, however, was her slowing emails. A fight broke out and we talked past each other then sat in silence. I wandered the house, seeking relief, but every comfort zone was occupied.

Tony, who had befriended a porn star, messaged me to say that he and his partner had a business plan. It would eliminate the viruses and data mining typically associated with watching pornography online. Tony then connected us on a call, where lofty revenue projections were discussed. In the end, they needed an investor.

The name of a multimillionaire I had recently spent time with came to mind. My brain went into overdrive as I spewed strategy. It caused Tony to say, "I've never heard you speak so fast." I wasn't finished. If the porn stars wanted my help, they'd have to give me equity in the business. Their agreement began unlocking a dream that I had been working on since grouping the initials "JTB" to lock the spreadsheet containing my finances. My thought had continued to be this is "Just The Beginning." I wanted to provide resources to people with business plans pursuing their dreams. I believed that I had just found the funding.

I got Jessica on the phone, and there was a tingle in the line. I could see the future unfolding in front of us and began telling her what I had planned. It connected much of what I had told her and she said, "You're blowing my head up."

While knowing that I needed a way out, Jessica wasn't enthusiastic about my new career choice. She conditioned her support on me not being on set. With her backing, I approached my parents. My dad didn't see a problem, but my mom disapproved.

MetLife scheduled me to represent them at a Morehouse ceremony honoring business and economic majors. At our table was the chair of the economics department. We began to catch up. Seated alongside us was a lady whom I vaguely recognized. She took interest in our conversation. During the course of dinner, she introduced herself as MetLife regional vice president of national accounts.

She had worked on the pitch to UPS, who had branded the slogan "What can brown do for you?" To secure the business, she printed her proposal in brown ink. I had heard about the sale from Cleveland and said, "That was you?" She confirmed and asked if I'd give her my opinion on national accounts. I alluded to the fact that I occasionally worked from home, which appeared to dampen her interest.

I could see my hard work was paying off as results accumulated. A webinar I had organized for the Caterpillar dealers yielded twenty-one participants. Considering I was only managing about ten accounts, this was a potential gold mine. Positive feedback came almost immediately with various administrators asking buying questions.

Skelley got the job with national accounts and was informed that I was working on Cherokee County Schools' renewal. She and I had butted heads when I first arrived, but then found common ground. The actuary was arguing his client's position and she wrote, "If you want me to do something to help you, I will… I'm not sure what I can do any differently than you… but if you want to gang up on him, we can try! Otherwise I am only responding that this is in your *capable* hands!"

It seemed that everybody was aligning to produce numbers except Jeff, who was often missing from the office. An administrator forwarded his email with the subject line "My phone is lost, send emails, as I will also be on Paid Time Off." On a hunch, I checked his calendar, which showed that he was scheduled for back-to-back meetings. He had either cancelled on four prospects because he lost his phone, or was more likely covering his absenteeism by calendar.

At home, I began hedging my bet on whether porn might provide a living and started to cover my bases. I bought a safe and began warehousing pictures and personal documents. To help me work, I played the rap artist Jay-Z's catalog on repeat. A security system came with the house, and to protect what I was imagining to be my new life, I decided to activate it.

My multimillionaire contact expressed interest in the porn proposal. It felt exciting as I envisioned hiding the origin of my new revenue stream while using the money for good works.

While preparing for an extended absence from the office, MiChaela, Fruit of the Loom's account manager, provided an update I was eager for. We had teamed well, and she sent me their annual survey. Just a year prior, the decision maker had described our relationship as *at risk*. She had upgraded it to *uncommitted*.

When previously asked about her account manager, she expressed a complaint. Her updated response was, "The account management team has made great strides in the handling of our account." Satisfaction with value was previously listed as "somewhat dissatisfied," and likelihood to renew all coverages was "somewhat unlikely." When asked why, she responded, "I have not been completely happy with the way our plan has been handled," Ultimately, she, "probably *would not* recommend" MetLife and found it, "somewhat difficult to do business with."

The current survey read, "somewhat satisfied" with value and "somewhat likely" to renew all coverages. Her likelihood to recommend became "probably would," and she found MetLife "somewhat easy" to do business with. Personal notes read, "Brandon has worked very hard to provide what we have asked… Last year I was ready to change from MetLife for both dental and life insurance. Brandon Rowell and MiChaela have worked to gain my respect of their effort to improve my experience."

With independent confirmation of my positive performance, I stopped by the cubicle of a rep who had warned me to be careful. I thanked him again. He reiterated that Robert had Machiavellian machinations. Having drawn him in to put things in writing that MetLife might frown upon, I interrupted with, "I got him."

When I had placed the call to Robert from Jessica's apartment, I knew that I was putting my career with MetLife in jeopardy. The porn opportunity was unexpected, but promised financial stability. At this point, I knew that I was leaving MetLife, but I had no idea of how my departure might unfold. After being out one night, I returned home and was heading for bed when my knee locked. In extreme pain, I saw no alternative, but to get on all fours.

For a documented record and to get the ball rolling on what was sure to be time away from the office, I emailed Jeff. "I hope you are having a wonderful weekend. I've had more problems with my knees lately… I literally had to crawl up the stairs,"

In direct contrast to his previous statements, and likely with Robert's help, he responded, "I'm sorry to hear that. Please take good care of yourself and realize that nothing is more important than your health. Given this and your past note, I think it wise to review all of your medical options regardless of workloads."

At that moment, Jay-Z came over my stereo saying, "Put this shit in motion, ain't no rewinding me back." With doors closing and new ones opening, I felt as though I had just entered into a gauntlet.

I went to bed that night with porn on my brain and was connecting the pieces to the puzzle as I fell asleep. Fireworks started to appear; then a jackpot's alarm began ringing ever louder inside my head. I popped up, saying, "Millions and millions and millions of dollars." I took selfies and looked for a pen to scribble my thoughts.

Hours later, I was visiting an orthopedic surgeon, who recommended consecutive surgeries to relieve my knee pain. It would require four months of recovery. The time was exactly what I needed. Knowing that I was ending my career, I had a hard time controlling my nerves as I composed an email to Jeff. I wanted to continue working the Caterpillar leads, but his response that included Robert and human resources said, "To be honest, I am not 100% sure on how we are supposed to handle this. By cc to HR, I would request their input."

Knowing that I had Robert's full attention, I shot back, "Sounds like a plan…"

Without Jeff or human resources copied, Robert emailed, "You must get this taken care of. You come first… health especially. Anything we can do, let me know."

It was Robert's last line that caught my attention, he didn't want his communications turned over to human resources. He was finally getting to know me, and it had come with a price. He was realizing that he was caught in my trap. Uninterested in picking a fight, I responded, "Honestly, the ability to take care of myself is the most important thing to me; everything else is secondary…"

I was continuing to put things in order, expecting porn to make me a multimillionaire when I heard the echo of my mom's voice. I said to myself, "It feels like I'm making a deal with the devil." I questioned if I would, and the answer was a stout "No!"

At that moment, I stopped in my tracks and reversed course to seek the light I knew had been guiding me since high school.

☮

While I wasn't as pressed to pursue porn, I needed to generate income and had already pitched my contact. He would be in Las Vegas, leaving my potential partners an easy drive from LA. Anticipating a celebration, I asked Tony to secure bottle service at the Playboy Club.

I appreciated how my broker, Bob, cared for me while I was in Cleveland, but I wanted Jessica at my side for the upcoming surgeries. As I saw it, she was already my wife. My roommates were moving out and Jessica's lease was expiring, so I made her an offer. If she agreed to feed me, I promised to pay the mortgage and utilities. She questioned what would happen if things turned sour. I promised to help her move.

Knowing that I was about to be sidelined, I hosted a gathering for our friends. Jessica and I moved her belongings in shortly thereafter. I became amazed at how things continued to fall in place. Her futon replaced my brother's love seat, her incomplete set of silverware complimented mine, and her two dishes made a nice addition.

The operation on my first knee went smoothly, and Jessica kept my mom informed by text. Afterwards, she helped me into the back of my car and drove us to the pharmacy. I slept off the anesthesia from the couch and woke to feel no pain. Jessica had planned to take care of me and was shocked to see me moving around.

After a flight to Las Vegas, I had a preliminary meeting with the adult actors to be prepared for the investor. When I thought we were ready, I reached out to my contact. We met in a lounge and the meeting was going as well as I could have hoped when the inevitable happened.

The actors' lack of business experience became apparent. My intervention prompted my contact to ask if I would be on set. According to my commitment to Jessica, I said, "No."

Progress of the meeting stopped and my contact said, "Someone like *you* needs to be present."

Jessica and I flew back to Atlanta with porn all but eliminated as a possible business when I learned that Stech would be in Hilton Head, South Carolina, visiting his grandmother. We coordinated a meeting time, and I thought about taking my BMW, but I was concerned about how Sharkie would react to her hair in the wind. She ran her fingers from her head, saying, "I don't care about my hair." With my leg still stiff, she chauffeured me to where we met my brother, Stech, and his extended family. Stech, my brother,

Jessica and I then went out for the night. Word later came that Nana "loved" my girlfriend.

I was used to earning a good salary and considerable commission, but the transition to disability payments increased pressure to find alternative employment. I called the regional vice president who had hired me into Cleveland and he promised to make a call. As the head of sales with the company I had spurned to stay with MetLife, he could resurrect the opportunity I previously had in Atlanta. I now had to wait.

Differences between Jessica and me began surfacing with how she treated what I had told her. We were slowly doing everything that I had promised when Sharkie got upset. She named a bunch of the things that we hadn't yet done. It helped me understand that I was living for life, while she was living for the moment.

Even having lived in Atlanta for a number of years, I still wasn't familiar with most of its attractions. Jessica and I discovered CityPASS, which allowed us to tour on a budget. We visited the CNN Center, Zoo Atlanta, Atlanta Botanical Garden, and World of Coca-Cola. We were in Centennial Olympic Park when she realized a discrepancy in one of my previous statements.

Through our courtship, I was entirely focused on

her and said that I hadn't been with anyone else in my bedroom. Speaking freely, I mentioned that there was another. Jessica had taken what I had told her to plan something special, and now felt our magic dissipating.

"It feels like it's over," she said.

"It's not," I assured her. I then did my best to repair the fracture.

The feeling was interrupted, though, as we traveled to the Atlanta History Center. Another source for the million-dollar porn investment had presented itself, and the entertainers called to discuss. I was already put off by the idea of working in porn, but I felt the need to run the lead to ground. They seemed to be working through things as we spoke and tried to renegotiate our deal. It caused me to get angry. I told them that they could abide to what we had agreed or we could "go back to whatever it was that we were doing."

I hadn't heard from my former regional vice president, so I gave him a call. I could hear him carrying on a conversation in the background. He said that he would call me back, but I knew he probably wouldn't. I next contacted my friend Tony to say that I was looking for a job. He reached out to his hiring manager, who responded, "I'm always looking for a good rep."

Tony had submitted hair follicles upon employment with his new company, and while I had never been concerned with drug tests, I knew failing was a real possibility. I told Jessica that I was taking a break from marijuana and planted a couple of seeds in the attic. Tony got back to me, saying there weren't any openings in Atlanta, and for the first time, I had no vision for my future.

Sharkie was still getting to know the area, and her job was largely dependent on agents who fed her gigs. In order to be in their good graces, she would have to be present. That meant taking classes in their studio, which came at a cost. Fortunately, they were advertising a sale.

I supported Sharkie's career, while knowing that it might conclude, and I didn't want any resentment. Without a clue of how I was going to afford them, I offered her several months' worth of passes. That way she could attend classes whenever she wanted. She objected.

We went back and forth until I looked her in the eyes and said, "Non-negotiable."

It was the first time that I had used legalese in our conversation. The phrase confirmed what I was doing, writing a contract for Jessica's heart.

CHAPTER 7

EXIT STRATEGY

Little by little, I told my mom what I thought of my new girlfriend and summed it up by saying, "She's amazing." More than that, I knew that my mom had wanted a daughter since she lost my two sisters. Knowing Jessica's ability to listen and contribute, I told my mom, "Jessica's the daughter you always wanted."

Her twenty-sixth birthday was approaching, and I thought about what to get her. I recalled the shark we had seen in the streets of Macau, then shopped online to find a white terrycloth and purple silk reversible robe. Embroidered shark patches would look nice on the pockets, I thought.

I settled on two designs, a grayish cartoon and a sophisticated sketch. I considered them appropriate and ordered the set to be shipped to Minnesota. My mom found a company to assemble the gift prior to my parents' preplanned drive to Atlanta. On Jessica's birthday, I brought her to Stone Mountain. We saw attractions, stopped to experience a four-dimensional movie, and rode a train around the mountain's perimeter.

It was a good day, and we returned to the house where Jessica's mom had sent her roses. We also had unexpected company. My brother's girlfriend was there visiting my mom. Sharkie held a grudge from the proposed introduction, and I did my best diplomacy.

The robe wasn't yet wrapped, and I went upstairs to ensure that it was done properly. I then returned to present Jessica with her gift. From her smile, I could see that she liked it, but I felt tension from the unwanted company.

Throughout my parents' visit, Jessica blended with my family as we spent time on the couch. I was surprised to see her do more listening than normal, and I appreciated her attentiveness. When my dad began helping me replace an under-cabinet light, she was right there, not wanting to miss a thing.

After my parents left for Minnesota, the time came for my second knee surgery. Upon discharge, I was in much more pain. Jessica made me a sandwich and attended to me with loving care. The two of us would soon be traveling to Chicago, where I would meet her family. I was grateful that my crutches would serve as an icebreaker. Her mom, dad, brother, sister-in-law, niece, nephew, and paternal grandmother welcomed me. I was the first boyfriend Jessica had brought home. Unsure of how to react, it was too cute when her mom said, "I don't know what to do."

She presented family photos. Jessica's brother, his wife, her sister, and her husband treated Jessica and me to a dinner cruise on Lake Michigan. I expected Jessica's brother to be a big guy, and we were about the same height, but he had pounds on me. I wanted to make an impression on him, but he left one on me with a stare at dinner. We went to a lounge afterwards, where I sat with my knee resting. Jessica's brother said that he had just one rule about his sister, "Not to put hands on her."

The following day I accompanied Jessica, her mom, sister-in-law, and the kids to her aunt's house for her maternal grandmother's birthday. On the third day, we went to Shedd Aquarium in downtown Chicago. Jessica carefully pushed me in a wheelchair. When taking a pause with her nephew outside the restrooms, another patron said that we had a beautiful family.

I knew that Sharkie was happy to be home, but I picked up on a disconnect. She had told me that family was most important, but she often played solitarily on her devices. At home, she was called "Jessica" and "Jessie." In fact, her family thought it was funny that I called her *Sharkie*, so I stopped.

They made me feel like one of their own and provided favorite foods and ones to try. Jessica's mom even prepared homemade tostadas. I was beginning to feel really comfortable, especially with her young nephew, whose favorite cartoon was about Thomas the Tank Engine. One of the characters had been injured, so he associated me with him and began calling me "Hero." I appreciated the nickname and took on the mission of making Jessica's family whole.

I traveled to my parent's house for Thanksgiving and to see the frequent holiday guests. Included were my paternal grandmother, two of my dad's brothers, their cousin, and his wife. I proudly showed my youngest uncle Jessica's picture, and he responded, "She looks like a movie star."

Jessica and I returned to Atlanta, where my marijuana seed had grown to maturity. I cut the plant down and brought it to the living room for processing. Hours later, Jessica could see that the work had become tedious. Knowing that a miscalculation could lead to disaster, I created a safety system. Marijuana would only leave the house as an edible or in ashes. The leftover foliage went through the garbage disposal.

I was beginning to settle in when Sharkie caught cabin fever. She claimed to have "been taking care of me for months." In disbelief, I tried telling her that I wasn't initially in pain, but she wasn't listening. The disagreement turned to an argument, which led to a dayslong fight.

No room was off-limits for tension, and without a breakthrough in sight, I lay down to rest. I then opened my eyes to see Jessica standing in the doorway. She asked how I could sleep while we had unresolved issues. The topic of my relationship with Melissa, the person with whom I had been casually intimate, came up, and Sharkie questioned how we could be platonic. She asked how I ended things, and I told her what I remembered. Sharkie recalled something different. The discrepancy led me to read my texts with Melissa aloud. They revealed a plan for a final fling, but I maintain that was because I couldn't get a read on Jessica.

Through the fights and resolutions, I picked up on something that bothered me. Sharkie changed her words just enough to accommodate her position. Despite both of us being under the same roof, I began preferring to argue over text messages. It gave Sharkie pause when I could point to what she had written.

In the gray area, however, was a greater lesson to be learned. Relationships inevitably have conflict. When people are pushed on our respective actions, it's easy to fall into a defense. By allowing the other to express their full point, we are able to find resolution. Jessica's primary complaint was that I often referred to *her* and *me* instead of *us* and *we*. She captured my thoughts by saying, "When everything is right with us, everything is right with the world."

She asked me a question that I anticipated. I was prepared to answer.

"How many women had I been with?" she wanted to know.

I looked directly into her eyes and responded as accurately as I could, "One."

We nestled together and stumbled upon an online IQ test. It seemed easy, but for any question that hung one of us up, the other had insight. It was no surprise that the results scored us as "genius."

I adjusted my standing wish from, "May all of *my* dreams come true" to "May all of *our* dreams come true." In turn, Jessica presented me with a handmade gift she had been working on. It was set on red cardboard paper and was decorated with hearts.

She said it was the best that she could do to capture her feelings. At the center was notebook paper with handwritten lyrics to Beyoncé's "Halo." I was her angel.

Our interactions were epic; every moment felt as though it might have been scripted. At the heart was truth. There was nothing to hide because we had come clean about everything we had ever done.

With basketball season in full swing, I watched games as she streamed shows to her laptop. When not looking at TV, we spent time on our respective computers. Despite the distractions, there was presence. I could see out of my periphery when she was watching me, and I often admired her. We agreed there was comfort in just knowing that each other was there.

Our relationship was approaching cruise control when it came time for the inevitable. I had no local job prospects and was still employed by MetLife, so I emailed Jeff and Robert.

> First and foremost, I want to thank both of you for supporting my time off on disability. As of my last doctor's appointment, it appears that I will be cleared to return to work on or around

January 1. Believe it or not, this time away has been extremely difficult. However, I can definitively state that this came at the perfect time. During the past few months, I have not only been able to address the issues with my knees but also *ALL* personal issues that have previously plagued me. I am eagerly awaiting my return to work and any additional responsibility that you may have for me.

Jeff and I spoke by phone the next day. He said that I would be transitioned to an account executive. It was a position I had eyed from Cleveland and knew that my large group experience would make me even more effective. In the back of my mind, though, was the series of events that nearly led me down a dark path. Those, and the dream that came with them.

I had emotionally won the lottery and wondered if all of the information I had collected would go to waste. I then made the commitment, whether it was on TV or a bumper sticker, to reference and catalog each and every Bible verse that came my way. The first was John 3:16: "For God so loved the world that he gave his one and only Son, that whoever believes in Him shall not perish but have eternal life." The life

I was beginning to build, I wanted forever, and the thought was comforting.

Even though Jessica's belongings were in Atlanta, Chicago was still her home and she traveled there for Christmas. Her aunt hosted an annual get-together on December 24. The kids opened their presents and the adults exchanged gifts. I traveled to Minnesota, to spend time with my family.

In anticipation of my first day back at work, I set my alarm the night of Sunday, January 3. I woke up early the next morning and did my best not to disturb Jessica. On my way out, I stopped to spray my favorite cologne, and then smothered her.

I timidly returned to the office and was pleased to see notes and pictures welcoming me back. Assistants came to talk, as did Jeff, who said he was unsure that I'd return. In my absence, he had hired another rep, Leweling, who was new to sales.

Robert came to talk basketball, and in closing he told me about missing a big free throw, which led to his focus on golf. At first opportunity, I walked across the hall into the break room. From the large windows, I could see Stone Mountain. My next verse, Psalms 109:8 came: "Let his years be few; let someone else take his position."

Jeff called a meeting to discuss my new responsibility. Because I had previously declined it, I knew that the previous offer wouldn't be on the table. I was shocked, however, to hear my new assignment. I was to work direct leads from a new campaign targeting schools, association business, MetLife career agents, and non-producing brokers. My case load was reduced, yet I was still responsible for advancing MetLife's diversity agenda.

The assignment was essentially for someone who was brand new to the business. Despite immediate doubts, I got to work. To see who was off-limits, I requested a list of assigned brokers. Blackburn had eighteen, no doubt, prime wholesalers. Leweling had eleven that were focused on larger cases. Vietri, whose dad reported to the CEO, was assigned eighty-nine agencies, and I got seven.

I returned home after a few days on the job to see a familiar sight. Sharkie was in bed with a bowl and a spoon. A box of cereal and a carton of almond milk were on the nightstand. The TV was on, and her laptop was open, but she was happy to see me.

As I prepared for the work the next morning, I asked, "What are you doing today?"

She stretched, smiled, and said, "Nothing."

I made calls and set meetings to see my new contacts in person. Aside from my black broker, Charles, just two of my agencies had eligible business. One of them had only a couple of accounts, while the other worked with a number of schools. Their representatives were friendly and liked my presentation on MetLife's retiree dental program.

In a follow-up meeting with Jeff, I presented my findings. Targeting schools directly would involve numerous brokers competing on public bids. Few of the associations had the organizational capacity, premium, or membership to meet MetLife's standards. The career agents focused on individuals and small businesses, so sizable groups were out of the question. The meeting became contentious, and Jeff said, "Well, if you think I'm fucking you, you're entitled to your own opinion."

With my career all but over, I wondered if I had enough ammunition to file a lawsuit for discrimination. To get an answer, I called the only female member of my dad's poker crew, who was the top lawyer at a large company. I opened by saying, "Everything I'm about to tell you, I have in writing." She didn't hear the case that I was presenting, saying only, "I know what they did to you is terrible… It'll take five years. Secure another source of income."

Aiming to wrap up my business in the office, I knew that I needed to spend time with Vietri. We had met upon my transfer from Cleveland at a Morehouse event. Our interactions had been mostly pleasant, and I didn't want to confuse our relationship. He agreed to double-date for dinner. I clued in Jessica, and when conversation turned to work, she and I went silent.

With a respectable windfall lining up, we lay in bed, and I snapped a selfie to replace the midnight photos I had taken when I thought porn was my future. As Valentine's Day approached, I woke up from a dream that included flowers. I knew that I wasn't going back to sleep, and snuck across the street. I went straight for the roses, made my purchase, and returned to surprise Jessica, who was still sleeping.

Seeking to reduce my cost basis, I listed my BMW for sale and got a call shortly thereafter. The man said he was interested in a test drive, but something didn't sound right. I asked how he intended to pay, and he responded, "We can work something out." When I pressed for clarity, he insisted, "I'ma get that."

Having avoided a possible car-jacking barely impacted my mounting stress. My body found an outlet through night sweats. They started slowly, but then gave way to sheets that were consistently wet. I knew the cause, but Sharkie insisted on a trip to the doctor. I chronicled recent events to the physician and noted additional hair loss.

I called my former boss and dad's friend, Larry, for legal guidance. Then, I visited the Equal Employment and Opportunity Commission (EEOC) to get a better feel for the process. They said that a charge couldn't be filed without adverse action. In other words, I would have to be put on a performance improvement plan or be terminated for the EEOC to investigate.

When the time felt right, I wrote Jeff to say that I felt like my opportunity was less compared to *others* in the office. He came to see me the next morning and said that I "had put a lot of thought into that note." He didn't realize that I put a lot of thought into everything that I did. I could see that he was under pressure as he listed several things that he expected from me. I retorted. He got visibly frustrated, turned to leave, and said, "I'm going to have to put you on a performance improvement plan."

The first two Bible verses came right on time, and the third was no less direct. Psalms 129 reads in part: "From my earliest youth my enemies have persecuted me, but they have never defeated me. My back is covered with cuts, as if a farmer had plowed long furrows. But the Lord is good; He has cut me free from the ropes of the ungodly."

Jeff followed up with an email on which human resources was copied. It listed several deliverables. He requested that I self-evaluate and turn over my prospect list of associations. The next morning, Jeff sent me a screen print of yellowpages.com with a note that read, "I thought this may help with your [new business] search." Vietri, the son of an executive vice president, was overloaded, but I was to go knocking on doors.

After being denied approval for the Cobb deal and forced to let the Caterpillar leads cool, I was expected to sell $4.5 million of new business in 2010 or have 60 percent of my annual objective by January 1 while being reduced to cold calling.

I followed up that afternoon in response to Jeff's request for deliverables and included a couple of my own. I asked him to provide the math behind my prorated goal and the name of a rep whom he had touted as having success with associations. At his request for self-assessment, I suggested using a tool that was brand new and the only one I was unfamiliar with. I categorized the association listing by how much progress I had made and then gave it to Jeff, who distributed it to the other reps. Any progress I could have made with them was now gone.

At the conclusion of his email he wrote, "I really want to see you engaged and passionate about your role here at MetLife. This opportunity is what you make of it, and I know that with some intense focus you can create opportunities that you *don't* believe exist."

I was a bit amused that he was just beginning to understand the war of words taking place in our emails and responded, "I am very engaged and passionate about the job that I do every day. I do, however, want to offer a point of clarification. I *do* believe opportunities exist! My concern is not the difficulty in finding opportunities, it's the ability to close these opportunities in a reasonable amount of time."

He was unable to provide the rep's name, suggested that I reach out to a third party to get it, and couldn't replicate the math. His justification was, "Please note, this is a very quick calculation. I may have used a slightly different starting point."

It didn't matter. I couldn't reach my goal and shot back, "I'll reach out to get the name myself and loop you back in. . . . I understand the math and agree that this calculation is fair."

Upon returning home a couple of days later, I saw Jessica was on the couch. She alluded to nothing and

I greeted her before walking upstairs. To my surprise, she had arranged the dying rose's petals on our bed. An eye was in the upper left corner, a heart was in the middle, and the letter "U" was at the bottom right. She loved me. I collected the petals, dried them, and added fragrance to the potpourri.

I was getting everything ready for a quick settlement, but knew I had more work to do. The annual Eagles outing in Phoenix was approaching, and the regional vice president who interviewed me in Houston, had moved there. I told him that I was a bit frustrated and asked to speak with him. Along with his wife, we met with my dad and his poker buddy, Woody, for drinks. I asked John what I needed to prove that I deserved more opportunity. He suggested that my online calendar reflect my activity.

John happened to have bought a house in the same community as my dad's friend, Beck. An invitation was extended, and we rode to the community's summit. There, Beck had cleared space for his multimillion-dollar home. We pulled in behind a few cars and a golf cart. The house included a synthetic putting green and was designed in a circular fashion. Each room offered a view and a retractable wall opened to outdoor seating. There was a room separated by a sliding door that was specific for poker, and at the center of the house was an infinity pool. The third level offered a loft-style room with more views. Solar panels helped to reduce expenses.

Before we left, Beck's wife grabbed me, looked me in the eyes and asked, "Are they bringing you along?" It was her way of asking if I was being properly groomed to have success.

The attention from all of the guests was on me and without hesitation I responded, "Slowly."

I was excited to introduce Jessica to everyone I knew, which led me to book a trip to Cleveland. My former office mates and I coordinated a happy hour, but Sharkie was booked on a conflicting gig. While having drinks, I hinted at Jim what I was experiencing in Atlanta. After I returned home, he called to say that there was a management opening in Minnesota. It offered a substantial increase in pay and ability to develop a team.

Given my hometown ties, I figured it to be a lucrative opportunity. The interview however, became disturbing. I confidently spoke to my prospective boss, but the conversation kept being redirected. He wanted to know more about a piece of business that I had lost. Clearly, Robert had sabotaged my opportunity. The interviewer said that he liked me and would hire me as a rep, but couldn't do so as a manager.

Knowing that I had difficult questions for MetLife to answer, I took Larry's advice and called human resources. I told them that I felt as though I had been discriminated against. Then, I returned to the EEOC. I completed the paperwork to file a charge and included the information their investigation should seek. Romans 13 provided guidance: "Everyone must submit to governing authorities. For all authority comes from God, and those in positions of authority have been placed there by God."

Feeling as though justice was at hand, I turned my attention homeward. My failing wireless router required periodic restarting, so I began shopping for a replacement. I discovered a suite of Apple products and created a wish list.

A box then came in the mail. Jessica had ordered me a new pair of sneakers. I reciprocated by enrolling her as my domestic partner and putting her on my health insurance. I also decided to make her the beneficiary of my life insurance. For that, I needed her social security number. She gave me the numbers,

3-2-7-8-0. More than a match to my birthdate, they confirmed her as my soulmate.

Bonuses for renewals and year-end business arrived in amounts corresponding to my wish list. I bought routers, a miniature desktop computer, and paid off my Acura. I invested in a vaporizer to give my lungs reprieve from smoke, and with the purchase of a grow tent, I moved plants from the attic to my closet. A bonus of several thousand dollars allowed me to get from under water on my BMW, and sell it to a dealership. Ultimately, I was working toward an engagement ring and wondered when I could afford it.

When I thought porn would make me an instant millionaire, I told my mom to plan a wedding. I asked her again. I wanted to get married on my thirtieth birthday, and it was just days away. I hadn't done right by Jessica's request though, didn't have the money, and tabled my urgency for her arriving family.

They were passing through Atlanta on a return from Florida and arrived on the twenty-sixth. After a quick welcome, I was happy to see them settle in. Her brother bought us dinner and the family gave me a large bottle of Hennessy with an attached balloon reading, "Happy Birthday from all of us."

We began to stretch out, and I queued LeBron James's movie *More Than a Game*. I hoped it would help them connect with the passion I had while isolated in Cleveland. On the wall behind us hung a painting that I purchased when at a low point. It included dull pastels with a little boy huddled in the corner. He was wearing a straitjacket and it was titled *All Alone*. Their presence was in stark contrast from what I felt in Cleveland. It's why I moved.

Jessica wanted her family to see Stone Mountain, but had rehearsal the next morning. I agreed to show her family the attractions. On our way to the exit, I was walking next to her dad. He spoke limited English, so I did my best to ask in his native language for his daughters hand in marriage. He acknowledged my words by shaking my hand.

Jessica joined us as we returned to the house for a group picture. Her family got on the road, and she told me about reservations that night at a favorite restaurant. We entered a secondary room, and I was surprised to see my brother, Rawle, and a host of others. Jessica had arranged my party.

I raised a toast to family and received a handful of gifts that included a scrapbook chronicling my first thirty years. Personal notes were inside, including one from Jessica. She referred to me as her best friend and said, "Get out there and *be* somebody!"

A familiar name then began popping up on social

media. I had listened to Shaun King's commanding oratory as a fellow student at Morehouse. Now, years later, he was launching a church. Jessica and I attended his Easter service.

The only real structure at the office was Monday morning sales meetings, and they gained formality. Jeff paid me increasing attention. It was almost comical as he finished a point, asked a question, then called my name to see if I could answer it. My training had started with fundamentals, which helped me to answer correctly.

Though being scrutinized locally, I got an email from a rep working my former territory in northeast Ohio. It read, "I started covering some of Akron/Canton back in September. I wanted to tell you that you are one popular guy up here! A lot of brokers always say how much they liked you."

Morehouse wanted to add a sales class to its curriculum and asked MetLife to participate. I was called on to teach and was joined by a senior vice president who flew in from New York. He was impressed by how well we worked together and suggested several trainings that would get me more exposure. I had already completed them. Knowing that I was seeing the best that MetLife could offer reminded me of what Jim had told me years before, that I could have eventually run the company.

As part of the performance improvement plan, Jeff and I had regular meetings. They revealed just how involved Robert was. Every time we wrapped, Jeff went directly to Robert's office for debriefing.

My frustration with MetLife was beginning to boil when my parents came to town for a friend's annual gathering. Sharkie was in Chicago dealing with home sickness as I began to feel that MetLife's forcing me out meant that nobody was safe. I decided to take a stand. My parents and I went out to dinner and I lit into a monologue. I was sure to deflect wandering ears by saying, "My employer" as opposed to "MetLife." I told my parents that with the information I possessed, I could change their stock price. I finished by saying, "They don't want a piece of me."

My parents left town, but not before my mom left a stocked freezer for both me and Jessica. The warmth of spring was starting to take hold, and I was eager to share a hobby with her. My mom's sister, Sharon, kept a garden and I was always excited to see what she had planted. I had a bit of experience in gardening myself, and took Jessica shopping. She was exited to pick things out.

We worked on the upstairs balcony as it started getting dark. Fatigue set in as she used her hands to shovel the soil. Jessica had moved past the surface of the activity and become invested in the process. The transformation was the sexiest thing I had ever seen.

Our first anniversary was approaching, and I had made plans, but was working overtime to minimize MetLife's ammunition. Sharkie nearly ruined the night, though, by accusing me of checking out a waitress at dinner. Afterwards, I surprised her with tickets to her first live play. The actors of *Cheaper to Keep Her* put on a powerful performance. It peaked with the main character, played by Brian McKnight, belting out lyrics from his hit songs. Work had clearly taken its toll on me, though, as I struggled to stay awake.

My efforts were paying off through personal relationships I had developed in the customer service center. An account manager wrote, "I truly want you to know that you are the best and easiest rep that I have worked with since I have been with MetLife. You always follow through and reach out to see if I need anything or can assist—and that is huge! Thanks again for everything!"

It was a rare Friday afternoon that I was in the office. Vietri approached, hoping for a better understanding of my role. He said something to the effect of "They're screwing the black guy." I knew he was in comunication with our coworkers, so I remained vague. Jeff, who normally left through a hallway adjacent to his office, took a longer path to stop by my office for conversation. It was the first time he had ever done that, and it felt like a last-ditch effort to save our relationship. He left, and footsteps then approached that quickened at the sight of my open door. Robert's tall frame leaped past.

Proverbs 22:16: "A person who gets ahead by oppressing the poor or by showering gifts on the rich will end in poverty."

I was back home on my couch about an hour later and processing the events of the day when I got a call from my Uncle Clifton. It was he who led the charge to get my mom's name changed when her dad died while she was at college. His wife had sent me the busting care package as a freshman.

More than a multimillionaire businessman, he was an inspiration. As a child I had seen him on TV riding on the back of a convertible in the Bud Billiken Parade, the largest African American parade in the country. He owned the building housing his accounting practice on the south side of Chicago. It was his black face that allowed Checkers fast food restaurants into the city, and he comped meals for my mom, brother, and me.

Even into his seventies, he was responsible for bar hopping with his nieces and nephews who were turning twenty-one. When my time came, the two of us and my brother were chauffeured by the basketball journalist Scoop Jackson.

Uncle Clifton's son met us at a bar, where I ordered the first of several Long Island Iced Teas. He raised the toast, "May you live to be one hundred, and I'm the last person that you see."

We hopped several bars and our adventure concluded with a martini, burrito, and my head out of Scoop's Pathfinder. As I vomited, I heard my uncle Clifton in his deep voice say, "I knew you'd make it."

He hosted a barbecue every year and summoned the men into his office, where we took shots of tequila. He went round for round with us, prepared my taxes, and upon noticing that I wasn't giving to charity said, "Open your wallet."

Now, I was thinking about how Vietri had assimilated, Jeff was doomed, and Robert was squeaking by when by phone I told my uncle, "Today's the day that everyone sealed their fate." He asked what I was talking about. I told him that I was suing my employer. MetLife had recently purchased Alico from the troubled AIG for $16.2 billion. Their expanded footprint included business in all but two continents, Antarctica and Africa.

To settle, I wanted all of my outstanding compensation paid and commission from my presentation on retiree dental given to minorities through scholarships. Lastly I wanted what they had paid when the State of New York fined them for charging black customers more than they did whites, $250 million.

I told my uncle what I would do with the money. He reminded me that taxes needed to be paid. With a lump sum exceeding $150 million, I intended to take a third for myself and then use the rest as an endowment. The gains would go to any and everybody with a viable dream who is willing to work for it. To ensure success, I would provide funding, counsel, and access to a network. He quickly caught on, saying that it would only fail if I "took my finger off the button."

For all of the swirling positivity, Sharkie couldn't see where our relationship was going. She questioned if it was genuine or if money was at the center. I reminded her that during our courtship she "never saw the garage." In other words, she didn't know how well I was doing. As we stood outside our bedroom, she asked how our story would end. I pointed inside and said, "We go to bed in there and wake up in heaven."

She continued to complain, and in disbelief I said, "You're gonna piss me off." I finally had my fill, acknowledged the points that she was making, and allowed her to finish. I then unleashed a series of unrepeatable words and watched her expression turn to shock.

She said, "I've never heard you talk like that before."

I turned to walk away while shooting a glance and replied, "You pissed me off."

The head of human resources sent a company-wide email reaffirming MetLife's commitment to diversity. About that same time, I was notified that representatives from the legal department would be coming to Atlanta. I was on time for a meeting that included a veteran attorney and his younger woman colleague. Other employees began to trickle in.

The seasoned attorney asked if meetings typically started so disjointed. I assured him that they did. The topic turned to lawsuits, which confirmed to me that their purpose was to take my temperature. Deepwater Horizon had recently exploded, and with oil still flowing into the Gulf of Mexico, I quipped, "You could be BP." The woman attorney cracked a smile and looked at her coworker. His and my face were deadpanned.

Taking a page from a previously disgruntled assistant, I stopped in the office after hours to clear out my drawers. When I was finished, what remained was necessary to do my job and a host of pictures. I printed a query from the Internet, forwarded calls to my cell phone, and closed my door for an extended absence.

Still interested in getting Jessica to northeast Ohio, we purchased tickets. Our visit began at the Pro Football Hall of Fame in Canton. We then drove north into Akron for lunch and were joined by representatives from a family agency I used to call on. They worked out of a converted house, and the matriarch warmed an apple dumpling for me whenever I wanted.

Jessica and I continued our journey to the Rock & Roll Hall of Fame, but I caught her in a funk. I learned while on disability that I had the power to put her in, and more importantly bring her out of, a bad mood. I was able to warm her up with special attention before we continued toward Sandusky.

My first time there was to conduct enrollment meetings at the water park. I made a return trip when Jim organized a regional meeting at the Lake

Erie island Put-in-Bay. Summer weekends brought a crowd of people to the local hot spot with their bars and restaurants.

Sharkie and I booked a room, explored, and came to a signpost. It pointed toward cities and included their distance. Chicago was listed. She posed for a picture, which should have tipped me off that another trip was coming. After returning to Atlanta, she stocked me up with groceries in preparation for her absence.

I didn't enjoy seeing her go, but was excited to vaporize and get some work done. On my list was a couple of doctor visits. The first was to an ophthalmologist who determined that each of my eyes required the same prescription. Next, for peace of mind, I confirmed through testing that I have no sexually transmitted diseases.

I knew that Jessica was enjoying herself, and I encouraged her to do so. We continued our updates through email. I began closing messages with "XOXOX." If she were to change each hug and kiss to a star, she would have a perfect five. We were speaking by phone when she was in a room with her family. A noise came from what sounded like the furnace. It brought silence. I paused as we waited for normalcy. In that moment, I feared losing what was becoming family.

When Jessica came back, I redirected the effort I had put toward my job into studying her. I learned which pieces of laundry she preferred to air dry, that she loved Target's dollar section, and I memorized how she liked her burrito bowls. She didn't know it, but I even reviewed restaurant menus for vegan items before finding something for myself. She was picking up on my likes too. When unloading groceries, I discovered that she had bought me REESE'S Peanut Butter Cups, my favorite candy.

Money wasn't generally a topic of conversation, and she surprised me by voluntarily paying the gas bill. I opened a retirement account for her and titled it "Jessica's Dreams." The intention was for her to create a nest egg, but she said, "One day, I'm going to turn all of my money over to you."

Knowing how hard she had worked, I didn't take that lightly and responded, "A lot people would be jealous of what we have."

MetLife's internal investigation concluded, and the investigator said that neither Jeff nor I would be happy. She didn't find evidence of discrimination and recommended that he go through training. For those paying attention, my absence from the office was a clue into the unfolding drama, but Jeff's subsequent resignation ignited interest.

An annual meeting was upon us, and every rep under Robert's supervision traveled to Atlanta. I didn't want to answer questions about my situation or be in his presence.

Second Corinthians 14–17 reads:

> For our present troubles are small and won't last very long. Yet they produce for us a glory that vastly outweighs them and will last forever! So we don't look at the troubles we can see now; rather, we fix our gaze on things that cannot be seen. For the things we see now will soon be gone, but the things we cannot see will last forever.

I found myself sitting in front of Remus, the rep who first warned me to watch my back. I thanked him again. He asked about the office tension and I said, "Look around." With representation from Houston, Louisiana, Mississippi, Alabama, Georgia, Tennessee, the Carolinas, and Florida, I was the only person of color. On a scheduled break, I walked to get away from the crowd.

I changed levels and was sitting outside on a bench when the Atlanta sales manager who first interviewed me was going to his car. He stopped to talk. I thanked him for seeing promise in me and for passing my name to his boss. He had no clue what was happening between Jeff, Robert, and me and asked what I wanted. My reply was simple, "A fresh start."

I began cleaning up at the house and brought loose items into my basement. With a focus on electronics, I sat with five computers, including an old desktop and the one that I bought after rupturing my Achilles tendon. It was a budget buy, didn't work very well, and I had used it to download pirated content.

I was sorting through my porn collection when I realized that nobody was more attractive to me than Jessica, so I deleted it. I then uninstalled file sharing programs and formatted the hard drive. I next turned my attention to the desktop, that had served me since college. From there, I transferred all of my files to a portable drive. With all of my files transferred and backed up for redundancy, I uninstalled the operating system.

With my former life deconstructed, I took the extraordinary step of walking to the fuse box in the garage. I opened the panel and flipped the main circuit, which ceased the flow of electricity into the house. In my mind, I was laying roots and waited a moment before restoring power. I then returned to my desk.

Blackburn, the top rep, to nobody's surprise was promoted to take Jeff's place. He called for a meeting with me and Robert. They came into my office and Robert's stress level was evident. He recoiled every time Blackburn said something I could use as ammunition. They asked where I had been, and I presented the queried list. I had eliminated non-producing prospects.

While walking through the office, I was joined by an African American woman who worked in national accounts. We had previously discussed entertaining, and she started asking questions that I spun with a politician's efficiency. Realizing that she had missed out on deeper conversation, she cornered me with a question that I wasn't prepared for. "Did it rain over the weekend?"

I had been engrossed in work so I smiled and laughed. "I have no idea."

I was confident that MetLife would quickly settle while I prepared for the long haul. I had started reducing my expenses, but was in need of income when Scott from Ohio planned a vacation to Atlanta.

He grew up in a trailer park, but had built a million-dollar business. I told him I wanted something of my own, and he offered to partner while paying me a draw. On July 4, I hosted a barbecue while keenly aware that it wasn't just the nation's independence, I'd be celebrating.

I wouldn't see a commission check for several months, so I set August 1 as my start date. Reps submitting their two-week notice were dismissed immediately. I was about to leave my resignation letter on my desk when Blackburn walked in. He was disappointed to learn that I was leaving.

I packed what was left, stacked it on my chair, and pushed it to the lobby. I entered the elevator as a handful of assistants asked where I was going. Before the doors closed, I said, "To pursue greater opportunity."

"I will execute terrible vengeance against them to punish them for what they have done. And when I have inflicted my revenge, they will know that I am the Lord."—Ezekiel 25:17

CHAPTER 8

NEW LIFE

I completed an expense report for my final months at MetLife and received reimbursement. Work emails had long since stopped coming, and I began focusing on other matters. My aim was to begin my new venture with a clean slate.

I set the mood in the house with my slow jam playlist. Jessica noted, "These are the songs you played when you were trying to tell me that you liked me."

We were later on the couch watching a sitcom. She was essentially in the fetal position, but on her knees instead of her side. I was spooned on top of her. A punchline was delivered and we laughed in sync. It prompted me to say, "This is how I want to spend all of my down time."

I often told her that I loved her and was sure to reiterate when things weren't going well. That's when she least wanted to say it, but the gesture allowed us to start fresh after an argument. We were standing outside our bedroom when I told her, "I taught you how to love."

She could openly discuss topics that most people are shy about, but she struggled with death. I could see it on her face when she was thinking about it, and Jessica required intervention to reset. It wasn't a topic that disturbed me, and more importantly, the Bible was teaching me that death is nothing to fear.

I was home alone organizing our bedroom when Jay-Z's remix for "In My Lifetime" came on. While I was high on marijuana, the chorus became hypnotizing. I locked into the lyrics and heard him say, "Medusa," the name of the character in Greek mythology who turned people to stone. It gave me pause. Then, a series of cryptic words followed.

Hebrews 4:16 had recently presented itself: "So let us come boldly to the throne of our gracious God. There we will receive mercy, and we will find grace to help us when we need it most." The reference allowed me to continue with peace of mind.

After listening to "When I'm Gone" by Eminem, I knew he was headed for a downfall. The song was essentially a goodbye to his beloved daughter. His following album was difficult to listen to, but the second track of his new one caught my attention. He opened by thanking his fans for their patience; then he chronicled the loss of a friend, turning to drugs, and eventually hitting rock bottom. The stage was set for redemption. I removed Jay-Z from my library and put Eminem's *Recovery* into heavy rotation.

Scott bought me a ticket to fly to Akron, where I was invited to stay at his house. We were typically up around 7 a.m. He drove us to his office as he puffed on a cigarette, and we arrived where coffee began to brew. He shared an office with his wife, and I wound up sitting between the two.

Scott paid for lunch, a family occasion that included his stepson, who was also employed as an agent. The Affordable Care Act was beginning to take hold, and Scott participated in conference calls as I started learning health insurance. I was accustomed to being an expert, so I felt a bit out of place. The thought of having my own clients, though, was refreshing.

The office shut down at five, and Scott's wife had dinner ready shortly thereafter. I changed clothes before taking a seat at the kitchen table. Their youngest son had health concerns, so the family adopted the recommended vegan diet. Our nights were spent together in the family room, down the hall, where Scott played his guitar, or in the basement.

We agreed that baby boomers would soon be retiring, which would create a fertile market. We needed a name for our agency and included what we thought were the necessary components to open doors: Atlanta Community Health Partners, or ACHP. Although I had incorporated JTB Capital, I had no idea what was necessary to make a business legit. Scott took charge of filing the paperwork, obtaining insurance, and making us eligible to sell products.

He started flying to Atlanta, where my basement became his bedroom and doubled as our office. I listened as he called companies from my prospect list, and did my best to mimic his approach.

I was returning to the EEOC when I began wondering what a powerful company like MetLife might do to keep me quiet. I gathered courage and continued into their lobby, where I found myself starring at a photo of the signing of the Civil Rights Act. Just over President Lyndon B. Johnson's left shoulder stood Martin Luther King Jr. I knew taking a stand against institutionalized discrimination was the right thing to do, but I wanted to maintain my anonymity. I looked closer at the room, which was full of white men. In the background I saw a brown face that I didn't recognize and said to myself, "I wanna be *that* guy."

With emails, surveys, and reports from my time at MetLife backed up to a mini SD card, I was due for a visit with Rawle. He had purchased a large house with his fiancée, and I made the drive to southwest Atlanta to see him. We found ourselves on his deck, where I presented the disk for safekeeping.

My EEOC investigator then notified me that MetLife was refusing mediation. They instead offered a $5,000 settlement. Keeping quiet about my overpayment upon returning to Atlanta would have netted me $60,000 more. Their offer was an insult, I declined.

Although my lawsuit against MetLife was the foundation for what I wanted to do financially, my focus was increasingly shifting to what was happening at home. The light coming through the windows of Sharkie's room had turned green. It caused me to step outside and observe the plants. When I next saw Jessica, I asked if she had seen them. She responded, "They're big."

We had a variety that she promptly referred to as *our kids*, and she insisted that I learn their names. They included "Billy Basil" and "Jose Jalapeño."

As normal, we found ourselves on the couch. She was sitting cross-legged and I was relaxing to the right. Almost as if in slow motion, Jessica set her laptop aside and unfolded her legs. She stood up and approached as I cleared space. She then crawled into my lap, where we came to a peaceful rest.

After my relationship with Jessica went public, many of the women from my past began to resurface. One wanted a familiar friend; another was reminded of me. A former classmate said that she'd be in town and suggested meeting for a drink. I didn't see the harm, but Jessica questioned her intentions.

I was invited—not her. The girl had a reputation, so I put Jessica's theory to test. I responded that inclusion of my girlfriend would be appreciated. It caused the woman to get angry. Jessica's instincts got me to that point, and I surmised that platonic intent wouldn't carry such emotion.

I continued, however, to defend my relationship with Melissa. She and I talked career, family, and sports. Sharkie wasn't moved, and at her request, I told Melissa that I needed space.

Jessica and I had our share of blow-out fights, which increasingly resulted in her leaving the house. We were getting into another when she turned to walk away. I wanted to finish my point and grabbed her wrist. She writhed. I was shocked by my action and let her go.

The pit of our battles came when we weren't communicating. We were upstairs when it had gotten late and she was heading to the garage. I heard a thump. I went to investigate and found her on the steps, crying. She had banged her head against the wall. Jessica argued that she never wanted a relationship. I knew that she was in pain and said, "It gets easier from here."

I worked methodically after every fight to reduce friction. After sourcing the problem, I engaged in prevention. It turned arguments into growing pains, but I also made Jessica accountable. I was reclined in the massage chair when she called. I sat up to listen to a story that was funny, but ran long. I looked at the phone and saw that she had been talking for nine straight minutes. I quoted the time. Although she was excited the next time she called, Jessica took a pause to ask if I was busy.

I was impressed with her resourcefulness and hard rule of no shopping until obligations were satisfied. She systematically organized her belongings with pouches hanging from a door and clothes ordered by color spectrum. I loaned her a rack which housed her shoes and a wall shelf for pictures of her family.

I was really happy with the direction our life seemed to be going when we found ourselves on the couch. The TV was on, and I was using my laptop while facing in her direction. I stopped to make a comment and looked to see that she remained focused on her screen. I knew that she had heard me, but I wasn't going to force her to respond. She had also stopped filling me in as fully after phone conversations with other people, so I went back to what I was doing.

By my estimation, I was honoring the *three-month rule* and working on laundry when Sharkie approached. She saw that it was hers and caught an attitude. I shut the argument down by saying, "I'll make your life really easy if you just let me."

Sharkie had befriended a group of guys that she referred to as "gay boys." They found a club they enjoyed. I wasn't interested in going, and Jessica gave me a pass to vaporize and play Xbox. I could easily game past 4 a.m. and often finished by taking a shower, getting in bed, and praying.

I had just gotten to sleep when Sharkie returned, looking to update me on her night. Then came a complaint. She liked parking in the garage and having a security system, but wasn't a fan of entering a dark house. I began lighting her way.

While I loved playing Xbox, my favorite way to end

a night was together. I had placed a couple of blankets over the back of the couch, which allowed me to creep into her late-night hours. The best nights, however, were when we shut down the floor and headed upstairs at the same time. It was a tantalizing feeling as we conversed, knowing that I was about to lie next to my best friend.

Jessica and I stopped at Sevananda, a natural foods store, and discovered a hot bar with vegan food. Their offerings changed daily, and we were impressed by their samples. As the store was located on the way back from my barbershop, I made a habit of picking up a meal whenever in the area.

I was later at home when Jessica showed up and was acting funny. She had been to Sevananda. We sat to eat the food she brought as she told me that one of the dishes was made with "seitan." We ate the rest, but that portion went into the trash.

We planned her first trip to Minnesota as another gig became available. A company wanted women to do promotions at the annual bike rally in Sturgis, South Dakota. I wasn't excited about the crowd, but believed Jessica could handle herself.

The job happened to coincide with my mom's return from Chicago. They planned to ride back together. I was already in Minnesota when the two arrived, and Sharkie entered the house wearing a track suit that I hadn't seen before. It was pink, looked to be made of velour, and was decorated with skulls and crossbones. It read, "Phucked Up." I feared that she might be facing an internal struggle, but believed she was strong enough to get through it.

Like she had done for me, I gave Jessica a tour of my old neighborhood. I told her that I wanted to visit a local lake, but first had a surprise in mind. It was nearly spoiled by her choice of outfit. When it came time to go, Jessica surfaced wearing shorts that were short. I had seen them multiple times, but my mom wanted her in something more conservative.

I wasn't interested in reliving a similar experience I had with my ex-girlfriend Mariah, so I defended Jessica. My mom had done business at the location and persisted. I reluctantly asked Jessica to change. Both she and her mood did, which lasted until we exited the car. We took steps toward our destination, and I turned to see that she had stopped. Unbeknownst to her, I had advanced the jewelers an image of the rings from China. We then sat for education as I anticipated a forthcoming quote.

Boys II Men was in town performing at the state fair, so my parents, Jessica, and I decided to go. We toured food stations and found seats as night fell to enjoy the concert. Space was limited on the articulated bus bringing us back to our car. Thinking that I wouldn't be seeing them for a while, I chose to stand near my parents. Leaving Jessica by herself produced another growing pain, and understanding that I was making the transition from being their child to her spouse.

One of the things I liked best about Jessica was how she valued relationships. That was a big deal for me, as my friends and family were most important to me as well. My friend Tonya, whom I had gotten to know in Cleveland, gave birth to a daughter and asked me to be her godfather. I was honored that Tonya would choose me, and I traveled with Jessica to northeast Ohio. Sharkie went to visit a dancer in the area, and I connected with Scott.

Jessica came to Scott's house on the day of the ceremony and talked about vegan recipes with his wife. We posed for pictures and Scott allowed us to borrow his new car. Jessica and I drove to Tonya's, where I met additional family and accepted the new responsibility.

The last quarter of the year was slow for Sharkie, and she asked about going to Chicago. I knew she wanted time with her family, and her absence would allow me to focus. In a matter of months, I had become a business owner, but I wasn't sure how to communicate from my new capacity. Not wanting to get caught uninformed, I started tapping various news outlets before making calls.

I began prospecting small companies with pitches that rarely got me traction. When someone entertained me, I didn't have much follow-up to my opening. The implementation of Obamacare presented a whole different set of challenges for gun-shy consumers.

Scott was better at opening doors and had our first success with a small accounting firm. He explained tax advantages to the owner, then enrolled him and his employee. My agreement with Scott was that all Atlanta business would count toward my $80,000 draw.

Scott had trained several agents before me and claimed responsibility for their success. I wanted credit for building my own business, which gave me motivation to work harder. A local printer provided business cards, and I established a weekly routine. Monday mornings were for organization, I made phone calls through Wednesday, Thursday was for door-to-door, and I finished the week at my desk.

I cold-called a company run by an older man. He

seemed friendly and gave me information to provide a quote. A lady at another business granted me entry and did the same. I returned to the older man with savings to show. He said that he'd pass it on to his current agent, meaning that my work would benefit someone else. I thought I had a sale with the lady, but she had been inundated by my competition. She asked that I try again in a year. In another businesses foyer, I waited to speak with a decision maker who approached then slammed the door in my face.

I was continuing door-to-door and started speaking with a man who dealt with fire station supply. He had a small group policy and Scott helped me land the account. He cold-called a larger company in Atlanta, whose HR professional happened to be from his hometown. The business added $20,000 in revenue.

I got an appointment with a firm specializing in legal technology and returned to present my findings. I wasn't necessarily confident, but I did my best to answer their questions. To my surprise, they agreed to my proposal. A surreal feeling came over me as I walked to my car. I was realizing that I had just closed my first deal.

☮

With Jessica back in town, I continued my pursuit of familiarizing her with everything that was important to me. Homecoming was upon us, and it required a backpack, bottle, and comfortable shoes. We met up with Rickey, Rawle, and Kareem, who was present when I met Sharkie.

She snapped pictures to capture what had become a sprawling event. Although Rawle had pledged Alpha, most of the people he was socializing with were Sigmas. They gave us seats, food, and drinks in their tent.

At the house, I was surprised to see Jessica had placed a package of REESE'S Klondike Bars in the freezer. On top was a note that read, "I Love You." A pan of red velvet cupcakes, also a favorite, appeared weeks later. The accompanying note said, "Yes, you can have one."

Of course they were all for me, but I was, more importantly, getting used to the notes she was leaving around the house. None left a greater impact, however, than the message she wrote in a card saying that I had become her life. The feeling was mutual, and like the rest of her writings, it went into the safe.

While we hadn't before, Jessica and I started to settle on a plan for the holidays. Thanksgiving for her family was disjointed, so we chose to celebrate in Minnesota. While there, she became amused by the central vacuum that my parents had installed in the kitchen's island. When kicked on, it sucked dirt to a canister in the garage. Jessica swept the floor to prove it worked.

In anticipation of Christmas, Sharkie went back to Chicago. I traveled to Atlanta. While grocery shopping, I saw a bin of discounted pomegranates. After a quick Google search for a recipe, I bought a couple dozen along with supplies.

A pot of water helped to prevent squirting juices from staining clothes as I separated the fruit from rind. Per the recipe, I layered the seeds with sugar and lemon juice in a pot. Heat dissolved the skin, and I used a strainer to skim pits from the top. Liquid pectin was added and I then filled mason jars with the pomegranate jelly.

My brother's dog, Charly, came back to visit, and I discovered her passion for the sun. She enjoyed the spot in the kitchen that collected light from a window, and I later found her sunbathing in Jessica's room. There wouldn't have been enough light to cover her whole body, except she positioned herself against the bed with her head tilted at almost a ninety-degree angle.

I took a seat beside her and started petting her as I looked into her eyes. The sun reflected against the back of her lens as I continued to gaze. The shape of a swirling star revealed itself, which caused me to look again. The star was gone, but it was replaced with a set of vertical diamonds. She was continuing to prove special.

I was beginning to shop for Christmas when I got a card from Scott. He included a note about our friendship, venture, and a cash bonus of $300. I had already ordered Jessica's gift, and was pleased to have the money for her family.

For my first Christmas away from home, I directed my energy toward the gift exchange. The year's theme was superheroes. Everyone had to wear a T-shirt of their favorite. I found a black one laced with green, matching eyes, and the phrase, "You wouldn't like me when I'm angry." I was representing the Incredible Hulk.

On New Year's Eve, I rode around with Jessica's dad and brother to pick up food for their house party. I later accepted what I thought was a challenge from her older brother. My favorite drink had been provided, and I started downing Hennessy and Coke with lime until Jessica pulled me aside. I already wasn't feeling good, and she explained that drinking in excess wasn't how her family celebrated.

I was clean-cut upon arrival, but had grown a beard during my stay. My shave before leaving measured how long I'd been there. After seeing me integrate with her family, Jessica's mom told her, "Jessie, I love him."

I returned to Atlanta and set Jessica's and my gifts under the tree to commemorate the holiday. She delivered on the ShamWows that I asked for, and I had given her a three-dimensional puzzle of Chicago. They sat alongside an automated soap dispenser, which came from her grandmother in the gift exchange.

Rickey was on leave, but preparing again for duty, so I invited him and a few people over. He stopped by with a young lady I had never seen before. She must have deduced that I owned the home, because as we sat on the couch she started rubbing my leg. The unexpected advance froze me in place. Jessica addressed my inadequate response and the growing pain helped me understand that I should have had a quicker reaction.

I later stepped outside and saw an armadillo. The critter was just to the left of my driveway and seemed to be digging in a circle. I appreciated how my new strategy to protect the most sensitive parts of my life in layers mimicked its armor and snapped a picture.

A couple of days later, a snow and ice storm rolled through the area. It shut the city down. There was a run on produce at the grocery store, and Scott was surprised that I wasn't making calls. Around the same time, Sharkie said that she wanted a vacation. I knew that she could budget, but I would be on the clock. I got the feeling that she was unsettled and figured that addressing her requests would help her relax.

A dancer whose family purchased a timeshare in West Virginia offered a cabin and a total of five of us committed. Sharkie mostly slept as I drove the first shift. It allowed me to take advantage of satellite radio. While she was awake, I tuned into the Chicago-based WGCI, hoping she would feel more at home. Strangely, it didn't matter what station we were listening to; a recently released single seemed to repeat. The chorus refrained, "I wish that I could have this moment for life."

Hello Friend

Family Portrait

Fourth Grade

Stech

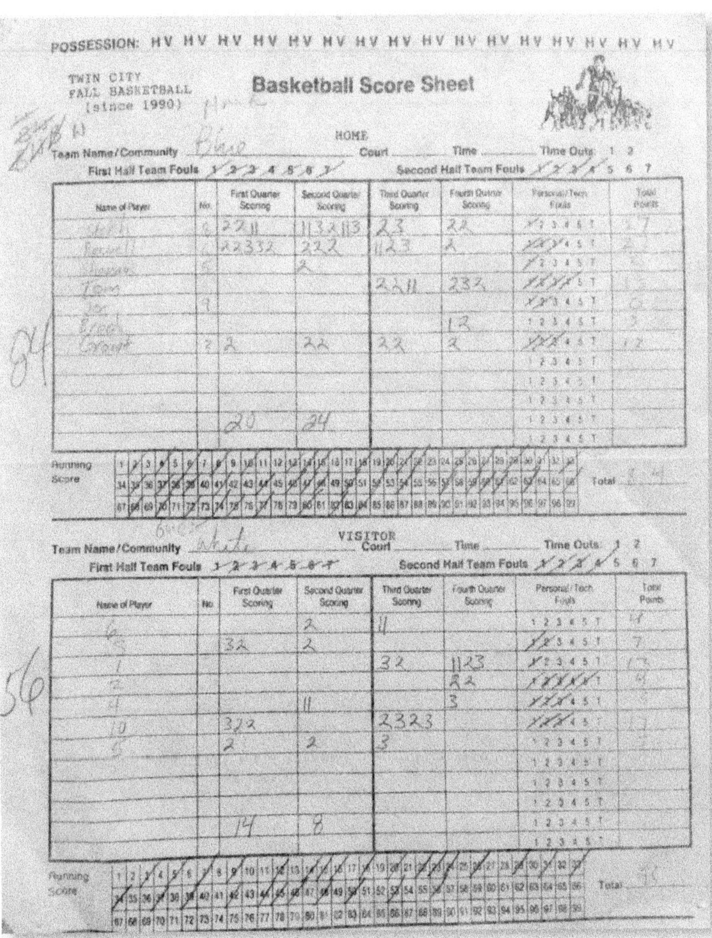

Box Score

A Seven Footer

Mumbling Through

End of the Line

Let It Ring

The Send Off

Japan

Picking up Knowledge

The Text

More Than I Could Eat

The Dream

Visiting Hilton Head

The Stare

Back to Work

Consolidation

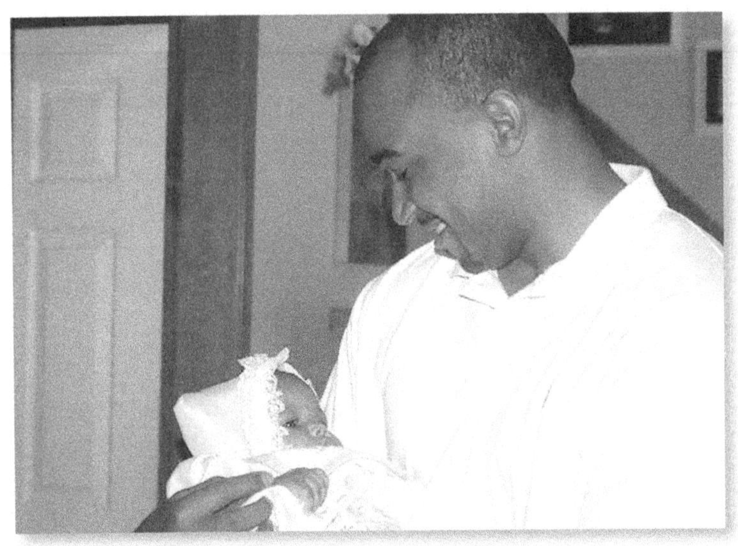

God Daughter

Homecoming

Charly

Armored

Act II

CHAPTER 9

THE STORM

Jessica and I did our best to split responsibility when we traveled, and our trip north was no exception. I drove the first leg as Sharkie slept, then got comfortable in the passenger seat about midway into our journey. After dozing off, I woke to near whiteout conditions and saw that we were on a back road. Jessica was tense at the wheel, and I did my best to say things that would keep her mind off danger.

We were first to arrive and proceeded to check in at the resort's reception. I wasn't expecting much, but was impressed by the dining room table, fireplace, and large gathering area. An open staircase led to our rooms.

Just as I allowed the surroundings to sink in, Sharkie's friend and the guy he brought with him arrived. Unable to contain my delight, I heard myself use a word that I had learned from Tony, saying, "This place is *über* nice."

The unknown man gave a curious look, then introduced himself as an arena football player. We were told that our host's girlfriend wouldn't be coming, making it three men and Sharkie.

My new cell phone carrier included a USB dongle that provided Internet to my laptop. The spotty reception was strongest in the kitchen, so that's where I set up my office. By way of instant messenger, Scott could see when his associates were online. I woke the next morning to log in.

At the end of my workday, the group said they wanted to go ice skating. Despite having only attempted it once, I agreed. We went to a rink that was mostly empty, and while trying to find my footing, I sensed Sharkie's attention being diverted. To test my feelings, I skated off, which allowed her opportunity to move around.

Her previous relationships had failed due to jealousy, so I was intent to give her space. We returned to the cabin, and with an early morning ahead I called it a night.

I was into my daily routine and making calls when the arena football player came to the kitchen. I acknowledged his presence as he eavesdropped before returning upstairs. Sharkie later said that they had spent the night drinking. The guys made a game of jumping over the railing onto the couch.

As night approached, Sharkie and I went to a nearly empty restaurant. The host sat us near a couple who struck up conversation that I entertained. Sharkie later complained of my talking to strangers.

Upon returning to the cabin, we gathered around a table when someone suggested playing Ring of Fire. I had never heard of the drinking game, but agreed and did my best to quickly learn the rules. A deck of cards was spread out facedown. Upon turn, each participant was to draw a card. An ace indicated that everyone was to drink; a deuce allowed the person who drew it to choose someone else for a drink, and so on.

Eventually a queen was drawn, representing a question round. Everyone had to participate. Questions were to be asked until someone failed to do so. It came time for the football player to ask Sharkie a question, and without hesitation came, "How big are your tits?"

I immediately said, "That's not cool." The table dispersed and with plans of a morning departure, I decided not to make a bad situation worse. As we prepared for bed, Sharkie defended the perpetrator by saying it was only a game.

She and I had previously argued over an interaction she had with her ex. They were in Chicago, and he touched her breast to get her attention. Sharkie dusted it off by saying they had "that type of relationship." I was more concerned about future actions, yet she failed to draw a line the next time she saw him.

Over the course of our relationship, I had indicated concerns which had mostly been addressed. A major one, though, hadn't. It was how we lay in bed. I typically initiated contact, which was okay until I needed to adjust. Sharkie complained that the bed got too hot, which made her keep to herself. That night, I was already upset, and the draft coming from the window didn't help. As the temperature dropped, I held my ground. Sharkie was just inches away, but I shivered throughout the night.

We woke the next morning to a fresh layer of white. Our housemates said that a blizzard was incoming and prepared their snowboards. With the chances of Sharkie and me getting on the road dwindling, we decided to join them at the slope. I had no intentions of renting equipment and was cordial, but curt, as we walked from our cars to the lodge.

Snow was beginning to fall, and Sharkie had just completed a snow angel when I decided to get a body board. I left her warming by a fire, rode the lift, and lay down face first. I used my feet to push off, which began an intense rush.

I reached the bottom, having expelled built-up aggression, and re-entered the lodge. Sharkie was shocked at my appearance. Aside from my smiling face, I had no idea what had changed. My outfit, made of dark fleece, was caked in white.

As we walked back to our cars, I was still upset about the previous night. Snow had been falling all morning, and I put my car into gear. It wouldn't move. Only three people around were capable of freeing it, and I reluctantly accepted the football player's olive branch.

The forecast showed the storm was passing, so Sharkie and I packed our bags. I was just feeling the relief of saying our goodbyes when Sharkie confounded me. She asked the football player for tickets to a game. He smiled and looked at his friend.

As soon as we were on our way I said, "TICKETS?!" Sharkie said that she was just trying to show support and didn't understand why I was upset. I drove while hoping that she would come to her senses as we sat in silence for as long as I could take it.

The issue remained a concern upon our return to Atlanta, but Sharkie continued to defend her position. Feeling defeated, I asked for the opinion of our host, which marked the first of our problems to be made public. At issue was the football player's behavior and Sharkie's response. When she and I started dating, she had told me that the easiest way to determine if someone had lied was to ask the question in a different way. She was sitting in the living room when her dancer friend responded. Sharkie read the message aloud and I was immediately confused. She had posed the question in a way that absolved her of any responsibility.

I ceded the argument and was getting back to work when more bad news came. I had tried seeing my Uncle Clifton when I was last in Chicago, but I was fighting a cold. He was dealing with pneumonia and couldn't speak above a whisper. My germs would have complicated his health.

He had settled into a house long ago, began gourmet cooking and continued to dabble in business. Upon a previous hospitalization, the staff began referring to him as "Mr. Wonderful." When we spoke on that fateful day, Uncle Clifton's final words echoed in my mind: "You're the one I want." To my knowledge, he hadn't picked a successor for his ventures, and I felt as though he was giving me his nod.

His body was donated to science. In lieu of a funeral, he requested a cocktail party. Sharkie and I traveled to Chicago, and while I asked for her to be invited, there wasn't capacity for his best clients, let alone Jessica. I put on one of my oversized suits and went to meet my family.

Upon entry was a table displaying two of his favorite things: a pipe and a Bloody Mary. I found a table with my mom, dad, and brother, as well as my Aunt Sharon and her husband. The obituary referenced a construction business that I didn't know my uncle owned. It wasn't a solemn occasion, but I missed his deep laugh as I wondered if he would help finance my dreams.

Upon return to Jessica's house, I found my way to a chair and plopped down. My clothes mimicked my relaxed posture.

Jessica's brother, who knew my uncle for giving away food in the community, asked, "Did you win the case?" It was a reference to my sharp dress and exhausted look.

I was growing increasingly closer to his kids, who enjoyed when I picked them up for a gentle shake. His son, whose head bobbed back and forth while I did it, especially liked it. Anytime I went for an errand, he asked to come along. I was unsure about taking him away from his family and always deferred. As I was preparing to travel back to Atlanta, I saw him playing by himself and got on the floor to join him.

While back home, I noticed that the bulging veins in my biceps that I identified as a sign of strength had faded. I was typically rolling out of bed just in time to activate my messenger, so working out in the morning wasn't an option. The gym got crowded after work, so I decided on Monday, Wednesday, and Friday at noon. I informed Sharkie, who, too, had a membership, and vowed to join me. I often found myself waiting for her to get ready.

On one of my days in the field, I bought a bag of rice crackers. As we sat on the couch, Jessica and I munched. Knowing they were a hit, I purchased more. I ate them by the handfuls, but noticed my favorites were becoming scarce. I glanced to see Sharkie pecking from a paper towel and return what she didn't like to the bag. The second time I found myself staring at leftovers, they went into the trash.

She asked for us to bake something together, and we decided on my grandmother's pound cake with vegan substitutions. The result was a dessert that looked similar to what my grandmother had mastered, but tasted markedly different. It wasn't bad, but I could see that Sharkie preferred the edges and left me with the center.

Jessica wasn't focused, and I could sense her growing anxiety. She wasn't a fan of the agents she had hired and participated in a recent audition that didn't go well. The opportunity was for an up-and-coming rapper, whose girlfriend she got to know while living in Los Angeles. After getting a direct lead, Sharkie showed up at a tryout, and was dismayed to see other dancers represented by her agents. Sharkie hadn't been included.

The artist had final say, and Jessica was notified that she wouldn't be getting the job. She came home in a sour mood, saying a spot went to a blonde who simply bounced up and down. The artist's album, *B.O.B. Presents: The Adventures of Bobby Ray* was edging *Recovery* out in my rotation, but Sharkie refused to listen.

She had started her career in Chicago, honed her skills in LA, and was trying to put everything together in Atlanta. She, however, was spending most of her time on the couch. I knew something in the house would inspire her and was pleased to see her assembling the three-dimensional puzzle I had bought her for Christmas.

☮

Jessica dreamed of buying into a soft-serve chain, and my interest piqued when a franchise opened across the street. I enjoyed the act of pumping my own samples and topping my treat. We paid based on weight for food that was really good, but their efficiency was even better.

My parents planned a visit, and I gave Scott, who was making a habit of staying into the weekend, a heads-up. He paused before saying that he had already purchased a ticket for the same time. We were invited by a wealthy friend of my dad's to dinner. The five of us rode through traffic in my sedan to a southern-style restaurant.

Scott and Francis bonded during cigarette breaks. When the opportunity presented itself, I floated the dessert business. Francis looked into my eyes and said, "Let's open a franchise." He then looked across the table to where my dad was sitting and said, "We'll get your dad to run it."

I got to work putting a proposal together, but began feeling as though I was making all of the effort. It was exactly the type of project that I wanted to finance, but I thought Sharkie would take a greater role. My frustration grew, and I placed the material in a binder before confronting her about balance. She disarmed me by reciting facts from the website. Although I couldn't see it, she was working.

Feeling better about our upcoming meeting, the two of us drove to Francis' house. We were given the floor, and I led with profitability. He asked a handful of questions, and I provided an application with prepaid postage. I knew the store would sell itself, so above all, I requested that he visit a location.

My business wasn't growing as quickly as I had hoped, and there were more stumbling blocks than I expected. I hadn't had much success since closing my initial deals but decided to stay the course. It brought me to the field on a Thursday. After hours of knocking on doors, I returned home. Sharkie welcomed me back, but didn't inquire about my day.

Rawle and his friend from Detroit wanted time at the shooting range. Jessica, however, wanted nothing to do with a firearm I had purchased in Cleveland. I accepted their invitation and went on a Friday afternoon. Sharkie then complained about me finishing my week with recreation. My work was complete, so I didn't see the issue. I had even cleaned floors, which she knew to be a pet peeve. Further complicating matters, she had left a maintenance request for her "landlord." Her recent actions fueled a beef that I was ready to levy.

The attentiveness and care-free attitude that caused me to fall in love seemed to be fading. It was replaced with distractions and complaints. I had made the phone call that changed my career, but I was working to pay *our* bills. Frustrated, I said, "I disappear for hours and you're not remotely interested." I wanted our time together to be quality, which is why I worked so hard while she was away. "You don't see me working, and that's not a coincidence," I ranted. Fed up with the quick dismissal and nonengagement of my comments, I finished by saying, "You have no respect for me."

Sharkie pressed me on issues that were concerning to her, but she quickly disappeared when she wasn't getting her way. Feeling as though we had reached an impasse, I reversed our roles and left the house. To help me relax, I queued a playlist of an artist whom I had been following since seeing his musical debut in the Digital Underground track "Same Song." It catapulted Tupac Shakur into the mainstream. I retraced my steps since arriving in Atlanta and reminisced about places that I had called home.

The mood was completely different when I returned to the house. Jessica wanted to know where I had been. Her openness allowed us to tour in a relaxed way. Instituting a new rule, I asked that we remain in the same vicinity until arguments were resolved. She agreed.

☮

Sharkie introduced me to a military vet who was in the throes of a divorce. He was looking to get away. I agreed to let him stay for a few days, and he made himself comfortable on the couch. In my downtime, I joined him and Sharkie, who remained plugged into her laptop, to watch TV, help sort out problems, and enjoy his company.

Jason, whom Sharkie had given a ride to the airport, was also spending time around the house. A group of us went for soft-serve, where he casually and continually dropped the N-word in mixed audience. I was already put off with his lack of filter, and we were later at home when I needed groceries. I asked if they wanted anything, to which Sharkie said no. Jason, however, told me to "get" him some Starbursts.

Sharkie joined a dance crew that was featured on MTV, but they would have to pay for studio time and asked to use our garage. I made every effort for her to know that it was her place too. They placed several full-length mirrors along the wall where she normally parked her car so they could rehearse. I was getting into a groove on my Xbox when Sharkie asked that I film their routine.

I put my controller down and began to assist.

After returning to my game, I was again interrupted. Sharkie asked that I continue to film, and I got up before explaining that my video game competition was happening live. I wound up in the kitchen preparing to cook as she and her friends began packing up.

Her body had mostly disappeared down the steps when I realized that she was leaving without saying goodbye. "Bendición," I called out. It gave her pause, but she continued without signaling the cross or giving me a kiss.

I woke up on a Saturday morning and was surprised by the number of people who had stayed over. I left to run an errand, and Sharkie could sense my displeasure when I returned. She asked why I was upset and I said, "There's always people in the house."

For the turmoil that Jessica and I were experiencing, we also had our really good moments. Whenever she was preparing for work, I often stopped what I was doing to spend time with her. It tended to be a moment of peace, but on one occasion there was an energy in the room. With the rapper Nas playing in the background, we embraced on her way out. He repeated the word "breathe," until we slowed down, and did.

There were three types of entertainment that Sharkie enjoyed: dance, comedies, and reality shows.

Bad Girls Club had been on for several seasons. It featured catty, half-dressed women. I, however, hoped that Jessica would re-watch the TV show *24* with me. She eventually conceded to one of the eight seasons.

Whether it was a music video, live performance, or award ceremony, Sharkie seemed to know somebody on stage. It was a competition, though, that produced a face that I had never seen before. Sharkie had a crush on the rapper Method Man, grew into liking the actor Michael Ealy, and caught [Justin] Bieber Fever. Because I had told her that no one was more attractive than her, I kept my feelings about Nicole Scherzinger to myself.

Aside from sports, I wasn't into any late-night programming and deferred to what Sharkie liked. She tuned us in to a couple of comedians, one she had met in LA, and another who was making a name for herself. I didn't think either was particularly funny, but Sharkie enjoyed their shows. To me, nights were better spent answering questions from notebooks that she had bought titled, "How well do you know your spouse?"

Scott asked that I spend time with him in Ohio, and after arriving, I began to understand exactly what that meant. We had grown close, and with the amount of time we spent together, I believed that I was his best friend. We golfed, played basketball, and stepped outside for hacky sack on cigarette breaks. I became accustomed to leaving for work, eating, and exercising when he did. I had also come to entertain his streaming thoughts.

He talked while I listened. I was beginning to decompress after dinner as we sat in his living room. One of his kids began acting up, and his wife responded with pointed lips and a finger in their direction. It was a sharp departure from the pleasant demeanor that she normally displayed. During the three-day trip, I had only talked for about forty-five minutes and was mentally drained.

I grabbed a meal and boarded my flight but was still stressed when Jessica picked me up. To no fault of her own, I got upset when she started talking. I couldn't take it and asked for silence. I knew my reaction was unexpected and attempted to explain. She dismissed Scott's behavior by saying, "He just likes to talk."

Jessica and I were in the house on a quiet afternoon when a noise came from outside. It didn't alarm, and Sharkie acknowledged that she heard it also. I approached to investigate and thought she might, too, be interested. I, however, found myself at the windows while she continued on her computer.

I was appreciative of the specialized cloths she had given me for Christmas and the warming weather presented an opportunity. I asked Sharkie to join me outside to wash our cars. She declined.

With our second Valentine's Day approaching, I woke up early and wondered how I might spark our relationship. I snuck out of bed and walked across the street for flowers. I set them on our kitchen counter, hoping to again surprise her, but after climbing the steps I found Sharkie awake in bed. I had to explain where I had been.

She asked about going to Chicago, and I said okay. Privately, though, I started questioning her open-ended visits. In addition to seeing family, she'd be going out. I asked only for a message before bed so that I knew she was safe.

While away, Scott came to town with his stepson. It became clear that he had gotten too comfortable. I hadn't appreciated his referring to my ex-girlfriend Leslie's breasts as "big floppies." In line with a recipe his wife had shared, he elbowed his son, asking if I ate "Sharkie's pie" for dessert. It was a reference to oral sex. He could sense that I was upset and made what was becoming a routine apology.

Sharkie was still in Chicago as my birthday approached. I didn't want to spend it by myself or explain that the Jessica I had come to know was gone. My brother's dog was smart, fun, and beautiful. He had adopted her from Atlanta's Humane Society, so I started trolling their website. I found a thumbnail of a similar-looking canine.

The two-month-old looked like Charly, but had a lighter coat. She was listed as a shepherd mix. I clicked the image and found two additional pictures, as well as a short video. In it, she was set back in a locker. I could tell that she was intelligent because she kept taking steps forward before retreating. She was probing.

I had a prospect meeting scheduled to end the week, but in my excitement, I shot over in the morning for an introduction. Upon entering the kennel, I could see metal lining the wall on the right, so I circled around to the left. After petting a few puppies, I turned my attention to the wall. That's where I found her.

An associate allowed us time together. I knew that I loved her, but didn't want her alone on our first day. I asked if they might hold her, but concern that potential parents wouldn't come back made that impossible. With no other choice, I began completing the paperwork for adoption. When it came time to name her, I thought back to my Spanish classes and wrote the feminine version of my class name, "Domema."

"Mema," was provided a crate. I picked out some toys and loaded them in my backseat. I continuously checked on her as we rode home and said, "We're going to have a lot of fun." Her incessant whine was only interrupted by a gurgle. I turned to see that she had thrown up. Luckily for me, she was eating again.

When we reached the house, I placed her in the grass. Then, I led the way inside. I had just about made it to my desk when I turned around to catch her looking back. She wanted a sense of where she had come from. I put on my terrycloth slippers, and she began nibbling on them. I swapped my foot for a tennis ball, finished my meeting prep, returned her to the crate, and informed Sharkie that I got a dog.

As we settled in that evening, it dawned on me that I had forgotten to buy her food, so I shared my chips and queso. I was instructed to be separated from her on our first night, but I was comfortable on the couch. She fell asleep on the floor and against my arm. I later needed to adjust, so I picked her up so she could sleep on my chest.

Dog parks were out of the question until her vaccines took hold. We, therefore, spent Saturday around the house. With downtime, I began thinking of my birthday dinner and flipped through *Morton's Steak Bible*. It was a Christmas gift from my mom, and I found a recipe for Steak Diane. It had me salivating.

I shopped for the missing ingredients and starting fielding birthday calls the next morning. Sharkie touched base an hour or two later. I relaxed on the couch with Mema before starting to cook dinner. As seven o'clock approached, I plated toasted French bread that I topped with filet mignon and a cognac cream sauce that included mushrooms. I finished cleaning the kitchen so that I wouldn't have to look at dishes while I ate and poured myself a glass of Cabernet Sauvignon. To that point, Mema had gotten the last of everything I was eating, and I had no intention of changing behavior.

The only dog Jessica liked was the one she grew up with. Sharkie was lukewarm, at best, when she met Mema.

I was determined for her to have discipline, and we started with soft treats that she could nibble. As she learned, they came as reward for successfully executing instruction. Sharkie complained of shedding and preferred Mema to sleep in the basement. I wound up enclosing the garage's entryway with a gate against the steps. A pee pad was placed in the corner, but sleep was difficult as Mema whined throughout the night. Breaking to retrieve her would only prolong the adjustment. We endured to find urine on the floor the next morning.

In preparation of Mema's next night, Sharkie lined the floor with pads and taped them down. Mema's pen was starting to produce an odor, so I placed an air freshener in the wall before bed. The next morning, I found the pads were torn up, pee was all over the floor, and the air freshener had been ripped from the wall.

Her housebreaking proved to be an unexpected challenge. I watched as she went where and when she wanted. I grew aggravated with a patch on the landing that was consistently wet. When not being watched, that's where she snuck off to. Sharkie also complained about urine on the steps.

I thought she was surely mistaken, as I couldn't comprehend how or why Mema would go there. I was later working in the kitchen when Mema was climbing the steps. I could see her through the railing as she got halfway up, stopped, turned to look me directly in the eyes, and squat.

I could tell the world was opening to her when she took notice of the gazebo across the way. My aim was for her to grow naturally, so I leashed her to lead me. She sniffed flowers, but also wanted to see the rest of the neighborhood. I trailed at her pace. We circled around, found the entrance to a boardwalk, and journeyed back to the house.

Stray cats picked up on her presence and began spying on us as we relaxed in the grass. Any indication that they might be friendly was put to rest when we found a plume of feathers on our trail. Not one for intimidation, Mema retaliated by digging up and eating their poop.

Sharkie and I were preparing to leave the house for an outing when she went to wait for me in the car. I secured Mema's pen and turned the security system on. As I attempted to exit, she blocked me with bobbing and weaving. I was forced to get light on my feet, scramble past her, and close the door in her face. Feeling as though I'd barely escaped with a victory, I took a seat next to Sharkie and exhaled a breath of relief.

Mema was coming of age, so we went for her first

experience at the dog park. She got roughed up. I convinced Sharkie to join us on the next trip, and with the back windows cracked, we were on our way. Not five minutes later, I turned around to see the back seat was empty.

"Where's Mema?" I asked.

I made a panicked U-turn as Sharkie tried to comfort me. Traffic was stopped and Mema was crying on the side of the road. A young couple was scooping her up. I advanced to inform them that she belonged to me, and with child locks enforced, we continued on our way.

Either from jumping out of the window or playing at the park, Mema got cut. I left Sharkie at home and took Mema to the vet. She later entered the house wearing a neck cone. Sharkie asked if she was hurt, and without hesitation I responded, "Just her pride."

For all of the grief Sharkie gave me about Mema, she had become a source of entertainment for her crew. Mema was welcome to hang out with the dancers, and I was notified when there was an accident. On one afternoon, I showed Mema some love by stroking her coat. She then went upstairs. It wasn't long before Mema returned.

I had work to do, but she was commanding attention. I started petting her again and the massage got deeper. She got sensitive, but wanted me to continue. The interaction didn't sit well. She darted up the steps, where Jason called her name. I could tell that she was in shock because somebody asked, "What's wrong with Mema?" It was clear to me that she was learning her identity.

Lying around on Sunday mornings produced guilt, so I began to regularly attend church. I wasn't going to make friends; instead, I hoped to hear a word from God. There were two morning services and I arrived just after the first. I always slipped into an empty chair in the back.

Pastor Shaun King presented the material in a relatable manner, but he was still learning the power of the pulpit. He encouraged thought, but wanted final say. He chastised a member who spoke up by saying, "I have the mic."

Once concluded, attendees were asked to help break down. I always stacked at least one chair before leaving. Realizing the first service would facilitate a shorter stay, I started waking up early. When it came time for offering, I made a nominal donation in an envelope that included both Jessica's and my name.

I emailed Shaun with a bit of my backstory, and included the settlement I hoped to receive from MetLife. He didn't respond. I was a bit surprised and followed up. He eventually sent an unengaging reply.

The church advertised baptism, and the thought stirred me. I didn't, however, want to further open up to someone who didn't seem to care. I ultimately decided that my commitment was bigger than him, responded to an inquiry, and received an immediate response from a young lady charged with baptismal coordination. She informed me that I would have to sit with the associate pastor to discuss my decision.

Assistant Pastor Broderick and I scheduled a meeting. I drove the ten minutes from my townhouse to his midtown office. Sitting across from him, I was immediately impressed by his openness and concern.

On Easter Sunday of 2011, I locked arms with another member of the church backstage. A few others stepped out ahead of me, then came my turn. I entered to Broderick's introduction and he asked whether or not I'd "walk with Him." I affirmed, then told those gathered about the circumstances leading to my choice.

I concluded, "For every step you take toward God, he takes at least one toward you." After thanking the audience, I pointed to Jessica, who was recording the event on her phone. I told her that I loved her, then climbed into the pool where I allowed myself to be lowered.

Tony had shared our movie script with a few of his friends, and he always received positive feedback. We knew that it needed to be polished, and urgency came when he said that his eldest brother was interested. He was married to the Will Smith's sister and was in the process of lining up a meeting with the actor's agent.

The last time I had tried working on the script was on a flight from northeast Ohio to Atlanta. I was just beginning to dig in when the plane started to shake. I put the script down and the flight steadied. I started to read again, and the turbulence returned. Thinking it wasn't a coincidence, I stowed the papers.

Leaving MetLife wasn't a difficult decision, but generating income was causing stress. The potential revenue sources from my agency, lawsuit, movie script, and dessert franchise made me feel secure.

Sharkie's career took a positive turn when she hired a new agent. He represented members of her crew, and they were scheduled to perform at Atlantic Station. I went to watch. Sharkie's new agent presented himself as professional, and I told her that I liked him. Her workload increased shortly thereafter.

The first job he booked for her was from the Georgia Lottery. Sharkie danced on their behalf during the halftime of an Atlanta Hawks game. She was then selected to dance on two separate occasions with Beyoncé. They were both for her new single, "Run the World." The first gig was at the Billboard Awards. The second was part of Oprah's send off after twenty-five seasons on television.

Sharkie came back to town and put a suitcase that I loaned her upstairs. She quickly fell back into routine. After a class, she dropped my backpack on a kitchen chair and began to settle. With her arms removed from the sleeves, her T-shirt was hanging like a necklace. She had peeled and was eating a mango in a way that I had never seen before.

It was intuitive, but my eye candy was interrupted when she spoke. She knew I couldn't eat it, but offered me some of her fruit. I reminded her of my allergy. Eating mangoes causes me to swell and is potentially fatal. I took greater issue, though, with her travel bags that she hadn't unpacked.

She told me about an NBA player who saw her in Chicago. He said that she was pretty. She retorted that he was wearing a pretty scarf. I took her at her word, but a friend later recited a different version of her story. There were other inconsistencies, too, and I figured that I'd set my concerns to rest by asking Sharkie if she had ever lied to me. She was taken aback and quickly shook her head. It was good enough for me.

I took Sharkie to the strip mall across the street where Mema and I had been frequenting the pet store. There was a female associate we had gotten to know. Sharkie didn't like our friendship, and showed the clerk an attitude. Sharkie's behavior continued on our walk back. I sensed her jealousy and parroted, "Don't judge."

Sharkie continued, undeterred, saying, "I judge."

While on a drive, I saw that a house down the street had numerous belongings set outside. Upon closer look, I concluded it was the home of a hoarder. I showed Sharkie, and on a subsequent ride, she pointed it out to Jason. Our conversation to that point had largely remained private. The leak made me wonder what else she was sharing.

With her frequent absences, late nights, and disinterest, I began keeping information to myself. She picked up on the change. Feeling shut out, she began lobbing questions. They came in a way that felt more like interrogation than conversation. It prompted me to say, "I don't do interviews."

CHAPTER 10

IN-DEPENDENCY

From watching the aftermath of Deepwater Horizon's explosion, I knew that I next wanted to visit New Orleans. I had fallen in love with chargrilled oysters served at a restaurant in the area and there was no telling how their habitat might be affected. I offered to pay for the hotel, and Sharkie agreed to buy our food. On our way to the airport we dropped Mema off with sitters.

In New Orleans, we stopped for beignets at Café Du Monde, walked the waterfront, and of course went for oysters. For additional exercise, Sharkie brought a pirated workout DVD. I worked out alongside her in our hotel room while conscious of her previously stated stance against bootlegged material.

My previous visits centered around Bourbon Street, but we explored and found an open-air market. We stopped at a vendor selling pralines, and I introduced them to Jessica. There was a basket set out front containing slips of paper for patrons to take with Bible verses printed on them. We bought Icees, stopped for pictures, and came to a man selling dresses. Sharkie found one she liked, but didn't want to commit. I offered to and bought it for her. We stopped to get pralines for her family on our way back to the hotel, and I was encouraged by the Bible verses I had received. Sharkie refused to tell me what hers said.

We came to a tourist shop featuring an upright alligator. It had its mouth open, and Sharkie put her head inside as she posed for a picture. I found it amusing, but she didn't like the pained face that she had made. She asked for another picture so she could have one of her smiling.

She had levied complaints during the course of our relationship, and most were legitimate. I learned to understand the impact of my missteps and made amends. I committed to adjusting, but felt like I was the only one trying to make a difference.

She was often first to break into an argument and focused on the minor, while I took a global approach. My hope was that we'd meet in the middle, and in a recent argument I said, "You can't blame everything on me."

Despite the challenges, I was determined to eliminate anything she could complain about. Sharkie was upset about posting pictures quicker than me, so I made a point of getting those from New Orleans online before she did. When we next came to tension, I vowed a fix, but was told that my concern had to wait.

Sharkie was interested in furthering her education, which I supported, and she told me of a course she had found online. I grew concerned, however, upon learning they were based in Chicago. She refrained the same defense, "They're online classes."

Sharkie's friend, nicknamed Butt Cheek, planned a visit to Atlanta. I was okay with the company, especially from someone else who got high. With Sharkie's permission, I went upstairs and turned on my vaporizer. Once warm, I set a bowl on top, flipped a switch, and watched a white cloud form. I returned to the couch, where I handed it over. After one pull, Butt Cheek said, "It tastes good."

Jason and another dancer were interested in getting together, so we met at a Waffle House. Shortly after being seated, I felt the conversation going in an uncomfortable direction. I went quiet and watched

Sharkie berate the people whom she spent the most time with. It was an effort to impress her friend. The subject turned to Beyoncé, and Sharkie's fellow dancers expressed negativity. It caused Sharkie to recalibrate and defend the person who had recently given her work.

The increasingly disturbing comments continued after Butt Cheek left. I was on the main level as Sharkie and I were engaged in discussion. It continued as Sharkie walked upstairs. As if she didn't think I understood, she said, "Capisce?" I tried to explain that the word came as an insult, but Sharkie said that she was "just joking."

The "jokes," as she saw them, continued. When she was relaying messages between me and her mom, Sharkie turned my words negative. "That's not what I said," I told her. Sharkie claimed that her mom knew that she was "just joking."

For all of the transient people in Sharkie's life, her brother and his wife were consistent. They were high school sweethearts, and Sharkie's sister-in-law was a person with whom Sharkie talked openly. Her brother had taught Sharkie how to keep secrets, and it was with him that she discussed her dance contracts. Sharkie complained that I didn't understand them, failing to realize that I built my career on insurance jargon.

After a long day, a favorite ice cream I had bought for Jessica still hadn't been touched and Sharkie was preparing to go out. That normally meant Xbox for me, but I was exhausted and lay atop our bed. Her once-penetrating words were slipping away, but Bible verses, song lyrics, and life coincidences were giving me peace and direction.

She crawled onto my back for affection and to say that she was leaving. It felt like manipulation. Our conversation turned to listening, and in reverence of what I was receiving, I asked if she was experiencing anything similar. Sharkie said that she wasn't. I suggested that she try, and for the first time began wondering how she acted while we were apart.

She typically got out of bed later than I did, and complained about having to make it. I began tidying my side after getting up. The nitpicking continued, and I was in the kitchen when she came home to complain about something new. I told her how I felt, and she turned to leave. The title of the song that she claimed to be using as inspiration came to my mind. As her head disappeared down the stairs I called, "Man in the Mirror."

I had been doing my best to establish the base of what I had hoped would be a happy, productive relationship. Our dysfunction, however, reached a head as the two of us were in the living room and she threatened to move out. I wanted to resolve our conflict, but Sharkie stormed up to her room. I knew that she wanted me to follow, but was more concerned about her honoring our agreement. She had promised to stay in the vicinity.

I could hear her screaming and throwing things around, but I remained on the couch as I tried to keep myself together. Mema sensed the chaos and got involved by bucking circles at my feet. I held my head as my eyes filled with tears.

The coming Fourth of July holiday promised relief. Sharkie's mom wanted to visit. I thought her independent voice would help. My parents' friends invited us to join them on Kiawah Island near Charleston. I was able to board Mema before we drove to Savannah, where Sharkie, her mom, and I stopped for lunch. We took a break to walk on the beach before getting to Charleston. From there, we caravanned with my mom and her friends.

We walked the beach on the island, which brought out a playfulness in Sharkie's mom that I hadn't seen before. As if not having a care in the world, she swam and dove like a dolphin. Sharkie stopped to write a message in the sand. Her name was on top, which was followed by a heart and my name was underneath.

Upon visiting the local clubhouse, we stopped for drinks and a view of the ocean. A friend of my parents', a successful businessman, offered me advice on my venture. He talked about liking to work on terrible weather days as those drove away his competition. On our way off the island, Sharkie, her mom, and I passed by African Americans farming the land. They reminded me of how slaves once helped to establish the community.

We arrived in town to face holiday traffic, which had us watching fireworks from the car. While waiting, Sharkie's mom asked about an experience. I answered, but without looking up from her phone, Sharkie gave her account. It marked the first time we came to a divide.

She and I were drama free as our relationship approached the two-and-a-half-year mark. It was uncharted territory for both of us, and we exchanged looks as if to say, "We made it." She was then booked for a gig.

A series titled *Playboy Club* would be filming in Chicago, and she was cast as a bunny. She would be living at home for six months. I told my friend, Tony, that it would be the biggest test of our relationship. A recent believer in extreme couponing, Sharkie prepared for her departure by taking me grocery shopping. I picked out beef, chicken, and pork that I intended to smoke, shred, and stretch into low-cost tacos.

Sharkie had begun dying her hair red, and re-upped on dye #36. Our final stop brought us to a drug store. Sharkie picked out three boxes of cereal at six cents each. It was at the house, though, that she told me what I least expected to hear. She said that we had grown apart. Considering how we met, gelled, and developed, I was dumbfounded. After a moment I said, "We were supposed to grow together."

With Sharkie at my side and Mema in the backseat, we drove to the airport and parked for ticketing. I got out and helped Sharkie with her bags. We embraced before signaling the cross and kissing each other's fingers. I told her that I loved her and watched as she turned toward ticketing.

Six months without her would have meant smoking a lot of weed, but I had recently turned a corner. When Jessica had been previously questioned about my habit, she indicated that my obsession would fade. I wasn't so sure. One night, however, she had gone out, and I decided that I didn't need to get high. It was a major step.

The timing was good because Jessica had recently expressed that my use was beginning to be a problem. What had started as recreation became stress relief and ended up as a crutch. To kick the habit, I set course to understand how it affected me. With plenty of seeds, I had a perpetual supply and knew that I could get high whenever I wanted. The switch on my vaporizer went *on*, and I rolled a blunt with each of my six remaining wrappers. I stashed them in ash trays throughout the house, which left only a short walk whenever I wanted to smoke. The sensation wore off after about four hours, so I watched the clock to avoid coming down. I used as much and frequently as I wanted until reaching a point where I could get no higher.

I finished my nights with a bowl before showering then woke each morning to greet Mema and vaporize. Our morning routine included checking the upstairs plants, preparing breakfast, and going for a walk.

I didn't want a collar on me, and figured Mema didn't want one either. It came off as we entered the garage. I opened the door to ready-made meals, stopped to say the Lord's Prayer before we ate and opened a window in the basement. I, then, took my seat to work.

With CNN in the background, I caught up on

email before turning to my prospect list. I hadn't closed a deal in a while, but felt as though I was making headway. On my radar was an exotic car dealership with a benefits manager who entertained me. I never did speak with the decision maker. A construction company allowed me to quote, then determined it wasn't time for a change.

Starting to get frustrated, I asked God for a sign that I was on the right path. Then, I walked into an office on a cold call. My research showed that the company had eighty employees, and a man named Chris told me to take a seat. He was responsible for the company's insurance and was unsatisfied with his current agent.

I later returned, and he bought me lunch. Chris insisted on switching and told me that his benefits and business insurance would come as a package. I estimated they would make me profitable. I wasn't licensed to sell everything he wanted, but I had several months to get appointed.

I had received an invite to a wedding and RSVP'd for two, but made the journey to rural Georgia on my own. A friend of Rawle's was getting married.

I took pictures to share with Sharkie, who was still in Chicago. Our conversation, however, had grown weak. She had befriended someone with a boat and was pictured in a bikini with a bunch of people on Facebook. Being surrounded by people I didn't know was less of a concern than my dwindling food supply. She failed to ask how I was holding out and concluded a phone call by saying that she was going to watch television.

I decided to drive to Minnesota for my mom's birthday and found myself in a Bentley. It was the car above all others that I wanted. The driver, whom I presumed to be an angel, introduced himself as the one who recruited Barack Obama. I was still trying to control my senses when we plunged over a railing. Instincts took hold, and after getting the driver's attention, I released a parachute with my fingertips. It allowed us to float to safety. We arrived at a market, and I continued to stumble. My companion greeted someone else before joining me in stride.

I woke up from the dream in a bedroom directly beneath my parent's room. Sharkie and I then planned to spend time at her family's cabin in Wisconsin. My mom offered to bake Sharkie vegan cupcakes, but was missing ingredients. After calling around, I identified a health food store that had them in stock.

My mom took the lead in baking several types, and I got on the road with Mema a short time later. I met Sharkie and her family at a gas station, said my hellos to her mom and the kids, then turned my attention to Sharkie. It felt like an eternity since I had last seen her. I gave her a hug before gingerly removing hair from her mouth.

It was a short drive to the campground, and we pulled up to a three-season porch that had a trailer attached. Family names engraved into wooden plaques indicated our arrival. After unpacking our cars, I leashed Mema to explore our surroundings.

Upon returning, I took a seat and started talking with Jessica's mom. We noticed her daughter wasn't engaged. She looked at Sharkie, who was, with the help of my Internet connection, using her laptop. Her mom then said that Sharkie was focused on "her life." I reminded Sharkie that my mom had baked her cupcakes. She reluctantly sampled one before complaining about my lack of affection.

I took Mema outside before bed and kept the kids involved with a game of Marco Polo. Jessica's dad surprised us the next morning with a visit. With Mema crated, we went on an amphibious tour that wound us through local terrain.

Sharkie, Mema, and I finished the day by going

with her dad to his friend's house. I was frustrated with Sharkie and excused Mema and me to the couple's backyard. I started throwing a tennis ball for Mema while wondering what happened to Sharkie's three-month rule. It was the baseline for her getting into a relationship, but she had ignored it. My arm started getting loose as it got dark, and I tested the yard's boundaries with a ball that Mema delivered every time.

Sharkie was hungry as we prepared to leave the next morning for Chicago. I suggested stopping at Subway, which had a veggie patty that I had seen her eat numerous times. Sharkie declined. We continued to drive and her family's vehicle exited a short time later. It pulled up to the chain, where Sharkie ordered the sandwich I had recommended.

I bedded down that night on a couch next to Sharkie and woke up the next morning to see that she had already left for work. My mom's sister lived about forty-five minutes away, and Jessica had twice previously accompanied me to see her. Sharkie picked a fight as we pulled up on the first visit, then again as we ate at a local restaurant before the second. I didn't want to see my favorite aunt while in a sour mood and told Sharkie, "This is the second time, and there won't be a third."

With Sharkie at work, I prepared to travel across town. Her nephew asked to come along, but I had gotten used to telling him, "Maybe next time."

The child with a grown-up memory replied, "You always say that."

Humbled, I left with Mema for the south suburbs of Chicago. We returned to Sharkie's house that night, which smelled of grilled beef. Her family found it strange that I shared my food with Mema, so I finished my plate. She approached me in search of her portion, realized it wasn't coming, and started to bark. Knowing that I had offended her, I said, "I know, I know, I know." One of the kids asked what was wrong, and Jessica's brother offered meat that she barely tasted.

As Mema waited for her next bite, I suggested that the two of us take a trip. We found a dog park. With the exception of a Great Dane and his parent, it was empty. The gentleman, a controlling partner of a law firm, and I engaged in conversation. The flow of discussion with someone I might have targeted for business came easily. It helped restore some of the confidence I had lost.

Mema and I stopped for treats on my way back, but Sharkie was still absent when we arrived. I sat down by her brother, and we talked as Mema chewed.

She had made herself at home and shared a moment with almost everyone in the house. The kids liked seeing her do tricks, but her playtime was cut short after biting Sharkie's nephew. I put Mema in her crate for punishment, and the kid's mom noticed Mema's remorseful face.

While on his way into the house one morning, Sharkie's dad was taken aback by Mema's protective barking. Sharkie's mom didn't like dogs, but sensed Mema's focus. I illustrated how she was *always* watching. There was concern about potential injuries to her grandmother, who responded to Mema's barging into her room by saying, "How pretty."

She commented on Mema's nonaggressive nature and I said, "She's like me."

The only person who had a problem was Sharkie. She said that I was trying to replace her.

She returned from work, and I told her I didn't appreciate that she left without waking me. She had also gone the whole day without sending me a message. I woke the next morning and felt my time in the house was coming to an end. I went into the yard in search of droppings, swept up loose hair on the floor, and stopped for a quick visit with Sharkie's grandmother. Sharkie's nephew had his toys out, but in my preparation to leave, I had begun fending for myself. I almost finished guilt free when I heard him ask his mom to play with him. It hurt my heart.

As the day wound down, Sharkie and I found ourselves sitting on the swing in her backyard. Neither one of us was happy. Our rules of engagement said that the first to speak would have their issue addressed. I broke the silence. It was the first time that I had beaten her to the punch, and I was feeling relief when Sharkie interjected, "I'm done on my part." She stood up, and walked in the house.

I sat for a moment, trying to understand what happened, then returned inside. No words were exchanged. I told her mom that I was leaving, but after looking at me and conferring with her mother-in-law, she said that I should rest. It didn't take long for me to pass out. I woke early the next morning to see Sharkie lying on the couch beside me. She was playing on her phone. With no acknowledgment from her, I packed my car and left.

Even after my return to Atlanta, Sharkie expressed no interest in mending our relationship. She instead wanted to know if I would be flying to New York for her cousin's wedding. I had previously committed and told her that I'd be there. I was also summoned for a visit with Scott, who had a new business partner. They talked in our meeting about streamlining services and presented a projection of my sales. I immediately recognized the point, but given how I'd responded to Scott's insensitive behavior, I couldn't count on him to protect me. I returned to Atlanta to await my fate.

I continued to prospect and attend church, where Pastor Shaun challenged the congregation to read the Bible in ninety days. He recommended divvying it up by length, but for continuity's sake, I began reading a book a day. I was past Genesis and into Exodus when I repeatedly saw the phrase, "stiff-necked people." It might have gone unnoticed, but my neck had grown tight.

I flew into New York, where I was met by Sharkie and much of her family. Before checking into a hotel, we ran an errand. While waiting, I found myself alone with her brother, who had become one of my favorite people. We started talking about my relationship with his sister, and having watched from a distance, he said that he was on my side.

Sharkie and I sat next to each other through the wedding events, but barely spoke. We got back to our suite, where she made it clear that I was expected to resolve our conflict. I had followed all of her rules and was still expected to cave. I knew that giving in would result in forever putting my happiness second to hers. Not ready to give up on our relationship, I shifted tactic and asked her to meet me halfway. She refused, and eventually went to sleep on the couch.

A get-together was organized for the next day, but Sharkie and I stayed at opposite ends of the house. Her family dropped me at the airport, and I figured that Sharkie needed to talk to me if she wanted her things. She messaged a few days later and showed up wearing headphones. Sharkie brought boxes to her room and locked the door. The next thing I knew, her friend Jason arrived to help.

I offered assistance, but she questioned my intentions. I reminded her that I had promised to help her move if things went sour. As she prepared to leave, Sharkie found me in the basement. I had just wrapped up business for the day. She came behind me for a hug and said, "I'm sorry things didn't work out."

Before letting go I responded, "My wish for you is that you find what you're looking for."

She contacted me hours later and asked for my help in returning the rental truck. I followed her to the facility, then she then got in my car so that I could drive us back to the house. As we came to a stoplight, the sun shone in our faces. I absorbed the warmth and said, "That feels good." Sharkie flipped her visor to shield herself.

Unsure of my next move, I called Tonya from Cleveland. She was the closest to a sister that I had ever known. Aware of my previous promiscuity, she had coached me about women's emotions. Tonya knew how much I liked Jessica and gave me words of strength. With Sharkie's belongings gone, I updated my Facebook status to *single*.

Scott had envisioned creating a Fortune 500 company with me on the board. Instead, he said that we'd be parting ways. His attorney drafted a separation agreement, which gave me the rights to ACHP and a severance payment of $10,000. Included in the verbiage was a restriction against us working together in future, and I signed it.

With a few months of living expenses and a promising account in the pipeline, I informed my dad of the change. My parents had depleted much of their nest egg by putting my brother and me through college and helping with down payments on our houses. The financial downturn had an escalating effect. My dad said that if I wanted to pursue my dream then I'd have to finance it myself.

Scott and I weren't really talking, but his wife started a game of Words with Friends. It happened to give us letters allowing us to express our feelings. Scott had promised that he would be at my side for as long as it took. I spelled "I-R-A-T-E." She countered with words having to do with expending resources. We were going back and forth when I placed the tiles "D-E-V-I-L." As soon as I pressed play, I lost control of the reflexes in my throat and swallowed uncontrollably. As I was trying to get the reflex to stop, all I could only think was, *I just made a deal with the devil.*

I was used to being away from Sharkie and had learned to compartmentalize our time apart. I figured that she would soon realize what she was missing, but was confronted with my economic reality. Each month cost me about $3,500, and after borrowing against my retirement account, I was down to $80,000.

I could get through business hours okay, but emotions were difficult to control during my free time. Knowing that Sharkie was monitoring Facebook, I started posting messages intended to facilitate a reunion. Just ahead of Halloween, she uploaded pictures from a party in which she was wearing a rainbow-colored outfit. I didn't feel like socializing, but accepted an invite to the house where I had previously turned down an orgy.

The periphery was dark, but the rainbow costume was unmistakable. We were separated by a barrier, but I was face-to-face with Jessica. I was finally able to complain and said, "Every time there was a fight, you left." She acknowledged my statement and faded away as I woke up.

The *Playboy Club* was cancelled, Sharkie was back in Atlanta, and I was desperate to see her. There was a video game that she had left in the house, but preferred that I mail it to her. I insisted on dropping it off and drove to the studio where she was rehearsing. She met me in the parking lot and gave me a hug. Still struggling to control my throat, I asked between swallows if she was having dreams about me. She said no.

From Facebook, I could see that she was planning to celebrate her birthday in Chicago. What irked me, though, was her request to be serenaded as perfect the way she was. At her party, she wore a shiny green dress and spent the night surrounded by people. In one of the photos, she was sitting with her legs uncrossed. I was miserable but attended a get-together nonetheless where a couple of guys were using their fingers to imitate a snapping camera. It was clear to me that they had seen the picture of Sharkie at the party.

With increased down time, I began reliving my relationship with Jessica and came to a point where I got angry. Sharkie and I were still in communication, but it was diminishing. I lashed out and complained about her failure to supply groceries and take out her waste. She came home sweaty from rehearsal, but didn't bathe before bed unless I ran a bath for her. Sharkie referred to Mema as a "bitch" and gave people she claimed not to like relationship status on Facebook. I was unacknowledged, and ultimately concluded what she had so often accused me of, I was out of sight, and out of her mind.

I attempted to change my focus to what was in front of me and allowed Mema to lead us to a drainage area in the neighborhood. Water flowed through the pipes, and her investigation took her away from my sight. Darkness was falling, and she had been gone for a while. I called her to return, but time passed without her showing. I thought she was testing my patience, so I went back in the house.

I returned and called her, but she didn't show. It made me nervous. After continuing to call with no result, I panicked and looked online for a map. I phoned the water department to see where she might have exited, then went to the freezer. I pulled out a package of smoked beef bones and used convection heat to blast them warm. I set the lure and prayed for Mema's return. I had never felt so alone and sat at the pipe's entrance to wait.

A moment later, I heard faint splashing. Then Mema's face emerged from the darkness.

CHAPTER 11

CALIBRATION

got a bad feeling and called Sharkie, who was prepared to lie. Our conversation turned to Facebook. She had seen photos of me at the gathering I recently attended. I was alone in the first, but the second included an attractive young lady. The third image had another woman and three grinning faces. With a tinge of jealousy, Sharkie said, "Nice pictures."

After everything we had been through, she said that she had ended our relationship because I couldn't get her into my Uncle Clifton's cocktail party.

While my online attempts to get her back proved unsuccessful, other women started to reach out. Hoping for reconciliation with Jessica, I slowed my postings while dismissing the women's advances. I was unaware that Milla, from Ohio, was paying attention until she commented. We then took our conversation private.

An email indicating unauthorized access to my Facebook account then arrived. The message included details of a device matching the one I had bought in China. The geotag was from Sharkie's neighborhood in Chicago, and the alert was followed by another. Knowing that she was still interested, I created distance with Milla and confronted Sharkie. She pled ignorance. A third message came, and I forwarded the evidence, but she said that her computer wasn't in her possession.

Pictures of her partying then began to surface. Feeling frustrated and betrayed, I posted that she "come clean." The very next image in my timeline was of her in a white dress, a sign of purity. I continued to monitor for updates and noticed a former classmate making light of my situation. I scrubbed my friends list and turned my pleas to Twitter, using an account that I had created for business. Only Jessica knew about it.

With little to no disposable income, I focused my energy on building the infrastructure to my business. The more effectively I used my day, the better I slept at night. The dreams, however, were just beginning. Jessica vividly approached to explain a disconcerting vision she had had. I couldn't, and didn't, want to shake from her presence. I worked through my days in anticipation of sleeping that night. My work began to suffer.

Dreams turned to nightmares with the general theme of being chased and cornered. I woke on more than one occasion to a TV playing a commercial for the Georgia Lottery. It featured Sharkie.

Charles, the black agent I worked with at MetLife, hired me to conduct benefit meetings for his client in Tennessee. It required several road trips, paid expenses, and brought compensation of $5,000. As I prepared to speak with employees, spiritual undertones began presenting themselves. Nearly everywhere I looked, I could see elements of both heaven and hell. When sitting in an auditorium, for example, I noticed that the architects had decorated the hall with upside-down crosses.

During my hours on the road, I felt the once debilitating head pains I had suffered in Cleveland be replaced by gentle clicking. Each advance of understanding seemed to unkink my brain. It was as if I was learning how to use more of it.

I sped home each night to retrieve Mema from daycare, but I had also been invited to a birthday party. It was being held at a restaurant named Steel, and our group was seated in a private room. Through conversation, I distinctly heard the number *six* called three times in succession.

An attractive young lady, whom I had never seen before, then entered. She paraded around the table while stopping to give hugs. I sensed that engaging her would be a bad idea and remained seated. She came to my side, then left as quickly as she had entered.

I kept quiet and buried my head in the menu. My behaviors didn't go unnoticed. Each of my comments drew a lively response from the party dressed in red. Their actions made me uncomfortable, so I excused myself for a restroom break. I counted thirty-six paces from the time I stood up until the time I reached the bathroom's basin.

The attendees' attention magnified as the bills came. Mine was $23.50. Thinking of the Bible verse that had first impacted me, I wrote $3.16 on the tip line. As I began totaling the numbers, I felt the parties' eyes converge. They erupted in laughter as I realized the last three numbers of my bill were 6.66. On the back of the receipt I wrote "Jesus Saves."

I had made plans with Sharkie to celebrate Thanksgiving in Atlanta and prepared as if we would. My parents were on their way to town, and I vaporized before bed. I was convinced that I could use marijuana and still get into heaven, but Matthew 22:37 told me otherwise: "You must Love the Lord your God with all your heart, all your soul, and all your *mind*."

Men in robes were all around, and they appeared to be signing contracts, but I refused. A man came closer and I noticed blue writing on his white clothing. It read, "unresolved evil." I woke from my dream, scared straight. The only thing I had ever really wanted was a wife, and to me Jessica, not Sharkie was the ideal mate. I looked toward God, and said, "If you give me another chance with Jessica, I'll never get high again."

About two weeks later, I opened Atlanta's paper. The Falcons had just clinched a playoff berth. Players wearing the numbers eleven and eighty-three appeared under the headline "Fifth Seed Secured." Her half birthday, as she liked to call it, was Cinco de Mayo, but Jessica was born on 11/5/83.

I thought I might be looking too deeply for assurance until I was running an errand after a trip to the barber. My inbox refreshed to show the subject line "Getting a Haircut." I was stunned at the title of my daily devotional and clicked the link to read about the prophet Hosea. He was forced to marry a prostitute, but by remaining faithful to God's plan, he helped deliver salvation.

☮

I prepared my trip to Chicago ahead of Christmas and told Sharkie that I'd like to speak with her. She called nine hours into my drive and said that she had been busy. I arrived at my Aunt Sharon's house in a depressed mood.

The following day, I joined my mom's sister to visit my Great Aunt Lucille. Aunt Cille, as I was coming to know her by, was in her nineties. We had spoken about the jelly that I shared, and she recalled pomegranate trees on our family farm. When I had previously attempted to introduce her to Jessica, she interrupted, "This must be the fiancée."

After suffering a fall, my Aunt Sharon and I found Cille lying in bed. She put me at ease by applying scripture to her story. Cille spoke with supreme confidence when she said that my relationship with Jessica wasn't over. She told me to "keep hammering" as "God didn't send the flood until the ark was finished."

The wisdom she provided seemed so basic yet profound at the same time. I shifted my mindset to continue handling the tasks before me.

After a brief stay, Mema and I continued to Minnesota. Sharkie sent me a text wishing me a Merry Christmas. I responded, but didn't get much in return.

On the way to Atlanta, I stopped at her family's exit for a meal with her brother. Unable to contain my frustration, I told him, "With the exception of leaving church early to resolve a two-day-old argument, I did everything she asked me to." I laid out my vision for the MetLife settlement, but told him that it meant nothing without the person who inspired it.

I knew my way home, but used the car's navigation to anticipate arrival. Mema and I were deep in Indiana and approaching a billboard that I had seen numerous times. It read, "Hell Is Real." At that moment, I checked my car's display to see our home was exactly 666 miles away. While it was par for the course in everything I was beginning to experience, I wasn't excited about my home being my own personal hell.

My savings continued to dwindle, but I earned the ability to sell the products Chris, my prospect, had asked of me. He was my best shot at turning profitable, but he said our business would have to wait a year.

I felt my house was in disarray. I normally organized while high, but I had quit cold turkey. Following my Aunt Cille's advice to *keep hammering*, I started going through my belongings and took mental inventory of everything I owned. Storage areas were opened, sorted, and rearranged. I went through digital media, sold my vaporizer, and used the money to buy a filing cabinet.

My church was also changing. Pastor Shaun decided that having service only once a month gave the congregation more time to serve. Scripture was offered as guidance, and I was struck by James 1:27, "Pure and genuine religion in the sight of God the Father means caring for orphans and widows in their distress and refusing to let the world corrupt you."

The congregation was introduced to Street Grace, an organization focused on helping victims of the sex trade. They were preparing to boost awareness at the state's capital, and I decided to join them. I was doing my best to stay quietly in the background, but a short, dark-haired lady introduced herself. She told me of another group named Out of Darkness that needed volunteers. I reluctantly provided my contact information, which led to an orientation.

Pastor Shaun spearheaded charitable ventures online. Most notable was his campaign after Haiti's 2010 earthquake. His celebrity auction was reported to have raised over $500,000. Shaun's shift in focus was apparent, but it still came as a shock when he renounced his religious title.

The congregation was dependent on the stability of our church community, and we were shocked. Unsure of our next move, people began turning to Associate Pastor Broderick. His profession of being a musician allowed him and his family to tour the world, but he then found himself at a crossroads. His wife had come from a line of preachers, and he decided to "answer the call."

There was a mass exodus of familiar faces, and depleted finances forced a change of venue. Our supplies went into a rental facility, and I joined a crew that setup in a movie theater each Sunday for service. When a new board needed to be formed, I volunteered. They initially named me secretary, but I eventually became the financial director.

In search of direction, Broderick said that he had something special planned. I was sitting in the middle of the theater when Jessica's named clicked into my head. To confirm God's presence in our mission, Broderick announced our first altar call.

The congregation filed up to the stage where Dorothy, our worship leader, began to pray. I had grown accustomed to her soothing voice, but in that moment, it chafed. She was saying things I didn't understand, and I realized that she was speaking in tongues. Her words then became very clear: "Hold on, my heart has not changed."

She returned to tongues and was recovering when Broderick made his way through the congregation. He placed hands on each person in attendance, praying specifically for their needs. My palms were stretched to the sky when Broderick came to me and said, "Ask God for anything you want."

I thought, *Show me your face, cover your people, and deliver Jessica's heart.*

Nobody knew my case better than me. MetLife had given me all of the training I could ask for, so I planned to prosecute them myself. In order to be sure that all of my bases were covered, however, I met with a local attorney. An investigator from the EEOC requested my reports and scheduled interviews in what was a slow-moving process. I was told delays were partly due to a change in MetLife's representation. Without the requested documents, my case was largely circumstantial. Citing privilege, MetLife declined to produce them.

I arrived for a settlement conference and sat across from their representation, Jamie Konn. My outstanding compensation was paid, so I outlined my plan for scholarships. The idea was immediately dismissed. My call for $250 million ended our meeting.

The EEOC employees asked me to wait outside. Jamie walked out a short time later, and I stood to wish him luck. The EEOC representatives protested my request, but I assured them that MetLife's behavior was both egregious and deliberate.

The supervisor suggested that I file a complaint in federal court, so I signed a release. I then returned to the attorneys with whom I had spoken. They, too, scoffed at my request, but recommended the investigation conclude. After updating the EEOC, I got a letter stating the case was being closed for lack of evidence. A window of time was provided for me to object, and I made a visit to provide additional documents. The EEOC then permanently closed my file and provided my *Right to Sue*.

The letter allowed me to get my case into the district court, but I needed help with the filing. I had paid minimal attorney fees and hoped my lawyers would work on contingency, but they reviewed the email where I had agreed with Jeff about my goal and considered it indefensible. I knew that I had chosen my wording for a reason, but sat in their office without the rationale.

My attorneys said that punitive damages would be capped at a $250,000, just one-thousandth of what I expected to receive. They estimated my case was worth $100,000, and after some contemplation, I agreed to pay them $5,000 for a court filing while they attempted to negotiate a settlement. They provided a letter that gave me access to the EEOC's investigation, and I drove to pick up the reams of paper.

I had just finished a work day when I was missing Jessica. My phone sounded. I looked to see that Sharkie had sent me a message. She wanted to know if I had given details to her friends about our breakup. I indicated that I hadn't, and our conversation ended.

I lay in bed contemplating what I wanted, what I had worked for, and what I was missing. An intense, deep, and unrelenting pain targeted my heart. I could feel flesh tear down the middle, and I texted Sharkie, "You broke my heart."

In what felt like a cold reply she said, "I hope you feel better."

Concerns of my circumstance were being addressed in my dreams, but I wondered how real they were. I saw pink flowers sprouting and woke up to start my day. Upon opening the balcony door, I stood in shock. My peach tree had sprouted the matching petals.

My birthday was approaching, and I had no plans. Milla, from Ohio, had coincidentally moved to a townhouse around the corner. She invited me out for dinner. I was confident that I would hear from Sharkie, but decided to accept. Milla brought me to a seafood restaurant and insisted on paying. She also provided a listening ear.

In return, I promised to cook her dinner, but searched for a reason to put distance between us. While she was en route to my house, I refreshed my Facebook page. Sharkie had updated her profile picture. In it, she was wearing a cream-colored outfit and looked to be standing on a runway. The photo came from a video shoot for "Ray Bands," a song performed by B.O.B. He was the artist Sharkie had refused to listen to.

Although a beautiful, intelligent, and hard-working woman was in front of me, I struggled to get my mind off Jessica. My words came with barbs. Upon seeing their affect, I quoted Broderick as I ended prospects with Milla, "Hurt people, hurt people."

I knew I needed time to think and booked a vacation to the Bahamas. Rawle agreed to watch Mema, and as the plane's door was closing, I thumbed through a catalog to see consecutive images that reminded me of Sharkie. There was a long-sleeve T-shirt on sale that had teeth along the arms. They made the shape of a mouth when brought together. Sharkie had recently bought one. The last message I saw in the magazine was, "It is what it is."

☮

My income-producing opportunities were stalling. The screenplay I had written with Tony, *War of Angels*, was on its way to Will Smith, until the actor shifted focus to the careers of his kids. My pursuit of opening a soft-serve store collapsed when my dad's friend said that he had "too many irons in the fire."

With spring in full tilt, I held out hope for a reunion with Jessica and set my sights on gardening. I bought thirty-five food-producing plants, but was most concerned about my lime tree. I had left it out during winter and it looked dead. I prayed for God to "breathe life into it."

The front steps got the most sun, so that's where I concentrated my garden. I addressed my wobbly railing with a layer of fresh cement and noticed a coincidence regarding my Morehouse license plate. It was MR1450. The digits matched my street address, and I liked the idea of being "Mr. 1450."

I toured the steps to see all of the vegetation and carefully examined each plant. Seeds from a cherimoya I had bought were beginning to sprout. The lime tree had fruit on its branches when I bought it, but the teaching of first fruits came to mind. If I decided to sacrifice the lime, the promise according to my understanding of the Bible was that the tree would multiply future produce. I had tossed the perfectly good lime into the woods for animals and insects to eat. I was now feeling annoyed that I wouldn't get produce when I looked closer. At the base of the plant, there was a shiny green shoot beginning to grow.

I wanted to speak with someone who could understand the struggles I was facing and approached Dorothy from church. We met at a café downstairs from my old apartment. She openly chronicled her personal trial before turning her attention to me. I was captivated by her emotion and wanted to share my experience. I got lost, though, in her eyes. The only thing I managed to say was, "It's crazy."

She gave me space, and I was then able to talk about the dreams I was having. Dorothy provided advice that I immediately found useful. The very next morning, I began journaling. Writing was followed by daily devotionals and a prayer to God for the ordering of my steps. A photo of Sharkie cuddled up with another man appeared on Facebook. I knew from when we first started talking that she had a lot of gay friends, so I didn't feel threatened, but seeing her enjoying life hurt my mood. I unfriended her and invested my energy into reading the lessons my parents' Sunday school teacher provided.

I looked forward to digging into my EEOC file, but was disappointed near immediately. Most of what MetLife had turned over was employee files. Scheduled interviews, never took place. There was contradictory correspondence, and I was able to see their defense was based on my loss of business. My attorneys contacted me the Friday before Memorial Day saying MetLife wouldn't increase my settlement above $8,000, produce further documentation, and to "have a nice weekend."

The remaining congregation of Courageous Church renamed ourselves *Mosaic*. It signified a group of broken people coming together to make something beautiful. Our lease was expiring, and Broderick proposed a move to a nearby suburb. The logic was for our ability to make a greater impact, but the move more than doubled my commute. With a month to prepare, leadership suggested that we visit other churches.

I was urgently walking Mema before work when I looked to see a sign saying, "Slow down." I figured it was for me, and after doing so, a young woman pulled up next to us. She offered prayer and an invitation to visit her church.

As the work week continued, I immersed myself in the business of Mosaic. Broderick became eligible for retirement benefits, which required me to complete paperwork. I was reading through it when I noticed something oddly familiar. The last four digits of Broderick's Social Security Number matched mine. It confirmed our partnership.

That weekend, I visited the young lady's church, but wasn't a fan of almost anything I saw. In a race to reach my car, I was almost to my door when I heard a man calling after me. He had chased me down to ask how I enjoyed the service. I told him how I felt. He invited me to a breakfast hosted by Christian Business Men's Connection (CBMC).

I showed up and was greeted by an older man named Luckett. We took our seats, and I was hoping for a quick exit when he circled around. He asked if I had participated in a discipleship program named Operation Timothy. I told him that I hadn't, and it became apparent that I wouldn't be able to leave without giving Luckett my contact information.

He later invited me to a Friday morning Bible study. I wanted no part of it but accepted the invitation. A handful of retirees paid for my meal and extended an open door. I couldn't refuse.

Another native of Minnesota who hosted Bible study on Thursdays attended the following week. He invited me to attend. I reluctantly committed and met another group of CBMC members. Their leader, in particular, amazed me with his teaching. I then made Thursday and Friday morning Bible study a regular occurrence.

My biggest project was still my settlement. In its pursuit, I made five copies of a binder I had built and shopped it to a handful of attorneys. I most wanted to work with a gentleman who declined for his lack of resources. I sat with another, who was unkept. He spoke with multiple words I was unfamiliar with and talked about how the daughter he partnered with liked "making big companies pay."

I eventually sat with a female attorney, coincidentally named Jamie. She had recently settled a case she thought was similar, and too thought my request was unreasonable. She noted, however, that Title VII cases don't have a limit on punitive damages. Along with a $5,000 retainer, she took one of my binders and began representation.

After a long day, I pushed away from my desk. I led Mema outside and looked into the night sky while thinking about how a $250 million settlement would get me everything except what I really wanted. I was with Rachel during a high school summer when I first saw a shooting star. It wasn't until that moment that I saw another.

Things started to wear out and break down. My dress shoes had lasted for years, but a crack exposed a gap in their sole. I went to a discount store and was able to get another pair. Then, my washing machine quit. I shopped in a scratch and dent section for a replacement. My portable gas grill caught fire, and a 10 percent off coupon helped me invest in a new one. A depression had formed in the middle of my mattress, so when a store advertised a sale, I went shopping.

My days were typically full, but I knew my office hours were over when Mema woke up from her nap. It was time for exercise. I met people who told me about other parks, which took us to a trail near a creek. After fetching her ball, Mema gave me time to gaze at the water. The serenity felt better than getting high.

Aside from using the phone and running errands, I wasn't talking much. The downtime allowed me to observe nature's harmony in action. There were no exaggerations to sift through or lies to deal with. Events happened, or they didn't.

Mema was mostly restricted to dry kibble in the morning, so after playing, she was ready for a hearty dinner. I prepared our meals and approached her bowl. While hunched over saying grace, I got deep into my words and questioned who I was praying to. I couldn't seem to find safety and said the only thing I knew would help, "Jesus, save me."

Mema developed a cyst on her back and a mole on her knuckle. I was confident they weren't cancerous, but wanted them removed. Having committed my life to God, I couldn't understand why I was facing such difficulty. Matthew 19:24 heartened me, "I'll say it again—it is easier for a camel to go through the eye of a needle than for a rich person to enter the Kingdom of God!"

A check arrived for Sharkie from the Georgia Lottery. I sent her a text to coordinate an exchange. She questioned whether or not money had indeed arrived, then directed me to leave it in the mailbox. I was losing my nest egg, constantly dealing with rejection, and was two years into a legal battle with more downs than ups. With no intention of accommodating her request, I did my best to prepare for our first face-to-face in nearly a year. I worked at my desk as the evening quietly passed.

Upset, I started questioning God's plan and asked for a sign that He was in control. Within twenty-four hours, my mom called to say that Rashad, my friend from high school, had been killed in a motorcycle accident. My thoughts immediately went to his son, and in the mix of emotions, I mentally committed that I would help to raise him.

Rashad's sister, who I learned was living in the Atlanta area, was helping to facilitate Rashad's funeral. It had been years since I had communicated with any of his family, and I was sure to seek out his mom, sister, and, of course, Brandon. I learned that Rashad had remarried and fathered another child. Rashad's mom was preparing a move to Atlanta to help with Brandon.

Sharkie's brother texted me, asking about my most recent interaction with his sister. I told him that I loved him like a brother, but that his sister had brought drama and told lies. I continued by saying that if she wanted her check, I thought she would at least ring my doorbell. He seemed to understand. I was later at Rashad's repass when she messaged again.

I texted back that I was at a funeral. She tried again while I was returning from seeing a cousin in Alabama. I told Sharkie that I was out of town, the check was on my desk, and she could come get it or request a new one. She asked why I was being difficult, and I said that I had already done more than enough for her.

I was later sitting at my desk when my doorbell rang. Mema shot up from her bed and ran upstairs. I followed and opened the door, expecting to see the mailman, but locked eyes with Sharkie. She asked for her money. I told her where she could find it. She objected to entering the house, but I led the way to my office. As I took my seat, her arm reached past me to take the check. By the time I turned around, she was gone.

CHAPTER 12

MISREPRESENTATION

A client with an aging father asked about Medicare, which spurred me to get licensed. At a subsequent orientation, an insurance carrier said they needed Spanish-speaking reps. They promised leads if I 'd provide my contact information. Commission checks for my client base came in, and while they totaled less than $500 for the month, I was pleased to have generated the revenue.

The real money, as I saw it, would be coming from MetLife, and it was time for my deposition. I brought my binder with a cover titled, "The People vs. MetLife." It had a photoshopped image of MetLife's mascot, Snoopy, whom I had airbrushed brown. The camera started rolling, and my attorney, who hadn't immediately noticed my artwork, asked me to conceal the cover of my binder.

Konn, MetLife's attorney, produced several documents that I had answers for. Then came the one I was awaiting. He pointed to the email I had sent to Jeff which said, "I understand the math and agree that this calculation is fair."

Konn then asked, "So you did agree with your manager that the $4.4 million sales objective for 2010 is fair?"

I had used the word *calculation*, not *objective*. The nuance was arriving at the goal, not the goal itself. With the reasoning I had previously struggled to explain intact, I confidently responded, "That's not what it says."

I had sold everything I could without telling my parents about the state of my finances. My secret revealed itself when I returned home from the law offices. I was several months behind on my cable bill, and my dad, who was in town with my mom, discovered my status when he turned on the TV. My service had been disconnected. He and my mom agreed to stake me for as long as they could.

I was preparing to leave for my second day of questioning when my mom stopped me. Konn had confiscated my MetLife name tags in our first session, so I traded business casual attire for a MetLife-issued golf shirt. My mom took a look at my outfit and gave me the heartfelt instruction, not to be "the angry black man."

Konn wrapped up his questions, and my attorney began her cross-examination. She asked me to name my "shit" accounts. The first one that came to mind was the Presbyterian Church in America. Given the spiritual battle I was fighting, I didn't want to implicate a faith-based organization in wrongdoing. I paused until I could think of another name.

The topic turned toward creating business. My attorney, Jamie, started digging into a report I had provided. It was the quote history of brokers assigned to me. She pressed to understand why it was important, and I explained that the past would help determine my future opportunity. More importantly, I couldn't compare numbers with my peers because the defense had refused to provide their reports.

Konn interrupted, "Just for the record, defense only received the document request last week."

My attorney, Jamie, replied, "Yeah, so you haven't had an opportunity?"

Konn continued, "So we have not refused to produce anything."

I then interjected, "It was part of the original request from the EEOC in 2010."

After my attorney, Jamie, rested; Konn followed up.

I sensed that we were coming to a close and threatened that MetLife would lose business if my story were to break. Tension grew. The most damning evidence showed the Atlanta reps alongside their numbers. Blackburn had 354 opportunities and Vietri had 316. I, the only African American, twenty.

The national close ratio was 7 percent, meaning that for every one hundred opportunities, we could expect to close seven. My twenty prospects would translate to 1.4 cases sold. The average coverage brought $400,000, and that multiplied by 1.4 equals $560,000. My anticipated revenue was almost $4 million short of my goal.

I was the lowest-producing rep, with $200,000 in sales. Leweling, who was assigned work with accounts producing larger cases, was next with $720,000. She had eight quotes, and Konn attempted to shape the numbers by saying, "You had more than twice as many sales, but a third or less of the total sales."

His logic didn't compute, and I responded, "You just contradicted yourself."

I returned home from my deposition much more relaxed after having spoken my mind. My parents were readying their return to Minnesota, and my mom took me grocery shopping. She made me promise to tell her if I was ever hungry.

The weather was turning cold, so I harvested dying plants before moving their remnants to a compost bin. Those hearty enough to survive the Georgia winter were consolidated on the front steps. I brought the tropicals inside, positioning a handful of the warm-weather plants near windows. The rest went into my grow tent.

Mema and I would again be traveling to Minnesota for Thanksgiving, so I began cleaning the house. I was able to condense the household chores into a three-hour process. With the night coming to a close, I packed, took a shower, and closed my eyes.

We got in the car before sunrise, and I left the seat warmers on for both me and Mema. She eventually curled up for a nap, and we were into Tennessee when traffic got heavy. I took a less-congested route that my dad had told me about.

We were about halfway into Illinois when I saw blue lights coming toward us. It had been years since I had received a ticket, and I was surprised to be pulled over. I had just got over the shock of my broken streak when another officer advanced. He issued my second citation in less than two hours.

Upon returning to Atlanta, I went to see my prospect, Chris. I had done everything I thought necessary to be named his agent, but he informed me that he was changing jobs. Chris scheduled a meeting with his replacement, who requested that I speak with the owner.

The replacement let on that Chris' transition had been in the works for about a year. I shot him a glance and noticed that he was trying to conceal a smile. Although I was upset that he had been leading me on, I still hoped for the best. His replacement told me to check back periodically, but with pressure mounting to generate income, I bordered on annoying with my follow-up. I should have expected it, but I failed to secure their business. The deal I was hoping would right my financial ship was now dead.

I got an email from my lawyer, who insinuated that she no longer wanted to work on my case. Jamie thought I'd have a tough time winning and recommended that I accept MetLife's new offer of $15,000. I was unprepared to walk away and told her that I wanted to see the requested documents before making a decision. I provided additional questions that I wanted answered, and she advised me that the information would be available on January 8.

It had been about a month since I completed my training with the rescue organization Out of Darkness, and I then got my first call to help. Another woman would serve as my partner and we agreed on a location to meet. I then drove her car to a run-down neighborhood. A large man, whom I suspected was our client's pimp, came to meet us and said the woman we were there for was inside. I cautiously climbed the steps of a dark house to find a young woman readying her bags. We packed them in the car and were about to leave when the man pulled her aside to offer words of encouragement. He was helping her.

En route to the safe house, we stopped at a McDonald's, where I paid for a meal. We were ringing the doorbell of a suburban house a moment later. The short-haired lady who recruited me answered the door. I was both surprised and happy to see her level of commitment. She introduced us to other women who had made the call for help and coordinated a group prayer before we left.

A day or two later, an Out of Darkness dispatcher asked me to provide transportation for the woman I had rescued. Feeling as though we had bonded, I agreed to pick her up. My partner and I drove into a parking lot, where a flash of white came from the right.

I felt the impact as airbags deployed. Once we came to rest, I checked on my passenger. She was okay. I exited my car to see about the other passengers, then focused on my Acura. The passenger doors were forced shut. As I collected the other driver's info, a car crept slowly by. In the backseat with her face pressed against the window was the woman I was there to help.

An insurance representative later called to say the other driver's policy had been cancelled for nonpayment. My uninsured coverage kicked in, but my car was deemed a total loss. Of all the vehicles I had owned, the TL was my favorite.

My insurance company issued me a check, and I already had three cars picked out. I drove to Stone Mountain, Decatur, and ultimately Austell to find my new ride. I updated my insurance to reflect the exact same year, make, and model.

I was in the shower when I was thinking about seeing God's face. I began surveying the tiling, wondering if it was hidden in the pattern. I examined the markings, locked onto an image of a head, then a pupil in the shape of a heart. Directly to its left was an eye that had a falling teardrop attached. The symbols most commonly associated with pain and love represented Christ as best I could imagine.

My attorney, Jamie, emailed me on January 8 to say discovery, a legal term for reporting, hadn't yet arrived. She reiterated her desire to be dismissed from my case, claiming that my $5,000 retainer was exhausted. She hadn't submitted my final information request.

MetLife revised their delivery date to January 14. I followed up that afternoon to find out when I could get my hands on the documents. Jamie sent me a note around 10:30 that night saying I could come by her office the next day. I stopped in around 4 p.m. and immediately began sifting through the stack of papers. Jamie wanted off my case and took a hard line. We agreed that if she drafted a template for me to pursue the discovery I was seeking, I'd release her.

At my mom's invitation, I agreed to attend ceremonies for Barack Obama's second inauguration. We were promised tickets to one of the many festive balls. My dad's eldest sister, who worked at the Pentagon, offered a place to stay.

My mom and I went sightseeing at the National Mall on the day before the ceremony. We stopped at the King memorial, where I read, "We shall overcome because the arc of the moral universe is long, but it bends toward justice." My mom was tired, so I walked ahead to the Lincoln Memorial. From there, I walked past the Smithsonian, Capitol Hill, and ultimately to the Supreme Court.

We entered a security line the next morning on our way to a luncheon. Food and drink were in abundance, and we watched the president's speech on TV. From there we migrated to the balcony for a view of his motorcade.

I returned to Atlanta in search of the draft Jamie had promised. She didn't have it, and claimed the delay was due to a doctor's ordered bed rest. I filtered through what MetLife had turned over and my frustration grew. The documents revealed my attorney's incompetence. Most of the material was duplication of my EEOC File. Further, Jamie had rewritten the questions I provided. As far as my reports were concerned, the names were omitted, so MetLife claimed they couldn't provide them.

In my experience, their legal team was careful to address all questions in an effort to avoid misinterpretation. They outright ignored mine. I took it in stride and redirected my emotions by restating questions that I knew MetLife didn't want to answer.

Going a step further, I used Konn's words against him. He had told the EEOC that *"Account executives* primarily sell group insurance plans to new customers, often working through or with independent insurance brokers to sell these plans. *Client executives* manage existing client relationships, working directly with current clients/employers."

Knowing there was no good answer to my question, I posed, "If Defendant contends this statement is true, please explain why Rowell was assigned a broker while working as a client executive, and why he was assigned the broker he was."

Konn also stated that Trinkwon made assignments "at his discretion," so I completed my first legal brief by asking him to explain the business reason for my assignments to Morehouse College and Atlanta Life. MetLife would have to reference my race in their response.

Four days from the time that Jamie emailed me the template, I was satisfied with the document and printed a copy. From there, I got in my car, drove downtown, and parked near the courthouse for Georgia's Northern District. I entered the building, cleared security, and took the elevator to the clerk's office. There, like I had done in high school for Larry, I filed the papers.

Konn, MetLife's attorney, then emailed me three attachments: a confidentiality agreement to release additional documents, a log describing them, and a letter stating my most recent request was late and wouldn't be honored. According to the court's discovery schedule, requests were to be made no later than January 16. That was one day after I sat with Jamie. With discovery being fundamental to my case, I reached out to Larry, who suggested that I appeal. I filed the next day.

I was wondering why I continued to suffer losses as I approached my bathroom. There, a pattern had been developing. Whenever I was most distressed, one of the lightbulbs in the vanity popped. Another one went.

Not a week later, Konn responded to my appeal with an objection, arguing that discovery had been extended twice already. I understood the first to be commonplace when counsel is changed. The second was due to my attorney, Jamie's, personal schedule. He decried my request to engage in fact finding by referencing the 1,400 pages he had turned over.

Having done my research, I wrote the judge that MetLife's attorneys had requested six extensions. Five went to the EEOC, as they appeared unwilling to cooperate, and one was a direct appeal from MetLife's in-house counsel. A seventh extension was granted when they asked for January 8 as a deadline, but submitted discovery six days later. I concluded my document by stating MetLife had failed to turn over promised documents and that my requests had been known for two years.

The judge denied my appeal.

He had rationalized that extensions would only be granted as a result of unforeseen circumstances. He went on to say that I had failed to show him why I needed the information, failed to act promptly, and implied that I procrastinated. In conclusion, he suggested that I should have conferenced with the court, but that opportunity had passed.

Larry suggested that I appeal again, which brought me to the courthouse days later. I opened my brief by acknowledging the lack of information and used a timeline for illustration. On December 17, my counsel had a complete list of what I needed, but I wasn't notified until three weeks later that she hadn't submitted it.

January 15 was when I realized that my former counsel hadn't properly submitted my questions, and I didn't get the template until January 28. Ten days passed from when I asked Konn for the additional information and he notified me that my request was late. That put me in court the next day. The heart of my argument was: "The outstanding information has to do with contradictions, false statements, and will show overall opportunity… The Defendant claims that [my] responsibility was based on customer complaints, but to date has not provided them."

Konn emailed me his motion for summary judgment about a week later. It was essentially MetLife's case against me. The eighty-four pages were statements by Jeff, the HR investigator, and exhibits. I was most concerned, though, about the three-week clock for me to respond. Defending myself wasn't a problem, but I needed ammunition to prove my case. So that I wouldn't forget about the deadline, I set a reminder in my phone.

My birthday marked four years since I had met Sharkie. I believed it would be the turning point for my promise that she would thank me in five years. Family and friends contacted me in the morning and I was still hopeful to hear from Sharkie as I walked Mema that afternoon. I wanted my phone to sound, but was aware of the hill Jessica would have to climb for reconciliation. In response, I tweeted, "The most painful thing you've ever done."

Rickey and Rawle stopped by that weekend to cheer me up. I instead took the opportunity to present my work. I offered them free range to look around my house; everything was in order.

Out of Darkness called at about 2 a.m.; a juvenile was in need. I got dressed and met my partner so we could travel to the local FBI office. An agent explained the victim had been taken into custody as a result of a raid. Transportation to the safe house went smoothly, but the next call helped me better understand the value of my service.

After agreeing to meet my partner at a bus station, I took a seat next to Beth, whose hair was dyed blue. She was open about being a preacher's kid who became addicted to methamphetamine. I had just got comfortable listening to her talk when she asked me a question that forced me to open up: "How long have you loved the Lord?"

I was talking about the chain reaction of events when we realized that our client was late. Beth knew her and said that she was coming from a potentially violent situation. We checked with a representative, who told us the bus had already arrived. Our calls to the client's number, however, went unanswered.

We notified dispatch, engaged a police officer, and I backtracked each number that we had for her. I got an answer from a relative who relayed our message, then said the woman would arrive shortly. A handful of people streamed past Beth and me as we stood next to a police cruiser. Beth recognized the woman and moved to embrace her. Our client was visibly shaken and pointed to the man who had called himself her boyfriend.

Officers moved to talk with him as Beth, our client, and I prepared to drive off. I then listened to the victim's story. The woman and a friend were kept in a shack, but she was allowed to accompany her pimp to the city. Upon arrival, he wanted to get high and took her to a bridge so that he could buy drugs. While there, he got annoyed and threatened to throw her off. Our calls helped bring her to safety.

While I was simply reacting to the environment around me and trying to make progress toward my goals, I noticed that my health had changed. It started with trying to keep pace with Mema when, and wherever she wanted to walk. It extended to my diet, which was sensible. At my heaviest I had weighed 240 pounds. Even when trying, I couldn't get below 220, but stepped on a scale to register 205. I felt in my core that I had begun anew.

I was later sitting in church as Broderick preached

about preparation and resources. He said that God puts us in a position that requires nothing more than what he's already given us. "Go into battle with what you have," he said.

I couldn't understand why it resonated until my alarm went off the next day. My motion for summary judgment was due. In a panic, I pieced together a defense against MetLife's accusations and cited missing discovery where I would have made my case.

Out of Darkness called me on a Saturday afternoon, and I was paired with a first-time rescuer. We were on our way to a hotbed for prostitution as I gave my colleague advice. I had only completed about a half dozen rescues, but knew enough to tell her that every call was different. We then pulled up to, and parked at a hotel. A woman came outside, carrying her bags as an agitated man trailed, screaming, "No, no, you're not going with them!"

Before taking a step to intervene, I was bolstered by the thought that I wasn't afraid to die. After all, I had lost the only thing I had ever wanted. I came at the man with respect as he shared his story. I separated the men from the women, and he explained she had been his girlfriend since before he went to prison.

He continued to say she was in no danger and had chosen to sell her body. He only learned of it upon his release. Omar was the father of two kids, but was helping to raise hers. One was in the state's custody, and the other was in her belly. He said that his girlfriend made the call with the hope of getting her child back, and Omar was upset that he looked like a pimp.

I could see he was trying to do the right thing. A relative promised to wire him money, but he had no ride to get it. Being born in New York, raised Christian, and then converting to Islam, Omar's journey paralleled Broderick's. On the condition they would join me for church the next day, I promised transportation.

I drove to Harmony-Leland Elementary, the site of our service, the next morning and began to set up as usual. Later, I went to meet the couple. Ten minutes passed as I waited and questioned the wisdom of my decision. That's when they came to the lobby. The congregation welcomed them, and afterwards I helped them run errands.

Sometime later, a persistent cold led me to schedule a doctor's visit. I immediately recognized the physician when he walked in to see me. He informed me that a virus was going around, prescribed antibiotics, and said that he still thought about the conditions that caused my night sweats. A quick story of what I was experiencing at work had stayed with a man whom I just met until years later.

I was getting peace of mind from tying off loose ends, and I began apologizing to everyone I thought I had wronged. Without realizing it, my actions were biblical, according to Mathew 5:23–24, "So if you are presenting a sacrifice at the altar in the temple and you suddenly remember that someone has something against you, leave your sacrifice there at the altar. Go and be reconciled to that person. Then come and offer your sacrifice to God."

I was conditioning my garden for the year and made the economical decision to supplement the rations my parents provided with food grown from seeds. I went to the nursery and picked out varieties, then returned to the house, where I got another call. Organizations had been soliciting donations, and I bagged up spare clothes. I placed them in a white bag and set it outside. With a blue marker, I abbreviated the nonprofit's name to "Hope."

CHAPTER 13

SURVIVAL

Upon returning from a morning walk, I entered my basement office to see my filing cabinet in the corner. Its hutch contained a multifunctioning printer, which was surrounded by binders containing my case against MetLife. The drawer beneath had clients' information, but prospects weighed the floor. Two statements taped to the side contrasted my financial history: my first commission statement as a broker, and my empty retirement account. Everything was where I wanted it.

The gentleman who invited me to his office on Thursday mornings asked me to attend a Christian luncheon. It occurred weekly, was a bit of a drive, and involved an unwelcome expense. I felt compelled to go and received a warm welcome. After listening to testimony, an attendee asked if I'd be back. I was trying to reimagine my schedule when a cohost stepped in. He said that one of the devil's strategies is to prevent fellowship. When that fails, he tries to overextend. Feeling as though I had earned a pass, I declined the invitation.

I returned to work on the infrastructure for my business, which was, with the exception of one major task, complete. I was still encountering apprehension around Barack Obama's Affordable Care Act. I didn't quite understand the mechanics myself, and with my friend Tony's help, I created a presentation that forced me to learn.

Feeling a bit ahead of the game, I took a moment to reflect. Mema joined me on the front porch, which overlooked the neighborhood. It was quiet. The sun was shining, my plants were growing, and Mema fell asleep at my feet. It was the first time that I appreciated peace.

The men's group at my church volunteered monthly at a food shelter. We planned on dinner afterwards and often went for pizza. Pastor Broderick had befriended the owner, Jay, who concocted a pie that tasted like a Big Mac. He asked an employee to bring one to our table and then sat down to join us. Jay shared how he was raised Jewish, read the Quran, and was ultimately born again as a Christian.

He had worked his way into being an executive at a large company that came under scrutiny for their business practices by the FBI. They approached him with a plea deal, but Jay had done nothing wrong. Despite a high conviction rate, he decided to fight. It cost Jay his marriage and millions of dollars.

As the trial was underway, he was encouraged by a woman who had been branded a prophet. She was at his side when the trial adjourned and gave a play-by-play of what to expect. The events unfolded as she predicted, and Jay was found not guilty.

I called my Aunt Cille with renewed faith, but was unable to give her the news she was hoping for. She gave me the sage advice to "follow my heart." I later returned to help Jay deliver pizzas to a community event. We made several trips to a warehouse that had been converted to host a carnival.

I told him that I was going through my own struggle and would appreciate meeting the prophet. Jay arranged a time, but warned me that she had an extreme personality. It was on display from the moment that we met. She recoiled as we shook hands and made a bunch of funny noises. I was skeptical and knew my feelings showed through. She paused and in a serious tone said, "*You* asked to meet *me*."

Knowing that she was right, I began to tell my story. The lady told me to go home and read the second chapter of Habakkuk. I was then to wait a moment before writing down everything that came to mind. Before our meeting adjourned, I was advised that I couldn't move forward without forgiving my ex, so I did.

I followed through with the prophet's advice then turned back to business. I was able to close a handful of accounts, schedule follow-up calls, and set meetings. A cold call to the owner of a newspaper servicing the African American community resulted in his asking me to lunch. We met at a well-known restaurant, and upon walking to our booth, I saw a familiar face. The last time I had seen Leonard, I was representing MetLife and told him that they expected "blood from a stone." He promised to circulate my résumé, but never got back to me.

We exchanged greetings, and I continued to my seat. Leonard came to me before leaving and said that he had joined a couple partners in a new venture. His new job was getting reps to sell on his behalf, and he left me his business card.

My parents stopped in on their vacation and my mom brought a care package. It included dozens of cookies that went into my freezer and a book titled *Proof of Heaven*. My parents explained that their nest egg was evaporating, and gave me the directive to find income.

I told my mom that I had encountered a former associate, but had no desire to contact him. She convinced me that I should, and on their way home, she expressed confidence in my ability. She bought a mat for the front door, left more dessert, and stocked my pantry down to bread crumbs.

As nights grew lonely, I yearned for female companionship and began replaying history with my exes. My status with some was best left where it was, but I reached out to a select few. They didn't return the interest.

I had found comfort in Romans 8:28: "We know that God causes everything to work together for the good of those who love God and are called according to his purpose for them." But, a recent Bible study made me question if I was qualified.

I knew that I loved God. My concern was whether or not I was called for His purpose. I prayed for a sign and got a message from Broderick. He came by in a funky mood and talked about a personal issue. I offered support, and our meeting reassured me that my future was, in fact, positive.

On my prospect list was a company that had grown significantly since their inception. They didn't offer benefits and were concerned about the impact of Obamacare. I put together quotes that required minimal employee contribution and made several trips to ensure participation. The final tally revealed that they didn't have enough enrollees. I lost the sale.

Of all my potential deals, I was counting on securing the business of a law firm. The lead seemed solid, as I was told in our initial meeting that they were facing an increase the partners wouldn't accept. Further, their agent wanted out of the business. I shopped around, put together a proposal, and was informed that they were staying put.

In disbelief, I could think of only one call to make. My nerves caused jitters as I dialed the businessman I had pitched porn to. I opened by saying, "This is the hardest thing I've ever done." I attempted to angle into becoming his agent, but sensing the quiver in my voice, he repeatedly asked if I was okay. He ultimately connected us with the person he had hired to make those decisions. I pitched the plan Scott had taught me to sell, but they had already implemented it. The call was a dead end.

I got off the phone, unsure of my next move, and checked my life insurance policy. It was just over twenty-four months old. Most carriers believed that two years is enough time to insure against suicide. Taking my life would provide enough money to satisfy my mortgage, but I wanted to avoid the perception that I had given up. I went to the grocery store as I continued to plot. Eating a few mangoes before bed would cause a fatal allergic reaction, but upon reaching for the fruit, I could sense that something was off. I considered pain pills, but worried about Mema being left alone with my body.

I went to bed and dreamed that I was beginning a joyous path. Days later, I was brought back to start again, but was instead forced toward a cave. I didn't want to enter, threw a stick into the darkness, and heard snakes shaking their rattles as they awaited my entry.

Broderick then called to say that he wanted to meet. I drove to a restaurant by his house, where he said that each of my parents had reached out to him expressing concern. Having kept the details of my struggle private, I sat quietly to see just how much he knew. He dug into much of the loss I had been dealing with and apologized for not having a better handle on my affairs. We agreed to remain in closer contact. I later opened my Sunday paper to see a banner reading, "Right Place, Bright Future."

☮

I woke the next day to see my daily Bible verse, journal the night's events, and read my devotionals. My work week started with recording the church's offering and a trip to the bank to deposit it. Tuesday's were for follow-up and a standing lunch with Luckett, of CBMC, to discuss the discipleship program Operation Timothy. Using workbooks, He was supposed to play the role of the Apostle Paul, who's credited with writing most of the Bible's new testament, mentoring his disciple Timothy. Luckett and I, though, found ourselves contributing equally to our respective growth.

I was down to forty-one cents in my bank account, but decided to participate in Morehouse's new student orientation called "Spirit Night." When I sat in the Martin Luther King Jr. International Chapel as a freshman, men in suits lined the halls. On cue, they greeted us in unison by saying, "Welcome, to The House." I took my seat as an alumnus and listened to several moving speeches. During a break, alumni were grouped with students who were free to ask questions. A current student, called "Man of Morehouse," asked how long he should study. Without hesitation I replied, "Until you can explain it."

We moved outside the auditorium, where new enrollees wearing white T-shirts formed two lines. Classmates' hands were placed on the shoulder of those in front. Elders led the way to the gym as the class of 2017 chanted, "I've got my brother's back."

A morning or two later I was traveling home from a Friday morning CBMC meeting. I was preparing to merge southbound on. an interstate when a Department of Transportation lawnmower cut across traffic. Brake lights flashed, but I couldn't stop to avoid the pickup truck in front of me. The worker turned, faced forward, looked again, then drove off.

I had hit a vehicle driven by a young lady. It was her first accident. As we waited for an officer, she gave me her perspective. We agreed that it was the worker's fault, but in his absence, I was given a citation. The afternoon was no better. I sat for the first of thirteen dental fillings.

Serving the food pantry was a highlight, especially when it offered leftovers that eased my hunger. I stretched my resources as best I could, but I often got hungry after dinner. I didn't have the luxury of snacks, so I ate seasoned bread crumbs by the handful.

Broderick wanted to camp before summer's end, and I had just gotten a commission check so I stopped in a sporting goods store to find a matching rod and reel were on sale, so I scooped them up. I added tackle and line to my purchase, then returned home to spool my reel. The line tangled. I attempted to pull it straight, which only tightened the knot. Determined not to waste resources, I began working with the free end. Hours later, the reservoir was clean and tight. I took and captioned the photos, "A tangled mess and a lot of patience."

My parents informed me that their support of my opportunity to become profitable was over. I wasn't concerned. I had developed positive rapport with a woman running human resources for an organization that helped African American farmers keep their land. I took the nature of their business as a sign that I, too, might keep my property.

My car insurance company informed me that my Acura was totaled, and another one was outside of my budget. The only other vehicle I desired was a Lincoln Aviator. I went to a dealership and began negotiating with a newly employed salesman. My offer was less than he was authorized to accept, so he got his manager involved. We agreed to terms.

When it came time to sign papers, the supervisor

reneged. I began to argue, but he held a hard line. I thanked him for his time, got up, and walked out. I was almost to my rental when I heard the *rookie's* voice calling me. Although I was confident I wouldn't find a better value, it was the yellow butterfly fluttering across my path that caused me to stop and turn around. The associate proposed a reduction of his commission, and admiring his hustle, I used my American Express to become his first customer.

I planned to use my insurance settlement to pay the balance on my Amex, but had no money for the mortgage. My food supply had again dwindled, and I stopped at the grocery store in search of deals. With a taste for soup, I picked up a pumpkin and discovered that the manager's section had nearly expired food. I took home packages of shrimp and lobster.

The congregation of Mosaic was healing, and Broderick held a service on forgiveness. He asked us to think of those we felt wronged by. On a given piece of paper, I wrote the name of the one I still hadn't forgiven. Outside, I attached my note to a helium-filled balloon. We released in unison and my message reading "God" carried into the sky.

Autumn in the south allowed my dad to extend his golf season. After traveling to Atlanta, my parents unloaded their car. Upon entering my kitchen, they discovered that both my refrigerator and pantry were bare. In fact, the only food I had was pumpkin soup. I told them how I used the bread crumbs and my mom angrily asked why I didn't tell her. My answer was simple: "I wasn't hungry."

She took me shopping the next morning, but I had another purpose in mind for their visit. Over the years, I had begun digitizing our family's photos with a program that identified faces. I recognized a great many and enlisted my parents' help with the rest. Per my Aunt Cille's advice, I was continuing to hammer.

As the exercise neared completion, I got more unwelcome, but not unexpected news. Liquidating my retirement account brought a heavy tax burden, which complicated my filing. The online tax software showed warnings, and a subsequent letter from the IRS confirmed that I was in fact, being audited.

Next, a large packet came from the Northern District of Georgia. I immediately began to sulk upon reading the summary judgment. I wondered what happened to my appeal, but later got a *Report and Recommendation* from a district judge that explained its denial. The reasoning was essentially the same as the preceding ruling, so I investigated the author.

According to therobingroom.com, Judge William S. Duffey Jr. "has no interest in thoughtfully and fairly weighing the issues. Instead, he makes up his mind about a case almost immediately and refuses to let the facts or even the law stand in his way. He'll find any excuse to dismiss a case, regardless of the merits… tends to side with corporate defendants… any civil rights plaintiff that draws Bill Duffey as the judge might as well just drop the case… He is more than likely a racist and also has a strong dislike for the disabled… shows a strong dislike for the underdog, especially the poor… should be impeached!" The revelation of the judge I had drawn did nothing for my case. Having come too far to quit, I began looking at the court of appeals.

Mema and I were well on our way to Minnesota for Thanksgiving when I realized we would again be passing by the billboard that had frightened me. Since seeing it, I had been avoiding the route. The ominous sign was set off to the right. On the side closest to my house was a much better message: "Heaven is Real."

CHAPTER 14

DREAMING

Things weren't going my way. I called the Department of Transportation and was informed that the cameras above my wreck captured live feed only. The young woman whose truck I hit said that she would help, but her family's attorney advised against her involvement. Due to the impact, I was experiencing numbness in my toes and went for an MRI. I tracked down the contractor who employed the driver of the lawnmower with hopes of compensation, but he stopped taking my calls. I wound up speaking with an attorney who agreed to work for me.

I reached out to my former associate, Leonard, who offered to buy me lunch. His new agency focused on property and casualty. It was an area of potential synergy, and we agreed to partner. The prospective collaboration made me feel as though my financial free fall was coming to an end.

Konn, MetLife's attorney, then emailed me requesting that I pay his client's legal fees. I was in disbelief. They had done everything they could to stymie my case and were now asking that I pay them for their efforts. I had no choice, but to continue moving forward.

My parents came for the Christmas holiday and left me with ingredients for meals. I didn't have money for January's mortgage or the bills that followed. My power company sent a demand for $200, but I knew of nothing else to sell. I dreamed that I was walking toward a shelf with a gun on it. I then woke up to sell my 9mm. The proceeds more than paid to keep the lights on.

In my next visit to the food pantry, the night ended with a large bag of unclaimed bread. The event's organizer, Diane, ordered me to take it home. I couldn't eat all of the bread before it went stale, so I put it into my freezer. Anytime I was hungry, I put a roll in the oven and prepared a plate of olive oil, salt, and pepper for dipping.

My struggle was ongoing, but I continuously found comfort in life's pleasures. The net effect was creating a dream that I wanted to walk into. Daydreaming started with having a $10,000 cushion. I was thrilled with both the location and layout of my home, but wanted to make improvements. I dreamed of swapping out the windows for energy-efficient ones, blowing out the home's vents, and updating the climate-control system.

A repairman investigated a drip coming from the gutter above my garage. It was eroding the concrete below. The persistent problem most likely affected the wood behind the pillars and I made allocating funds to fix it a priority.

Mema's house training, toys, and treats had left marks all over the carpet. I planned to replace it and the dark, grainy hardwood floors. The living room was ideal for quality time and doubled as a theater when the curtains were drawn. It, however, lacked surround sound. After updating my stereo, I'd soundproof the walls.

The builder chose two-tone faucet accents instead of my preference of brushed nickel. To switch them out would be easy. I found a tilt for the blinds on the upper levels that allowed light in during the day and privacy at night. The basement blinds, however, needed to be fully open in order to take advantage of the sun. Sheer blinds would enhance privacy.

My plant-growing season could be extended and

the outdoors further enjoyed by enclosing the upstairs balcony with screens. Cooking on the porch would be easier with additional lighting. The gutter running to the side of the house could feed a rain barrel, and I'd add plumbing, then set a timer to irrigate plants on the steps. I'd also extend the back deck and enclose the porch beneath.

Shelves in the garage would get home improvement supplies off the ground. The freed space would accommodate a deep freezer and kegerator. An under-stair, walk-in closet next to the entryway would be perfect for a wine cellar.

My brother loaned me dining room furniture that I'd replace with a convertible pool table. I'd buy proper nightstands to replace the plastic roll-away drawers in the guest bedroom. The owner's suite could use a new TV, and I'd swap out the bed's metal frame for one that held curtains.

Other homes in the neighborhood provide four floors of living space, but my attic was only accessible by pull-down stairs. Presuming that I'd one day father children, I planned to build two more bedrooms that would prevent my kids from sleeping two floors away.

Despite my daydreams, I had to deal with the reality of making my legal appeal as a pauper. Further, MetLife was granted a $7,000 judgment.

I learned about the Atlanta Business League, which was dedicated to minority businesses development. Their program, Tuesday Talks, was designed for members to get exposure with local CEOs. A session with the *Atlanta Business Chronicle* was first on their list, and I figured its publisher could help me network.

Upon entering their conference room, he asked, "What's your story?"

Knowing that it was a loaded question, I replied, "A long one."

I had the floor, but consciously made the decision not to intrude on the preplanned discussion.

I went to Grady Memorial Hospital the following month, the state's largest facility, which also serves the impoverished community. Our Tuesday Talks group was greeted by subordinates and led to a room with refreshments. The majority of attendees were trying to secure vendor contracts. I thought their lobby would be a good place to station enrollees for the Affordable Care Act, but held my comment.

The hospital's new CEO then entered and introduced himself. After his presentation, each participant was given an opportunity to ask a question. I mentally crunched some of the numbers he had presented and gave my calculations. I could tell that I had moved faster than most people could follow. The CEO was with me, but had pause. His reaction gave me the confidence of knowing that I could sit in a room with anybody.

Leonard invited my input on a growth strategy for his agency. I gave my thoughts, and he asked if I'd consider compensation to pay for the implementation. Considering its scalability, I requested minority ownership and a sustaining salary. He wanted to speak with his partners about the equity, but said the money was doable. We stood, shook hands, and I did my best to contain my excitement while driving home. I kept thinking to myself how I'd finally become independent.

I started to get a better feel for Leonard's partners in subsequent meetings. One of them spoke about his prior success with government contracts and the millions he made. There was talk about connections with nationally known figures, who for a price would sway bids. I planned to remain grounded in my morals, but was told that the principles wouldn't pay for my services.

Creditors with *blocked* and *unknown* numbers started calling my cell phone. I had no answers, so I turned off the ringer, which led to persistent vibration. I had no money for a haircut or desire to attend church. I made the decision not to go until my circumstances improved.

I spent my thirty-fourth birthday eating from a pan of jambalaya and drinking a glass of three-dollar wine. Commission from a client arrived, so I trimmed off my beard for Bible study. I went to see my barber afterwards, who inquired about my absence. I produced a photo of my furry face and told her that I was broke. She said that we were supposed to be friends, repeatedly called me "sir," and ordered me, money or not, to be back each week at our scheduled time.

My former partner, Scott, had wanted me to find office space. We looked at a few locations, but I didn't see value in adding the expense. My opinion began to change, however, when he suggested that it be within 250 yards of my home. My sights shifted to a row of commercially zoned houses.

Mema occasionally walked me past one that was for sale, and we eventually stopped to investigate. The outdated fixtures piled in the backyard indicated the space was going under contract. A for sale sign at a much larger and better-conditioned property next door popped up.

After some remodeling, I envisioned a welcoming

receptionist and offices for an account manager and intern. There would be space for meetings, filing, and a kitchen. My workspace would be in the back with access to the yard. My daily activities could range from insurance to tending grapes to make wine. A hot tub was already there, and a fire pit would help make a place where friends and family could enjoy a night.

I was four months behind on my mortgage when my parents told me to make a decision. They proposed that I sell my house or find another job. Neither choice felt fair. The thought of a movie I enjoyed as a kid came to mind. While scrolling through the TV guide I saw it listed and felt as though I needed to take a *Leap of Faith*.

Still getting nibbles on business, I figured there was time to catch up. I was walking toward Bible study days later and saw a row of welcome mats matching the one my mom had bought me. What I perceived as signs of hope didn't make bank deposits.

I began feeling like Montgomery Brewster, played by Richard Pryor in *Brewster's Millions*. The character was notified of his great uncle's passing and that Montgomery was the sole heir to $300 million. He, however, would have to learn a lesson about money to get it. Montgomery had to spend $30 million in thirty days while accumulating nothing. While scrolling through my TV guide, it, too, was listed.

A letter arrived advertising relief for homeowners. I responded to learn about a program that President Obama enacted as a result of the financial crisis. For a fee, the intermediary promised collaboration with my mortgage company. Seeing a way forward, I returned to church and asked Broderick for the microphone.

I started by thanking the congregation, then acknowledged their stability which I had drawn upon in a difficult time. It was ironic, considering how I wanted to keep my distance. I hoped to tell my story, but didn't have the words. My frustration set in as I gave the mic back to Pastor Broderick. I was preparing to resume my duties when he must have thought about how my struggle paralleled a famous character in the Bible. He, too, had lost everything, and I heard my pastor say, "There's a modern-day Job."

My plants were starting to bloom, but none made a bigger impression than my lime tree. While still in the tent, it produced masses of flowers. Most had fallen off, but eleven fruits were beginning to swell.

While Georgia's weather is mild compared to

Minnesota's, I dreamed of a reprieve from the cold. I fell for a mansion in South Florida, but it went off the market. A second had a large yard and covered inlet for a boat. It, too, became unavailable. I didn't see a house with everything I wanted, so I started compiling images that I liked.

On a lot with beach and intracoastal access, I planned to build a house with symmetrical layout large enough for two families. The landscape would be dotted with plants producing tropical fruit. The driveway would lead to multicar garages, split by a courtyard. Upon entering the house, I envisioned a foyer with dual staircases leading to the residence's wings. My office would be located immediately left of the foyer and have a chef's kitchen in front. I saved pictures of indoor/outdoor eating areas leading to a lagoon-style pool. There would be swim-up seating at the outdoor kitchen. I couldn't find a grill capable of rotisserie, roasting, grilling, and smoking, so I designed my own.

At the heart of the house would be a media room served by chaise lounges. Opposite the north wing would be a game room, bar, and golf simulator. The second floor would have a playroom, gym, reading area, and kids' bedrooms. On the third floor, I planned dueling suites and additional bedrooms.

My daydreaming was interrupted by a tailoring company looking to improve their healthcare. I was with Mema and en route to their business when I smelled poop coming from the backseat. I turned around to see her butt pressed to the cushion and active streaks of brown rolling down. I stopped so that she could relieve herself, and cleaned up as best I could. We had just parked for my appointment when the skies opened up and rain began to pour. I continued on to meet the prospect, who confirmed that my tailor-made suits, with the arms too large, were a total loss.

From the basement in my house, I could hear the mail being delivered and went to the mailbox. I shuffled through papers to find a letter from my dad. Inside was a handwritten note and a $500 check. He had gotten a part-time job. Later, during a morning walk, I looked up to see the mark of God's promise, a rainbow.

My laptop wouldn't boot. A diagnostic told me that the hard drive had crashed. Fortunately, most of my documents and calendar were backed up. I was learning to rely on my tablet when my router went down. By now, I was living by Murphy's Law, "Anything that can go wrong, will go wrong."

Mexico was experiencing a lime shortage, but mine were ripening. The store price of the thirty-nine-cent fruit had surged to a dollar. I, however, was harvesting limes the size of tennis balls.

With my love of agriculture, I planned to develop the family farm in Mississippi. Although currently the subject of dispute, it was given to my great-great-grandmother through an affair. The white man she fathered kids with wanted us to have property, and one of their sons Robert E. Fouché aggregated nearly 400 acres.

To develop the main tract of almost 350 acres, the land can be shaped through logging and retrieving of minerals. I imagined a separate, twenty-acre parcel as an orchard. I'd dedicate the vast majority of the space to raising heritage livestock.

My reality, however, was preparing to target business that I almost secured the year prior. I also happened to develop a new lead. My proposal was sound, but I fumbled my prospect's invitation to happy hour. The pressure I had put on myself to handle every situation perfectly left me in a place where I was socially awkward.

☮

Hard rains turned the neighborhood drainage area into Mema's personal pool. She had grown to love swimming, and while I entertained purchasing a yacht, the idea of having a boat just large enough to entertain was more exciting. I found one with a cabin and platform from which I could dive for lobster.

My brother had found job security, and I asked for a month's worth of expenses. He instead sent me a shot glass and $50 in cash. My mom secured a consulting gig, and to my surprise, pledged to me her compensation of $7,000.

The tennis shoes I used to walk Mema had become soiled. The left sole peeled back to my arch. I had learned to love walking, but I was also fascinated by luxury automobiles. I settled on a few, including the Bentley, a Tesla, and a new Acura NSX.

While still dealing with summer heat, the air conditioning in the house went out. The lower levels were tolerable, but heat was trapped upstairs. I could more comfortably sleep on the couch, but it gave me nightmares. With the fan on high, I lay down in eighty-nine-degree heat.

My online bank account came with a $500 line of credit. I was using the bank's money to keep my utilities on. They sent a letter requesting that I bring the balance positive or face legal action. I would have been happy to pay, but both of my local accounts were overdrawn.

My dreams of wealth continued. I have no qualms with flying coach, but the thought of Mema being locked away in the cargo hold made me consider other options. Chartering a plane would get expensive, so I'd train for a pilot's license.

Money always seemed to arrive just in time. Checking my commission report on Thursdays became a habit. With Friday morning Bible study at a restaurant, I depended on a deposit that morning to place an order.

Not having gas money was an obstacle to attending church service. I told Broderick, who acknowledged my efforts and gave me permission to use church funds. Our congregation was dependent on every contribution. We always seemed to get the money necessary to cover Broderick's housing and his weekly stipend of $250 to provide for his family of six.

With a windfall, I'd deed him the house, buy a church building, and construct a community center. The congregation would be responsible for upkeep, and their offerings would support missions.

The financing for my dreams came from a $250 million settlement. After paying taxes, 10 percent of the remainder would fund a foundation. I'd ask the most frugal person I know to run it. The interest on two-thirds of the remainder would support my organization and provide investment to entrepreneurs. The last third would go to my family and leave enough so that touching the principal would never be a temptation.

No matter the state of my finances, I made cooking breakfast on Sunday a priority. My meal normally consisted of bacon, hash browns, and eggs. I ran out of meat as a weekend arrived and only had a couple of dollars in my account. I pooled loose change to buy the cheapest package of bacon available.

Broderick asked the leadership team to meet with another church that had successfully established. We gathered for the drive and stopped along the way for BBQ. The most economical order was a sampler plate. With plenty left over, the tray was given to me. Upon finishing my next helping I arrived at the unfamiliar feeling, of being full.

I was anxious to shed the remaining connection to my former business partner. After getting a check, I contacted Georgia's Department of Insurance to get approval on a new name. With written confirmation,

I left Atlanta Community Health Partners behind to form Indemnity Partners.

☮

Once my income exceeded $100,000, I told my mom that I was finished with higher education. I changed my view upon learning about a PhD program for entrepreneurship.

When my work finished for the night, I used TV programs to escape. I became a fan of a celebrity chef whose adventures brought on cravings that I fulfilled in my kitchen. I steamed mussels, sautéed shrimp, had plates of cured meat, boiled crab, and fried conch.

My dad's mom, who made her living as a cook, gave me her culinary book. My mom has been collecting recipes for decades, and I'd like to spend my free time in the kitchen.

In my reality, Mema began to limp. I examined her paw to see her nail had been cracked sideways. It caused her pain with every touch. I didn't have the money for a vet, hoped it would fix itself, but ultimately told my mom. She insisted that I have it addressed and called in payment for Mema's corrective surgery.

My initial court date for the car accident was postponed. I met my attorney in the lobby on the rescheduled date. He was negotiating with the prosecutor when the judge asked if anyone was there to speak on my behalf. A hand went up in the back. I welled up upon realizing it was the young woman whose truck I had hit. She had defied her family's attorney, followed my hearing date, and told her story. With my legal charge reduced, the lawyer I had hired considered his work finished.

I have detailed plans about how I'd like to spend the rest of my life. They include a wedding and retiring in the heavens. Instead of taking the fast track, I worked through pain and agonizing defeat. Whether or not I'm able to live my dreams rests largely on my brief to the Eleventh Circuit Court of Appeals.

CHAPTER 15

THE ELEVENTH CIRCUIT

My Appeal to the Court
(Abridged)

I. SUMMARY

Ignorance of the court's rules is not a proper defense. I would imagine, though, that you might provide relief to a plaintiff who has struggled to secure counsel.

I've prepared to fight this battle since I first began documenting my performance in October of 2007. My history with the defendant is well-noted, along with my battle through the Equal Employment Opportunity Commission.

The request before the court is the ability to obtain

information that was originally requested through the EEOC in February of 2010, again on February 11, 2011, through counsel in March of 2012, and finally on February 1 of 2013.

Rowell, during the first six of his eight years of employment, worked in Cleveland, Ohio, and learned the trade of group insurance. He was able to "master" the skills of underwriting while growing in his sales and service capacity from groups of two employees to 25,000.

Rowell worked every assignment given to him, but after his relocation to Georgia, he was unable to accept a position because of his knees. After his employment was threatened, he elected to have surgery so that he could return to work at full strength. Upon return, however, opportunity was removed, and he was forced to maintain the role of a brown face in the market.

Ultimately, there is sufficient documentation to prove that while in Ohio, Rowell earned a strong track record of success. Documents show this carried over to Atlanta. What is missing, however, is the reporting that illustrates his opportunity as compared to his peers.

II. THE REQUESTS

Having secured emails, surveys, and reporting, Rowell approached the EEOC, but was rebuffed when MetLife refused to comply. Without having the ability to determine whether or not discrimination occurred, the EEOC dismissed the claim and provided a letter giving him the right to sue.

Having secured counsel, Rowell approached his attorney with a list of needed documents. After rounds of negotiations, MetLife offered a $15,000 settlement but again refused to provide documentation. Rowell provided yet another copy of the document list to counsel, during the discovery period, which was submitted to MetLife incomplete.

III. THE EXCHANGE

On January 15, 2013, Rowell, without information necessary to prove his case, counsel to guide him through, or more than a basic understanding of the legal system, agreed to separate from counsel on the condition that she provide a request-for-discovery template.

The subsequent illness of his counsel forced Rowell to wait until January 28 to receive the agreed-upon draft. He submitted a final copy to the defendant on February 1, 2013. On February 11th, MetLife notified Rowell that the requests were untimely. On the 12th, Rowell filed Motion for the Extension of the Discovery Period, referencing counsel's failure to properly request documents.

MetLife filed opposition:

"Rowell, with only three days left in discovery period, complains that he needs an additional sixty days for discovery because he believes that his initial discovery requests were not sufficiently drafted to inquire about or obtain the information he now wants."

MetLife had known, per the deposition on November 13, 2012, in addition to previous requests, that this information has always been desired.

On March 4, 2013, Judge Russell Vineyard issued an order denying Rowell's motion, stating:

> Plaintiff has failed to show why the additional discovery he seeks is necessary for his case and why it could not have been obtained prior to the close of the extended discovery period. Plaintiff consented to

the withdrawal of his counsel in this case on January 15, 2013, and he assumed responsibility for prosecuting his case *pro se* [without an attorney] with knowledge that the extended discovery deadline was looming. However, it does not appear from the record that he acted promptly to rectify the alleged failings of his prior counsel about which he complains in his motion. Instead, Rowell waited until just days before discovery was scheduled to expire to seek another extension. Even in his current *pro se* status, Rowell must bear the consequences of his own delay.

As Judge Vineyard indicates, Counsel was withdrawn on January 15th, but he assumes Rowell was aware of the discovery deadline. As an untrained litigant, Rowell was hardly in a position to read the 1,391 pages submitted, catch up on the local rules, and properly submit a request for Discovery... in one day.

Despite the complications, Rowell, with the exception of his first filing, turned briefs around within twenty-four hours.

IV. THE APPEAL

On November 18, 2013, Judge William S. Duffey Jr. wrote:

> Rowell had failed to properly show why the additional discovery he requested could not have been obtained before the close of the already-extended deadline. Judge Vineyard also noted that Rowell had not attempted to arrange a conference with the court to resolve any discovery disputes, but instead waited until discovery was about to close to file a request for his third extension.

While Rowell would have ideally allowed more than three days' notice, Local Rule 26.2 (b) states, "Motions requesting discovery extensions must be made prior to the expiration of the existing discovery period." Rowell abided by this rule.

V. SUMMARY

The last thing Rowell wants to do is burden the Court with a request, but is requesting that you see the circumstance in which he was placed. Nine extensions were granted to MetLife. This is the first request from Rowell, therefore, a Motion to Reopen Discovery and suspend summary judgment is warranted.

MetLife's Response

STATEMENT OF FACTS

MetLife sells group life, dental, and disability insurance plans to employers. Rowell, an African American, began working for MetLife as a Sales Representative in 2002 in Ohio. After a few years, he was promoted to the position of Account Executive. In 2008, Rowell requested and was granted a transfer to MetLife's office in Atlanta, Georgia, where he was employed as a Client Executive. As a Client Executive, Rowell was responsible for managing MetLife's accounts with employers having 500 to 25,000 employees.

In 2009, Rowell achieved only 10.6 percent of his sales goal. That same year, MetLife incurred over $3 million in losses resulting from clients assigned to Rowell who cancelled their contracts.

Two thousand ten was no better. Although Rowell

was expected to reach a sizable percentage of his annual sales goal within the first quarter, he had achieved only 6 percent of his goal after the first two months of the year. Rowell's sales were markedly lower than those of his coworkers. In addition, MetLife received several complaints from customers regarding Rowell's job performance.

Because of his performance issues, on February 23, 2010, Rowell's supervisor placed him on a Performance Improvement Plan. On July 30, 2010, Rowell resigned his position at MetLife to start his own insurance agency.

SUMMARY OF ARGUMENT

The District Court's decision denying Rowell's third motion was not an abuse of its discretion. The District Court did not make a clear "error of judgment" or "apply the wrong legal standard." Before the Court denied Rowell's third request for additional discovery, Rowell had (i) requested and been granted two extensions of the discovery period, totaling an additional six months of discovery; (ii) submitted substantial requests to MetLife (twenty interrogatories and forty-one document requests); and (iii) received comprehensive responses to those requests, including approximately 1,400 pages of documents.

The District Court's denial of Rowell's third motion to extend discovery should be affirmed because that ruling did not result in "substantial harm" to his case. The District Court granted summary judgment in favor of MetLife on multiple grounds. An additional sixty days of discovery would not have changed the facts or result.

My Reply

I. PURPOSE

The gist of MetLife's brief, as far as Rowell can tell, is that the court's decision to not allow additional time for discovery wouldn't have affected the outcome of this case. Rowell will demonstrate why that isn't true.

II. NEED FOR DISCOVERY

Discovery went on far longer than necessary. Defendant had ample notice and opportunity to provide documents that Rowell was seeking.

*The following quotes come from
Plaintiff's deposition, under oath.*

Konn – "But as you sit here today and when this complaint was drafted, do you have any evidence of specific 'key contacts and accounts' that you were excluded from?"

Rowell – "I have names of brokers, not clients, because we've requested those through the EEOC since this investigation started and you haven't provided them."

~

Konn – "Let's talk about Leweling's sales opportunities. What sales opportunities was she offered that you were excluded from?"

Rowell – "I haven't seen her case list because it wasn't provided."

~

Konn – "You allege that the performance ratings and customer reviews were fabricated. I'm saying, look, I'll assume they were fabricated. I'm not going to admit it yet, but I'm assuming they were for the purpose of this question. What evidence do you have that Trinkwon and Johnson, who are the individuals we've talked about in this paragraph, fabricated those ratings or reviews with the intent to cause you emotional distress?"

Rowell – "Like I said, I haven't seen any reports."

Konn – "So you believe that customer complaints were fabricated?"

Rowell – "I haven't seen evidence to the contrary."

Konn – "And the remaining reports have not been provided because you don't have possession of them or because MetLife has them?"

Rowell – "The latter."

Konn – "(Reviewing a document) So this is quote activity for each of the brokers to which you were assigned; is that right?"

Rowell – "The same report I requested for my peers, yes."

III. THE NUMBERS

MetLife contends that Rowell was placed on Performance Improvement Plan largely based on sales and persistency, but fails to disclose the entire story. In 2009, Rowell achieved 10.6 percent of his annual sales objective, incurred $3 million in losses, and sold 6 percent of his goal in the first two months of 2010.

When entering a new market, there is a ramp-up period, which is the basis for a guaranteed first-year salary:

Konn – "And doing the math, you were guaranteed from July 2008 through the end of June 2009 to receive a minimum payment of $12,000.83; is that right?"
Rowell – "Kind of."
Konn – "Why only kind of?"
Rowell – "They paid me too much."

As noted, Rowell notified MetLife that they were scheduled to pay him an excess of $65,000. During this time, he transitioned into his new role, where he wasn't expected to achieve his 2009 sales goal:
Rowell – "I tried every day to do what was right to the best of my ability, and what I'm telling you is Jeff told me that he didn't expect me to hit my first-year goal."

Three million dollars may be the top line number, but MetLife's own exhibit shows a lesser number of $1.6 million based on transition:
Konn – "All Right. What was your responsibility at Gwinnett County Schools?"
Rowell – "They wanted something MetLife had only done once before."
Konn – "And were you able to make that happen?"
Rowell – "Not really... By the time we had got the issues resolved, they had transferred to National Accounts."

Rowell's losses were further reduced by "shit" accounts assigned with management consent:

Konn – "Who told you that Ryan was giving you his shit accounts?"

Rowell – "Remus."

Rowell was assigned accounts designated as "at risk":

Konn – "You acknowledge that your persistency rate was low?"

Rowell – "I'll give you an example. Caterpillar Dealers has a nationwide trust. If you know anything about association business, you realize that some supplement others. In other words, groups with good experience are going to help those with bad. From the time I got that account, the account manager determined the case was falling apart."

Rowell warned management about troubled cases:

Rowell – "I approached Jeff Trinkwon after resolving all their service issues to let him know that Children's Healthcare of Atlanta was at risk because they were unhappy with their dental rates."

Konn – "Okay. All right. I'm just trying to confirm the account was lost because there was refusal to lower rates on behalf of MetLife?"

Rowell – "By Jeff Trinkwon, yes."

A case management assigned to Rowell was bought out:

Konn – "What about Choice Point?"

Rowell – "That company was bought out by a larger one."

According to MetLife, Rowell's placement on Performance Improvement Plan was based on customer complaints. He has yet to see them:

Rowell – "I was told there were customers that complained about me, but I wasn't provided anything."

Konn – "Trinkwon also told you that some customers complained about your performance; is that right?"

Rowell – "Yes."

Konn – "Do you have any reason to doubt the veracity of those complaints?"

Rowell – "As we talked about before, I haven't seen them in writing."

What the defendant claims to be customer complaints are actually internal reviews and are mostly positive:

Konn – "A partner was asked if you negotiate collaboratively between sales and service to arrive at business solutions best for the client and MetLife. At least one said they disagreed. Do you see that?"

Rowell – "I see three neutral, two somewhat agree, five agree, and two agree strongly."

Konn – "But at least one disagreed?"

Rowell – "I see one, yeah."

Rowell had a track record of success working with the same customer service center while employed in Ohio. He, however, is unable to compare ratings with his Atlanta peers:

Konn – "Had any of those individuals, Vietri, Leweling, Blackburn, or Ryan, received customer complaints?"

Rowell – "That's confidential."

Most large companies renew their benefits on January 1. That puts targets for someone in Rowell's position to achieve 25 percent or more of their sales goal by January 1. Rowell, however, was forced to take disability in the fourth quarter of 2009:

Rowell – "I requested the ability to work at home as opposed to going on disability."

Rowell was rebuffed on the one sales opportunity that would have allowed him to achieve his goal:

Rowell – "There was one opportunity that would have eclipsed my goal."

Konn – "Tell me about that."

Rowell – "I ran through all the numbers from every angle, and New York didn't want to do it."

Rowell's objective of $4.4 million in new sales was unrealistic:

Konn – "Okay… So explain how the twenty quotes in comparison to your comparators means that you have less opportunities for your business."

Rowell – "One point four is what I would have closed, based on the national closing ratio."

Konn – "Okay."

Rowell – "One point four accounts at $400,000 as the average-size account, would put me at $560,000."

Konn – "And what were your goals?"

Rowell – "Well over $4 million."

Konn – "And who set those goals?"

Rowell – "Jeff Trinkwon."

Konn – "So are you stating, based upon the number of quotes you received, that there was no way to reach the $4 million goal?"

Rowell – "It's mathematically impossible."

IV. EXTENDING DISCOVERY

By enlarging the discovery period, Plaintiff hopes to further address issues, such as adverse job actions:

Rowell – "I considered resigning because they threatened my job."

Konn – "How did they threaten your job, sir?"

Rowell – "They told me I could take it or find a new one."

~

Rowell – "The rep was put in a position where it was best for him to take another opportunity."

Konn – "And that's the same thing that you believe happened to you?"

Rowell – "Reducing my accounts to the point where I can't reach my goal, yes."

~

Konn – "You allege that MetLife affirmatively made a decision to constructively terminate your employment. What facts do you have to support that actual decision was made by MetLife to constructively terminate your employment?"

Rowell – "When Jeff gave me my new assignment, it was something I immediately recognized as bogus."

Konn – "What new assignment?"

Rowell – "Calling on associations as well as cold-calling from the *Yellow Pages*."

~

Rowell – "They were riding me pretty hard… Any time the meeting opened, the first questions, the hardest ones Jeff could think of, came to me."

~

Konn – "So you have no facts to establish that an actual decision was made by somebody at MetLife to constructively discharge you."

Rowell – "When you walk in one day and everything's all of a sudden different, you have less than a little to work with, you feel like something's happened."

Konn – "But no evidence that some decision was made by somebody?"

Rowell – "I mean, that assignments are given at discretion, and all of a sudden mine was very little. Yeah, I feel like that's evidence."

~

Konn – "What was your expectation when you accepted the position?"

Rowell – "That I'd have an opportunity to succeed."

Konn – "And did you ever have a discussion with anybody in Atlanta about that?"

Rowell – "With Jeff Trinkwon."

Konn – "Okay. And what was that conversation?"

Rowell – "He told me, 'If you think that I'm fucking you, you're entitled to your own opinion.'"

Rowell hoped for a comparison to his peers:

Rowell – "Vietri had eighty-eight brokers assigned to him, from south Georgia up through Tennessee… I had seven. Eight, maybe."

Konn – "And you're not complaining about specific clients, brokers, consultants. You're complaining that you had less?"

Rowell – "Correct."

Rowell – "There's a document here that's top twenty brokers year-to-date from 2010 and all of 2009. The total between the two years is $110 million in revenue, of which I wasn't assigned any."

Konn – "So is it your allegation that the fact that you were not treated the same as Blackburn, who was historically the highest selling rep in your office, racially discriminatory?"

Rowell – "That, in and of itself, no. You can make a case for giving a rep who's had success additional opportunity. Where I find fault is that you gave Vietri about as much as Blackburn. He had about a year and a half of experience."

~

Rowell – I'm alleging that I was treated differently than everybody else in the office, and in fact, the southeastern United States."

~

Konn – "And you were also assigned every other non-producing broker in the Atlanta area?"

Rowell – "Correct."

Konn – "It was hundreds of other brokers, wasn't it?"

Rowell – "Absolutely not, I may have uncovered five."

~

Jamie (Rowell's Attorney) – "Okay. And when I'm looking at the number of quotes, Rosenfeld had 345, Blackburn had 354, and Vietri, 315."

Rowell – "Sixteen."

Jamie – "Three hundred sixteen, excuse me… and all of these individuals are white?"

Rowell – "Yes."

Jamie – "Do you know of any other account executive who was assigned to look for accounts by cold-calling through the *Yellow Pages*?"

Rowell – "There was none other."

Rowell – "If you count the number of contacts working in agencies, you'll see that I had fifty-one people to talk to."

Jamie – "And what did your, I'll call them, comparators—how many did the white executives have to talk to?"

Rowell – "Leweling had 166, Blackburn had 129, and Vietri had 343."

There was pretext for discrimination:

Rowell – "My assignments were based on race and out of my job description."

Konn – "Were you assigned any white brokers?

Rowell – "No."

Konn – "So what evidence supports your position that the opportunities you received were based on your race?"

Rowell – "I received opportunities that singled me out as an African American when it came to MetLife's needs, but I wasn't allowed to share in the greater opportunities."

Konn – "So you believe you were discriminated against because you were asked to help MetLife recruit individuals from a college you went to?"

Rowell – "I had done work with Morehouse prior

to transferring to Atlanta, and that in and of itself is not why I filed a charge. It's that in combination with the fact that I was also assigned to Atlanta Life and an African American broker."

Konn – "And how was your assignment to work with the broker different?"

Rowell – "It wasn't in my job description."

Konn – "Okay. And you thought your race was singled out prior to moving from Cleveland to Atlanta, a move you requested. Jeff Trinkwon said that he wanted to increase the diversity on his staff?"

Rowell – "He also told me that he saw an attractive African American woman in the building and that I should approach her."

~

Rowell – "Race was an issue before I set foot in the office… When my move to Atlanta became official, Jeff told an office assistant that he had just hired somebody from Morehouse. He repeated, 'He went to Morehouse.' According to her statement, she got the impression that he was referencing the fact that I'm African American."

~

Rowell – "I received the black treatment in Cleveland, as well… I was assigned a black broker thirty miles outside my territory."

Rowell – "I told a friend that I was being discriminated against. Because he's not in the industry, he couldn't understand how. I described it to him as having three additional people in the office and everybody's got a hundred opportunities. You have ten, and you're the only black one."

Konn – "So brokers were not removed from you when you returned from disability?"

Rowell – "No. The one that they assigned me, Charles, the African American one, I kept."

Konn – "So are you telling me that your assignment to Pinkney-Perry is the basis for your racial discrimination complaint filed in February 2012?"

Rowell – "It just adds to the modus operandi."

MetLife's work environment was hostile;

Konn – "So what specifically are you alleging that the Regional Vice President Robert Johnson did?"

Rowell – "He put me in a position where I was in a real hard place to make a living."

Konn – "What facts support your allegation in paragraph thirty-six that MetLife and its agents intentionally harassed you?"

Rowell – "I feel like being singled out because of my race was pretty intentional."

Konn – "What are the emotional injuries you suffered as a result of MetLife's alleged failures?"

Rowell – "Stress."

Konn – "Tell me more."

Rowell – "I went to a doctor because I was sweating heavily at night."

Konn – "I'm going to go to count five of your complaint, which is the final count and good news for those of us who want to go home sometime soon. Count five of your complaint alleges intentional infliction of emotional distress. What facts support your claim for infliction of emotional distress?"

Rowell – "I had my salary cut in half."

Konn – "You allege the Performance Improvement Plan was fabricated. So I'm asking you, assuming it was fabricated, what evidence do you have that Trinkwon or Johnson fabricated it to cause you intentional emotional distress?"

Rowell – "It's the first step to termination."

Rowell – "I was back from disability a month. The next thing I know, I'm on PIP."

Konn – "And on what basis are you asserting that the process was fabricated?"

Rowell – "Because I was completely blind-sided from returning from disability to an assignment which was far from appealing after being offered a promotion."

Konn – "How did the conduct you allege cause you emotional distress?"

Rowell – "I was facing termination after giving my all to a company for eight years."

Konn – "And the emotional distress for you was that you would potentially lose your income in July?"

Rowell – "In addition to the night sweats and exceeding loss of hair."

Konn – "And how did Jeff treat you in the meetings?"

Rowell – "He tried to pick me apart."

V. SUMMARY

Rowell continues to need additional documentation to close this case and chapter in his life.

CHAPTER 16

HOME

I opened the slot to my PO Box and retrieved an envelope from the Eleventh Circuit Court. My heart immediately began to race. I knew after the first few lines that I had again suffered defeat. The judge thought I wanted to prove I could do my job, claimed I procrastinated, and didn't see why the lacking information was relevant. The EEOC considered my placement on PIP "adverse employment action," but the judge didn't agree. In the end, he wasn't "persuaded."

Finding myself fighting against both MetLife and the legal system, I called the court's clerk, seeking resolution. They said that if the judge had misstated facts, I could petition for a rehearing. I immediately began writing to resurrect my case.

With 2014 approaching its close, I again reached

out to the law firm whose business I had almost acquired. The funding vehicle I recommended promised savings—$60,000, in fact—for the company and their twenty-eight employees. My contact began asking questions that led me to believe they would choose my proposal.

While waiting for confirmation, I reconnected with the lady assisting black farmers. I was feeling good about my prospects as Thanksgiving neared. My dad sent travel money, and on the Monday before the holiday, I was in Minnesota, working. My parents asked about my sales opportunities, but I didn't want to jinx them, so I didn't share much.

I was back in Atlanta when the law firm told me that they liked my presentation. The partners, however, needed more time to understand the mechanics. They directed me to follow up in a year. The rejection shattered one-third of my anticipated revenue.

Time continued to pass, and I followed up with the farmer's organization. The lady said that she didn't think I would be providing a proposal. Shocked, I told her that I had already sent it. She checked her inbox, apologized, and asked for time to review it. On a follow-up call, she said that my proposal was good, but that they had already made their decision. She invited me to "try back next year."

With nothing in my pipeline, I faced the realization that I had failed.

A letter from the court of appeals arrived with only one word: "Denied." The rejection caused me to employ what I considered to be my nuclear option. I knew the US Supreme Court was unlikely to hear my case, but I was more interested in keeping it alive until I forced MetLife to settle.

While preparing my argument, I attempted to reach the author who had written about my home search in Atlanta's paper. She had moved on. The editors weren't interested, nor was the man I met for soul food, the publisher of the *Atlanta Business Chronicle*, or the Associated Press. Undeterred, I filed with the US Supreme Court as a pauper.

Out of resources, I contacted a real estate agent who came with everything necessary to sell my home. We took a seat at my breakfast counter. With contractual papers in front of me, I could think only of Sharkie. I was perfectly happy when I had met her, and now I was loosing my house. It took great strength to keep my composure as I signed the papers.

My mom asked what significance the money I expected to clear held. "None," I told her. She recognized that I had been through a great ordeal, proposed that I lease my house, choose a destination, and teach English for a year. My mom had just offered me a way out.

Grateful for her support, I began researching Spanish-speaking countries with cities on the coast. The reprieve was followed by news of an approved loan modification. It wiped out my late fees and reduced my mortgage payments.

I cancelled the realtor's contract, reimbursed his expenses, and listed my place for rent on Craigslist. A prospective appointment was scheduled by a white woman, but two black men came to my door. Bo introduced himself and said that I had spoken with his real estate agent partner, Debbie. Bo's companion, "Bull" was wearing a cap low on his head. He said that he was shopping for his family. When we finished our walkthrough, they stepped away. Bo returned to say that Bull wanted a lease.

Debbie supplied a background check for who she said was Bull's wife. My dad paid for new carpet and I started to pack. Hoping for a quick return to the home I had settled, I stashed my belongings in storage areas and a rental unit down the street. I began cutting down my plants, but had grown attached to those that I had started from seed. Bo said Bull's wife would appreciate them.

Bo gave me a set of money orders, I gave him keys, and with a packed truck, Mema and I were on our way. We stopped in Kansas City, where my brother was living, to return his furnishings. I then fought whiteout conditions in Illinois and finally arrived at my parent's house.

Bringing so much luggage felt markedly different than my previous visits. It was humbling. Aside from memorabilia that I had brought for safekeeping, there was nothing in my possession that I didn't need.

I knew there was purpose in my being home, and intended to focus. I had learned through organizing my home how much smoother life could be when everything was in place and my goal was to help my parents along. After spending business hours looking for work, I began purging their house of both old and unused goods.

With inspiration from an uncle, I scheduled an interview to deliver food. Top drivers earned in excess of $20 per hour, and I marked myself available for ten weekly shifts. Weekdays were geared toward corporate orders, but the rest focused on residential. I returned the next afternoon to be trained by a kid in his early twenties. Work that night brought excitement with every $3 and $4 tip I earned.

The money was allowing me to pay outstanding bills when American Express called. Having won default judgment for my failure to pay the $11,000 balance, they wanted their money. My dad stepped in to satisfy the obligation.

The weather was approaching the coldest of the season, and it registered nine degrees below zero. I kept warm by concentrating my thoughts on getting away. I looked into the Dominican Republic, but it appeared too commercial. The capital of Costa Rica, San José, didn't have beaches. Cartagena, Colombia, seemed to offer everything I wanted.

My weekly schedule started with a double shift on Monday and alternated with singles through Saturday night. With fifty-one weekly hours of making deliveries, I reserved Sunday to recuperate. The depression of my economic fall nearly got the best of me. After finishing a shift, I was driving on the freeway and nearly yanked my wheel to roll my truck and end my misery.

Mema greeted me when I got home, and I always had a present for her. I walked in on my dad's Friday night poker group, who knew I was capable of more than delivering food. As an independent contractor, however, I set my own hours, and more importantly, had no boss.

I encountered a setback upon learning that schools in Cartagena wanted in-person interviews. My brother suggested that I speak with a cousin who had taught abroad. He recommended placement programs. My goal was to start my trip in July, and I applied to each organization with reasonable fees. I thought my first interview went well, but I was later informed that I wouldn't be selected. I didn't connect with my second interviewer, but was confident after speaking with the third. Their supervisor then informed me that my application had been rejected. A bit dumbfounded, I asked why, and she told me that their company policy was not to provide feedback.

My dad thought I should find a better-paying job more quickly and introduced me to a vice president of human resources. He offered to buy me breakfast. Our conversation led to the question of what I wanted to do. I told him about my case against MetLife and said that I wanted to get it attention. He recommended that I meet with his contact from Minneapolis's newspaper. In that meeting, I received the feedback that my story was "too complex" for the daily paper.

My mom told me that a family friend and local judge, Pam, wanted to take me to lunch. The timing was good; Konn had just put me under pressure by filing a counter to my submission as a pauper. In order for my case to continue, I would have to resubmit at a cost exceeding tens of thousands of dollars. His move effectively ensured that my case would never be heard again in the legal system.

Judge Pam was focused on my well-being, but she was also interested in my argument. She was the first from the bench to recognize that sentencing guidelines for crack cocaine unfairly targeted low income individuals. She revealed to me that judges read each other's opinions, and in a conservative jurisdiction, I was never destined to win.

Judge Pam asked what I planned to do. With thoughts of taking my case to the court of public opinion, I pointed toward the binders in my backpack and said, "I'm going to turn this into a book."

I received an unexpected email from a Colombian placement agency. They scheduled me for a second-round interview and then offered near immediate placement. I was still behind on my bills, so I deferred.

The newfound lead time gave me better odds at preferred geographical placement.

I prioritized repayment of my bills, saving MetLife for last. While netting about $2,000 a month, I was eliminating debts and was on trajectory for a surplus before my trip. Being recognized as a reliable delivery driver came with better orders, and my financial cloud was starting to lift.

Bull, my tenant, then sent a video of rain coming into my basement. He also complained of a broken lock, so I hired a contractor to make repairs. Bull was paying his rent with cash deposits when my mom asked about him. Having recognized his tradecraft, being the discreet conversation, multiple money orders and cash rent payments, I said, "I think he's a drug dealer."

Notification came via email of my placement in the Colombian city of Santa Marta. It was a four-hour bus ride along the Caribbean coast from Cartagena. The metropolitan area had three major beaches and a lifestyle described as "laid-back." A national park was close by, and the hot and humid weather gave way to snow-capped mountains. It was one of the most biologically diverse places on earth. Given the opportunity to choose again, Santa Marta would have been my top choice.

Bull paid the first three months of rent on time, but had since fallen behind. He was past due. I shifted money reserved for MetLife to my mortgage, as he promised payment the following month. It didn't come. I was forced to begin eviction.

After covering months of mortgage, HOA, and storage fees, I again listed my property on Craigslist. Debbie, the agent who had placed Bull in my house, contacted me to say that she had another tenant in mind. They wanted to see my property as soon as possible. In my absence, she arranged a locksmith to let them in.

Upon entry, Debbie texted me that my place had been trashed. She suggested not only a cleaning crew, but new carpet. My belongings, which were in my attic and closet garage, were still in place. So that they would stay that way, I asked Debbie to have the locksmith install a lock on the closet door.

As I prepared a road trip to Atlanta, I started checking into Bull's background. A neighbor had given me his birth name, and I was able to extract his surname from the email address he used. Google returned an article from the DEA's website. It detailed Bull's arrest as an affiliate of the Black Mafia Family

(BMF). BMF was a trafficking organization associated with Mexican cartels. I continued to dig and saw that Bull was suspected of the murder of Sean "Puffy" Combs' bodyguard.

So they wouldn't worry, I didn't tell my parents about Bull's background. After staying in a cheap hotel, Mema and I drove to my townhouse. Her excitement turned to fear when I opened the door. Even after a professional cleaning crew had come by, my place reeked.

Mema waited in the truck as I tended to the mess. My plants were dead; there was pet feces on the deck and a sizable hole in the living room wall. I opened the windows and began shifting items to the garage. I went shopping for supplies, began making repairs, and then spent the day cleaning. Mema eventually joined me.

Night fell, and I hadn't heard from Bull, so I moved his stuff to a dumpster. Then, Bo called. Fearing how his partner might respond to his things being placed in a dumpster, I sent Bull's government name to Rawle. He would know where to start if something happened to me.

I spent most of the next day painting, and my dad bought more carpet. The night was almost over when I started to drive and found a hotel. Late the next night, Mema and I were almost in Minnesota, but I was exhausted. I stopped several times in Wisconsin so that I wouldn't fall asleep behind the wheel. After expenses, my credit card was maxed out, and I only had $1.43 in the bank. It was good to be home, though, and I hurried to bed for a double shift the next day.

My time in Minnesota was well spent. Through persistent and deliberate interaction, I was beginning to shake the feelings of being socially awkward. Even better, I had made huge strides in getting rid of my parent's junk. I still had plenty to do, and when my mom asked what I was most looking forward to I pointed to my head and said, "Clearing this thing out."

CHAPTER 17

FINDING PARADISE

R eal estate agent Debbie Winfield Farrell promised me $100 above my asking price, but required repainting of the garage. She said the applicant, Tequila, earned her income from cosmetics, and I Googled her name for verification. I was uninterested in dealing with my property from Colombia, so I hired Debbie to manage it.

My brother had a Colombian coworker and asked if I wanted him to make connections. The goal of the trip, as I saw it, was to get away. I passed. After two weeks of training in Bogotá, I traveled to Santa Marta, where I had secured a studio apartment. I took inventory, then walked to the store to get supplies and my bearings.

Monday was the first day of school, and I rode a bus to the entrance of Inem Simón Bolívar. From there, I walked the driveway to a pedestrian gate. Commotion was coming from the colosseum, and I entered to get a view of the school's assembly. Another fellow then arrived and introduced me to our supporting teacher.

I joined the other fellow as we walked to my first class. The group was studying electricity, and their classroom was fitted to match their future professions. The teacher, Sideleine, began the familiar first-day introductions. After the class, I was with the other teachers in their lounge when Aristides approached. He was assigned ninth-grade English, showed me his day's lesson plan, and invited me to accompany him. I was happy to tag along, and watched as he masterfully worked the room.

Sitting with Aristides helped me better understand our school, Inem. It was one of a series of technical schools made possible by resources from the John F. Kennedy administration. It happened to be the school Aristides attended as a student. His dad was involved in the agricultural program on the once-expansive property. Produce and livestock were plentiful, along with workshops designed to teach trades. Many of Santa Marta's elite had studied there, but poor management led to its deterioration.

A portion of Inem's land was taken by a business to build a mall. The air-conditioned classrooms sat condemned, and the library was rat infested. After studying in Canada, Aristides left a much more lucrative job in a private school to return home.

Colombia, I learned after selecting it as my destination, celebrates more holidays than any other country. Each special day's recognition comes the following Monday, which provides numerous three-day weekends throughout the year. My first day off coincided with Carnival. Barranquilla, just a two-hour bus ride west, is known to host the world's second largest gathering. That Saturday morning, I gathered my gear, hailed a taxi, and then rode a bus forty-five minutes in the opposite direction. Road signs and the bus driver's call indicated my arrival at Tayrona National Park.

After sitting for the mandatory video, I began walking a trail that led into the rainforest. The dense terrain gave way to the sound of crashing water. The clearing marked my arrival at Arrecifes, where violent waves gave credence to the hundred lives they had taken.

The path led me back into the jungle, where natives wearing their traditional white outfits populated the land. The next landmark was "La Piscina" or "The Swimming Pool." Its name came from a rock barrier that broke waves and stilled the bay.

I pressed on until reaching the opposite end of Cabo San Juan de Guía. There, I took my shirt off, unpacked my lunch, and prepared to settle. Included with my belongings was a snorkeling set that my mom had given me for Christmas. After settling in on the beach, I attempted to use it, but my excitement led to a smile that kept me from breathing underwater.

I woke from a hammock the next morning with thoughts of La Piscina. While on my way to swim, I noticed a resident raking sand. Their care helped me appreciate just how pristine the area was. My skin was starting to burn, so I booked return passage on a speedboat.

I was just beginning to settle into Santa Marta when my rent started coming late. Debbie was supposed be coordinating it, but she was dismissive and refused to enforce a penalty. The responsiveness she showed to earn the job was gone, so I listed my home on the professional Multiple Listing Service. Then, I emailed, called, and eventually mailed a letter to my tenant. There was no response.

A neighbor, who described herself as "nosy," then wrote me to say that for the second time in a matter of months, police had raided my home. She texted me a picture with patrol cars, along with an image of the back door. The lock had been chiseled off. She said that the *James* living there had been charged with pimping. I called Tequila at work, who said that she had never moved in. I recommended that she get in contact with the person in my house. My cell phone rang a moment later. It was Bo. He explained that Tequila had never taken possession of my home.

I demanded answers and threatened charges of fraud, which generated a response from the real estate agency's owner. He said that James would be moving out within days, but according to the law, I was unable to enter until he did. I told my nosy neighbor that James would be out, but she took the initiative to see for herself. After walking into my house, unannounced, James charged her with trespassing.

I wanted to lean on my dad or Rawle for help, but the reality was I needed to fly back to Atlanta. My dad purchased a ticket, and I packed my bags for a Friday-night departure. I flew to Medellín, where I spent the night on an airport love seat. My next flight was delayed, and I arrived in Atlanta late that night. After putting so much care into my home, seeing its condition was my priority. I took public rail and bus to the entrance of my gated community.

I went to the front door and peeked through the blinds to see furniture. My house was still occupied. I needed to collect my thoughts and walked across the street to an all-night diner. I eventually used Uber for a ride to Rawle's and entered with a key he had left. After being greeted by his dog, I lay down on his couch in the wee hours of my thirty-sixth birthday.

Rawle returned later that morning. He dropped $100 in front of me and said, "No backsies." The money was mine, and there was nothing I could do about it. Rickey booked a flight to join us, and I organized Rawle's cabinets while preparing our dinner.

He offered to take the train to work so I could borrow his car for a trip to my neighborhood. The next morning, I parked in the visitor area with a direct view of my house and began to wait. Nearly a week had passed since I was told that James would be out. Debbie assured me that he was moving that same day.

With no visible activity, I requested access, but Debbie asked for more time. I threatened eviction; she pleaded for patience. A moment later, the gate opened and a car pulled up to my driveway. My garage door opened and a tall man with dreadlocks exited my house. He spoke with the driver before the two left. I then contacted attorneys for advice on how to proceed.

The man returned about an hour later, and I asked

Debbie for permission to enter. She said nobody was home. With that, I started the car and drove to the courthouse. There, I used the cash Rawle had given me to file the papers for eviction.

The next morning, Debbie said that James was in the process of leaving. I arrived to a moving truck and walked past two guys who were working inside of it. Then, I came face-to-face with James. He complained that my neighbors were harassing him.

He walked me inside. It was strange to see someone else's belongings in my home. I walked upstairs to evaluate its condition. There was a hole in the ceiling of my bathroom and water damage in the kitchen. James said the hole came from the police and the water damage was the result of a broken toilet. The police's forced entry left the door frame leading to the garage busted. James apologized for the damage and offered to pay me for the damages.

As we were in the garage, I went to the closet and was surprised at how easily the knob turned. I pushed into the room that was full of my belongings three months prior. It was now empty. I asked James what happened to everything inside, and he said that's how he had found it. Gone were my household goods, including my extensive shot glass collection.

I was calling for quotes on repairs when James

claimed he had business down the street. Fearing I wouldn't see him again, I offered to tag along. Upon reaching his friend's SUV, James extracted a Louis Vuitton clutch, unzipped it to expose a wad of bills, and counted off a quick $500. I was astonished at the amount of cash he was carrying. He said that he was good for the rest, and I went back to my house.

The closet in the garage had a fresh layer of paint, which required removal of my belongings. Being that Debbie had requested the paint job, I determined that she was responsible for the theft. I asked her for my property, but she denied having it. I was forced to file a police report and insurance claim.

On my way back to Colombia, I was laid over in Orlando, where the gate agent offered to check traveler's bags. My backpack was heavy, so I removed my electronics and turned my luggage over. The next stop was Bogotá for an overnight layover. My mood, however, sank upon collecting my bag. Sharkie had left it by a light during a rehearsal, which had deformed the zipper. My bag was split wide open.

I didn't have to search long to know the last of my Colombian money was gone. The 35,000 pesos could have bought three meals. Instead, I used the last of my credit to buy chips, a baked snack, and a couple bottles of juice. A row of chairs served as my bed, and I saved leftovers for breakfast.

Upon arriving in Santa Marta, I exchanged the dollars I was saving to share with my students. Then, I pressed James for the money he promised. He complained about my attitude. James said that his friends wanted to "beat my ass," and he had stopped them. I explained that my "attitude" was a result of having to sleep in an airport because he didn't respond to my correspondence.

My homeowner's association notified me that my water bill hadn't been paid since December. The balance was $400. Between that and the repairs, I owed $1,500 more than I had. Notices reminding me of my outstanding bills started to populate my inbox. My mom asked how I planned to handle the situation. I replied, "I'd sell my soul, but I don't think it's worth much."

Knowing that my parents had given their all, I reached out to Rawle, who looped Rickey in. They pledged $850 and more if necessary. I thanked them for the loan and said I was disgusted at the state of my finances. I told them that everything I had was tied to my house. I was counting on James, a new tenant, and an insurance settlement from my missing property to right me financially. I pledged to sell my home before seeking help again. Rawle responded with a fiery email. Among other things, he said, "We don't loan." Rickey piled on to say that after seventeen years, we weren't friends, but family.

I hired the property manager whom I worked with on Broderick's housing. He said that he had a solid lead on a new tenant. I was feeling as though things were coming together when my bank account balance fell below zero. Unexplained fraudulent activity caused it to overdraft. The fees were refunded, but my card was deactivated. I had a backup, but a new pin wouldn't immediately arrive. I couldn't access what little money I had.

Even with the deposit from my new tenant, I was two months behind on my mortgage. Although I hadn't spoken with Tony in a while, I knew that if he had the money, then it was surely mine to use. Despite having a newborn daughter, he pledged his support. I updated my dad, who said that Tony is a really good friend. Knowing how they had stepped up when I needed them most, I responded, "I've got a few of 'em."

☮

About my friends, my relationship with Stech grew strength on the basketball court, where he consistently beat me one-on-one. I was disappointed when he decided to skip our senior season to pursue other interests. I knew that he could play a pivotal role in our championship run. Instead, he used the time to work on cable-access television. It helped him prepare to chase his dream of working in the entertainment industry.

Rawle has a tough exterior, but his sensitivity helped me to understand people individually. Among his strongest qualities are loyalty and his willingness to call things as he seems them. Coming after two accomplished sisters, he had huge shoes to fill. Rawle has found his footing and continues to thrive.

Rickey, who is sometimes too smart for his own good, undoubtedly makes experiences more enjoyable. He draws you in with his country accent, tags you with his humor, and corners you with his charm. "Pretty Rickey" is what they call him. Already a military man, he's ideal to ensure no one is left behind.

There's been no friend that I've grown closer to than Tony. He was always the perfect complement to anything I was engaged in. We started talking small, but our conversation expanded to create life that I had never imagined. He taught me the value of articulation, and his distinct voice helped me to conquer mumbling and find my own. If *War of Angels* becomes a feature film, I'm already prepared to complete the trilogy.

I was taken by Tonya the first time we met. I marveled at her genuineness and appreciated her tough love. She's someone you just want to sit and talk with. Through her, I gained insight into emotions and feelings. When Jessica asked if I was close to any woman whom I hadn't been physical with, I pointed to my sister.

I knew I liked Broderick when I saw him working with urgency. I most appreciated that he didn't claim to be perfect. Instead, he tasked himself and those around him to be better in the next moment than they were in the previous. He's my friend and pastor. It's a position that comes with much scrutiny. I, for one, will never question his heart.

My summer break in Colombia was coming to an end. A man whom I had bought food for said I needed to visit Palomino. After the hour-long bus ride, I walked on a dirt road until I reached the ocean. I spent the day reading and writing.

A massage therapist solicited me the next morning. The adult acne on my torso that I had suffered from since the age of fifteen was embarrassing. I had rarely taken my shirt off in public as the scars from pimples lasted months or years. The sun I had begun soaking in at Tayrona helped do something doctors hadn't. It blended my skin. I didn't decline her offer because I was ashamed; I didn't have any money.

The massage therapist started rubbing me anyway. As she worked, she told me about her hometown of Barú. Although I had researched it prior to traveling, it was she who convinced me to go. There, she said, people looked like us.

After a day's rest in Santa Marta, I took a bus to Cartagena. After a night's stay, a speedboat took me to Playa Blanca, named for its white sand beach. I knew to escape the crowds and walked until the sound of waves dominated the environment. A woman sitting outside a cabana priced an oceanfront room at $15 per night. I unpacked my gear and attempted to snorkel, but the strong winds carried water into the tube.

Without conventional hotels, most people cleared out by 3 p.m. The result was what the locals called *paradise*. My host secured several small lobsters that we cooked in her kitchen. I bought us beer, and we sat feet from the ocean while we refreshed.

It didn't take me long to realize I needed more cash, but the closest ATM was in town. The only way to get there was by motorcycle. I would be forced to confront my fear of open-air vehicles. After tightly holding the back bar for thirty minutes, I began to appreciate the freedom on our return.

That night, I learned of the political mess engulfing the area. The land had been passed down for generations, but developers wanted to build hotels. The proprietors organized to keep it, but some had lost their lives protecting their property.

When the discussion ended, I excused myself to buy a cup of ice. I poured Hennessy from my flask on top, squeezed a lime, and topped my glass with coke. With music playing through my headphones, I observed the star-filled night, then began to write.

I woke up early the next morning to find the bay to myself. With my snorkel gear properly fitted, I submerged. The water was calm, and the visibility was good. The sights were incredible, and I was increasingly comfortable. I spent the day in and out of the water. Whenever I was hungry, a local vendor happened to appear, selling everything from fruit to crabs and oysters. I had a plate of fish for dinner and sat in front of my cabana, where I watched the sun sink into the ocean.

In the morning, I swam a couple hundred yards into the bay. The still water and pleasant temperature made it feel like a giant bathtub. I could see people beginning their day back on shore; under the water's surface, fish were going about their business. After hours of tranquility, I decided to head in. The sea life surrounding the corals dispersed as I approached the waving sea grass, which gradually faded to white.

CHAPTER 18

REFLECTION

I was in my freshman year of college when my Spelman Sister wanted to set me up with her friend. While in their dorm, I stood up to shake the young woman's hand then sat back down. The lady I was there to meet then turned to leave. My Spelman Sister later said that her friend wasn't interested because "I was the type that you bring home to your parents."

I thought that I had met my future in-laws when Jessica brought me to her house. For all of her qualities, though, she lacks empathy. Of all the people I've come in contact with, she became the third of my friends, after Andrew and Johnny, who decided to stop returning my messages. I kept tabs on her via social media, where I saw her continue to do things she had previously refused to do. Sharkie's career blossomed. The updates began putting me in a bad mood, so I stopped checking. I went through hell for Jessica, but wound up with Sharkie. She had caught my attention when she parroted my words, but like that burger in Macau she proved to be a hypocrite.

The basis of any relationship is truth; they're built by following through on your word. My most important one was established when I was seventeen. I'm not much for jewelry, but I'd like to swap the cubic zirconia and faux gold in my state championship ring for white gold and a diamond. The inscription inside would remain the same, "Only with God."

I had no idea what awaited me after high school, but in retrospect, Morehouse was predestined. It was no mistake that I had a pastor directly across the hall from my freshman dorm room. Despite my attempts to avoid it, I wound up joining him in Bible study. Seeing the word "angel" in Spain could have been a coincidence, but the title continued to show itself when I needed to see it the most.

A former CEO of Atlanta Life told my parents that Atlanta had a deep talent pool. He recommended that my brother and I leave the city for development. Having a girlfriend in the Ivy League helped my confidence. Yet, I was unsure of what the world would offer. I know now that stopping into that professor's office and the interviews that followed were secured in advance.

My time in Cleveland often felt depressing, but in hindsight it was an incubator for the skill set that serves me today. I learned to navigate relationships, solve problems, and take on responsibility. The news of Rickey's deployment was tough to swallow, and his time away created depth that wasn't previously present.

While playing basketball in high school, I realized that I had a tendency to lose drive after accomplishments. When I was born again, everything became new. What was easy became tedious and forced patience. Once into life's gauntlet, I realized I was on the path to self-actualization, or living in the moment as the best possible version of myself.

I was never in danger of going under, and now I understand that a lack of funds created discipline. While I may need it, I don't much care for money or the material things it buys. I prefer good company and experiences. Every problem creates an opportunity, and the fewer resources available boosts the creativity necessary to achieve the desired result.

My credit score has fallen almost two hundred points, but I instead set my sights on heaven. Contrary to popular belief, it's reachable before dying. Heaven is complete harmony with your environment, knowing that everything works out if you just stay the course. It takes sacrifice to get here. Until I unpack my storage unit, I won't be entirely sure as to what I still own. Most important are my journals, which are safely tucked away.

My favorite rap artist, Tupac, guaranteed that he would spark the brain what would change the world. Even with bad knees, I endeavor to leave every situation better than I found it. You're only as strong as your name and the reputation that proceeds it. Mine is a profitable business, ability to invest in others, and a wedding away from being whole. While I prefer basketball shorts and a T-shirt, I'm equally comfortable in a suit and tie. I consider all of this growth.

While I hope to give Santa Marta as much as it's given me, I'm troubled by the thinning of classes over the year. The poverty is a concern, and I fear seeing former students who didn't take their education seriously. I know the future is in good hands, though, with teachers all over the world who sacrifice to raise kids that aren't their own.

Inem Simón Bólivar gave me an average work week of twenty-five hours. That's far less than the ninety-plus that I had grown accustomed to. With the heat and conclusion of this book, I've learned to live life at a slower pace. I've commonly heard "chill," when I'm in a rush. I've lost the weight that I gained by eating dinner after double shifts, and I am closing out the school year by hosting a basketball tournament.

I've learned that angels aren't born loyal; they become so through testimony. While I am unable to say for certain that I am, I certainly wouldn't be alone. A pillar of my Thursday morning Bible study explained the trinity as a corporation. God is the chairman; He oversees activity. Jesus acts as the CEO, and handles day-to-day functions. The Holy Spirit serves as the chief operating officer, making sure everything works from within. When we accept God's son as our savior, He works out everything displeasing to the body. It's all an effort to build the Kingdom.

With just a few weeks before returning stateside, I'm again at a crossroads. I have an idea of what I'll do when I get back, but I first need to see Mema. Although many would refer to her as a rescue, I've come to learn that she's my guardian angel. I next need to spoil Charly, without whom I wouldn't have Mema. Then, I'll spend time with my parents and my new sister-in-law. I look forward to meeting her and my niece. If the timing is good, I'll be back for my favorite holiday, Thanksgiving.

I need to put some money in the bank and will return to delivering food. I raised their bar on income potential, but don't expect to work as many hours.

Should the time come when I've re-established myself and my prospects for earning money with this book fail, I'll most likely go back to the insurance industry. I'd settle for placement just about anywhere, but I'd hope for a warm climate near the ocean.

To me, the worst-case scenario would be working for someone else while knowing that I've sacrificed at least equally as much to not only have something for myself but also provide for others. My preference would be to follow the publication of this book with a nationwide tour.

I have no desire to run for, or hold, public office. It's not my calling. While I haven't closed the door on marriage, I won't bring life into this world unless I can look into my kids' eyes and say, "You can have everything that you work for." Five years have come and gone, but I live every day with reminders of Jessica.

When I shared how much I expected to get from MetLife, most thought I had lost my mind. I had been surrounded by craziness. Only Tony understood the business. Attorneys knew the law. Nobody grasped the politics. If MetLife, like after 9/11, is again compelled to do what's right, maybe all of these dreams will come true.

Continue the adventure via **jtbcapital.com**.